Rediscovering Your Authentic Self vastly expands our perspective of who we are and why we are here. Moreah's illuminating wisdom, love, and compassion shine through every page of her book – a powerful tool for conscious living.

Simone Gabbay, Book Editor and
Author of
Nourishing the Body Temple and
Visionary Medicine: Real Hope for Total Healing

Rediscovering *Your Authentic Self*

by **Moreah Ragusa**

Angels Answers Inc.

This book is lovingly dedicated to all those in conscious pursuit of their spiritual path – in particular those seeking to understand and practice the teachings of *A Course In Miracles*.

Angels Answers Inc.
Box 1672
Okotoks AB T1S 1B5 Canada
Cover Design by Tim Auvigne
Author Photo by Kelly Mulner
Copyright © 2002 Moreah Ragusa

The Final Analysis
(Based on the Paradoxical Commandments by Dr. Kent M. Keith)
is reprinted with the permission of the author.
(c) Copyright Kent M. Keith, 1968, 2001.

Reproduction in whole or in part, in any form, including storage in memory device systems, is forbidden without written permission . . . except that - portions may be used in broadcast or printed commentary or review when attributed fully to author and publication by names.

First Printing October 2002
Printed in Canada

ISBN 0-9732110-0-8

Inquiries, orders, and other requests should be addressed to:
Angels Answers Group
Box 1672
Okotoks AB T1S 1B5 Canada
Phone 403-995-0095 Fax 403-995-0093
Email info@moreah.com
Website www.moreah.com

Table of Contents

Introduction ... 13

Part One - *Who Are We?* ... 27
- Spirituality ... 29
- Who is Satan? ... 33
- Organized Religion And Spiritual Organizations ... 35
- Free Will ... 37
- Spirituality And Karma ... 39
- The Idea of God ... 45
- Understanding the Son of God ... 47
- Understanding the Dynamics of Ego ... 49
- Each Soul is a Part of God ... 51
- The Christ Mind and The Dreaming Mind ... 53
- Atonement and Miracles ... 57
- Understanding Dilemmas ... 61
- Corrective Procedure of Atonement ... 62
- Atonement as Defense ... 65
- Love and Light ... 69
- What is Intimacy and Love? ... 73
- Fear ... 77
- What Is Sin? ... 79
- What Blocks Love? ... 81

Part Two - *The Power of Choice* ... 87
- Choice ... 89
- Inauthentic and Authentic Power ... 93
- Relationship Levels ... 97
- Transcending Defense Mechanisms ... 101
- Cause and Effect ... 107
- Reflection and Projection ... 111
- Heaven or Hell? ... 117
- Creating Heaven on Earth ... 119
- To Live in the Moment ... 127
- Solving Time Conflicts ... 133
- Miracles ... 135
- The Mind's Role in Illness ... 137

Part Three - *Relationships* — 141
- The Holy vs. Special Relationships — 143
- The Separated Dreaming Mind — 145
- Three Levels of Relationships — 149
- The Special Hate Relationship — 155
- The Special Love Relationship — 161
- Transcending Our Fears — 165
- The Dynamics of Special Love And Hate Relationships — 169
- The Dynamics of Attraction — 171
- Healing Our Wounds and Filling the Void — 175
- Transcending the Ego — 177
- Summary of the Special Relationship — 181
- Finding Our Inner Power — 183
- Our Relationship to God — 187
- Our Relationship to Our Parents — 189
- Transcending Archetypal Patterns — 193
- When Is It Time to Leave a Relationship? — 197
- Our Relationship to Spouse and Children — 203
- Healing Archetypal Defense Mechanisms — 205
- Nurturing Our Children's Self Esteem — 209
- The Holy Role of the Stepparent — 211
- Love Asks No Reward — 215
- Nurturing Our Relationships — 219
- Surrendering Feelings of Guilt — 221
- Love In Abundance — 223
- Our Relationship to Outer Relationships — 227
- Remembering Our True Identity — 231
- Our Relationship to Prosperity — 233
- Creating Abundance — 237
- The Unhealed Healer — 239

Part Four - *The Purpose of the Body* — 241
- Understanding the Body — 243
- Balance — 245
- The Purpose of Illness — 247
- Magic vs. Miracles — 253
- The Forming of the Body — 257
- The Seven Chakras — 259
  - Chakra One — 261
  - Chakra Two — 264
  - Chakra Three — 268
  - Chakra Four — 270

Chakra Five	271
Chakra Six	273
Chakra Seven	274
The Seven Chakras Working Together	277
Addiction	281

Part Five - *Expanded Consciousness* — 287

Perception vs. Knowledge	289
Reincarnation	293
Karma	299
Grace	303
Self-Love	305
Prayer	309
Illness and Healing	311
Prayer and Our Relationship to God	313
To Begin Again	315
The Final Analysis	319

We live in an eternal now.

Moreah Ragusa

Preface

    This book is intended to be a reflection on, and an interpretation of, the principles introduced in *A Course in Miracles,* a scribed book first published in 1976. Since that time, it has been published in different forms. The original Course consisted of three books — Text, Workbook for Students, and Manual for Teachers. For convenience purposes, these three books have been combined into one volume. Because there are different print editions of the Course, one might own a copy of either a numbered sentence-by-sentence text or an earlier version that was not numbered. My personal copy is from the 1992 soft-cover edition. Throughout this text, all quotes from *A Course in Miracles* are followed by a footnote to indicate the exact location of each quote. For example, if the quote comes from the Introduction of the book, it is signified by "In." If the quote is derived from the Text, a "T" precedes the chapter, part, section, paragraph, and sentence. In the case of a quote coming from the lesson book, the quote is followed by "W" (for Workbook). If the quote is derived from Part I of the lesson book, the symbol is "PI," and for Part II, "PII." Following this are the lesson, paragraph, and sentence. If the quote is derived from the Manual for Teachers, it is followed by "M," and then the question, paragraph, and sentence. If the quote is from the Clarification of Terms, which are found opposite the lessons in Part II of the lesson book, "C" is followed by term, paragraph, and sentence. In all cases the book, chapter, part, section, paragraph, lesson, term or question, are clearly identified as follows:

Rediscovering Your Authentic Self

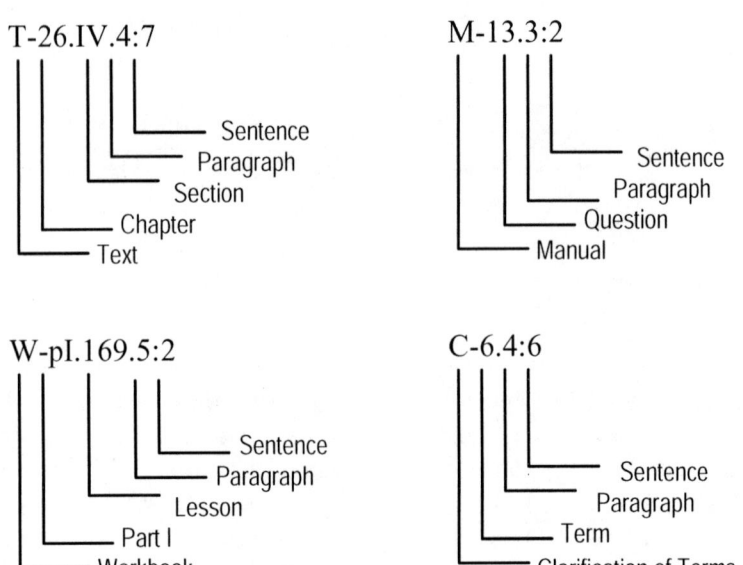

Moreah Ragusa

Introduction

  The day marking the beginning of my awakening arrived in the early part of the 1990s. I was watching an Oprah Winfrey program. For years, I had felt victimized, a prisoner, entrapped within life's struggles. At that particular point in my life, I had endured a tremendous amount of emotional and psychological suffering that had been mystically softened by miracles. In their wake, the miracles left transformative ways of thinking and feeling that would change my life for months to come. What exactly was behind these transformative thoughts and outlooks that had the power to set me free? This is what I had to discover. I had learned that if I was pushed far enough psychologically, some divine power buried deep within me would emerge. I was both starving and searching to become engaged with this power — only this time I hungered for it not through desperation, but instead through inspiration.

  Oprah introduced the author of the book, which she claimed was, at that point, the best book she had ever read. My whole being became animated with an unexplained joy as my body felt weightless; my spirit seemed to be celebrating a long-awaited marker towards my awakening. On that very day, I purchased Marianne Williamson's book, *A Return to Love*, which was the catalyst that launched me firmly on my journey towards freedom. I simply devoured it line-by-line and page-by-page. In this, her first book, Marianne shared her reflections on another book, *A Course in Miracles*. She reflected on, and explained how, its principles and theories had transformed her life and restored to her a sense of peace she had not been able to attain in any other way.

I extracted the teachings of the Course from Marianne's book and passionately began living them. Eighteen months later, I would purchase a copy of *A Course in Miracles* (ACIM), or "the Course," and make the same discovery that Marianne had made. The reading and living of its teachings caused an awakening that continues today. Since that day, I have learned, practiced, and taught its teachings, discovering also what thousands of people have recognized — that the Course has the power to restore perfect peace of mind.

Helen Schucman and William Thetford, Professors of Medical Psychology at Columbia University's College of Physicians and Surgeons in New York City, scribed ACIM. Although Helen and William were the scribes, the author is undoubtedly the spirit of Jesus Christ, who, the Course teaches, was the embodiment of a fully actualized Christ Mind, which, we're taught, is the Son of God. The Son of God is the collective of all people referred to as "the Sonship."

Through the Course we are encouraged to explore the idea that the Christ Mind is within us all and is revealed to be the actual place where all is one. These teachings touched my life so deeply, and continue to do so today, that I committed to God to make it my life's work to learn and demonstrate them with each person and every event in my life. Strangely for me, these teachings seemed somehow to be remembered rather than learned.

This book is dedicated to the purpose of making the reader aware of the blocks that we have placed before our awareness of love's presence, in addition to the guidelines that I call Universal Truths, such as: Thou shalt not kill; love thy neighbor as thyself; to defend is to attack; as you think so shall you be; and, both giving and receiving imply having. These truths are not meant to conflict with any other spiritual doctrines, but rather to enlighten the perception of the reader to better understand the goal of all religions. I believe that goal to be love and forgiveness. With the theories outlined in this book, you will be able to draw from the knowledge within your own being — to help guide you on your sacred spiritual path. The majority of the ideas and principles offered in this book are derived from the above-mentioned book, *A Course in Miracles* — a self-study course dedicated to the psychological retraining of the way we think. *A Course in Miracles* is published by The Foundation For Inner Peace. It is not a religion. In my opinion, the goal of *A Course in Miracles* is to relinquish fear, guilt, and judgment from the human mind, which will prompt the releasing of a perceived state of separation. This releasing causes the mind to return to its natural state — the state from which it originated and that, in fact, it never left. That state is an all-encompassing love. Therefore, it becomes clear that to identify ourselves with the Christ Consciousness is to accept our natural state of being.

Throughout the study of the Course, I realized that if I wanted answers, I needed to first ask. This realization changed my life. When we think we know, we are not teachable. Our mind is closed to considering other possibilities. But when we are willing to ask for understanding about the mystery of life, answers always follow. Subsequently, we become open to ideas that may have been previously unquestioned and unexplored. With an open mind, and what felt like a love-starved heart, I asked.

Rediscovering Your Authentic Self

I try not to confuse excellence with perfection; Excellence I can acquire; the perfection part is up to God.

Einstein

Moreah Ragusa

Asking and Receiving

    In 1987, I began surrendering my belief that I already knew what there was to know. I began asking why I felt such a gaping void in my heart that nothing I had tried seemed able to fill it. I questioned, why did I have to endure the painful experiences that I had in my life? Was there a lesson in them all? What is the real meaning of love and forgiveness? And why does life hurt so much?

    As a child, I was introduced to many religions as my mother searched to understand the truth about God, as well as her purpose in life. This was a blessing, for it gave me the opportunity to experience several different spiritual doctrines and practices. It also allowed me to observe that the search within all religions was, in fact, a search for a relationship with God. It seems that we have all felt at times as though something were missing — as though there were a void that nothing in the physical world could fill. That thing is our awareness of, and conscious connection to, our Creator.

    Through learning this lesson, I was able to more clearly comprehend who I was — the holy, innocent, perfect child of God. From that identity, I would learn that my purpose on earth was to do God's Will, which is to think and act only through love.

Rediscovering Your Authentic Self

*When the body is used to communicate love it becomes holy.
When the body is used to replace communication,
it becomes ill.*

Moreah Ragusa

Guidance from Within

Inherent within me is a strong inner knowing that has always spoken clearly and directly of the universal truths explored in *A Course in Miracles*. These universal truths, I have learned, govern life perfectly. When I was a child, I naturally and frequently sought the guidance of my inner voice to better understand my unhappy parents, who constantly created pain-filled, difficult experiences. In my adult years, miracles have become an essential tool in life. In choosing the path of self-reliance, I have learned to ask for, and receive, answers from within that allow me to perceive my experiences differently. I have always believed that each and every one of us has access to this inner guidance. The question is, why don't we always rely on it? *Most often, it is because of fear* — because we're afraid of making a wrong choice! We're afraid that the wrong inner guidance is answering us, and we're afraid of our inability to act out the guidance that is offered.

To tap into our innate inner guidance, we must first surrender all of our fears and ask for help. We must put our goal first and in so doing, become clear on the path to attain that goal. The meaning, and the deeper understandings we seek, will follow, but we cannot be attached to the outcome; genuine answers are not always easy to accept. They will, however, return us to our authentic self. Answers will come to us — if we ask.

But what happens if we receive answers that we don't like, answers that we do not feel empowered enough to embrace? In these instances, the truth that accompanies the answer will generate fear, and so we must ask to be joined with the power of God, which is within us, to act on the guidance. Fear can, and often does, prevent us from asking in the first place. We may feel individually unable to deal with the truth that guidance brings, so naturally the strength needed comes from unification with God. Ultimately what we come to understand is that the truth will always liberate us. The truth reflects our brilliance and our resilience to overcome what we perceive as obstacles.

In my travels, I discovered that although there were many religions, each religion in its origin was founded on the desire to commune with God. The Course principles reflect universal truths that I define as the laws of love. Love and its meaning, we are taught, are not teachable, but are, and must be, experiential. The thoughts that generate the experience of fear are what obstruct our awareness of the separation from love's constant presence. The skill of recognizing these obstructive thoughts is teachable, and it is towards the accomplishment of that goal that this book is written. In my opinion, all religions strive towards, and desire to expand from, these laws of love. It has become clear to me that all people, in all religions, are praying to the same God or as my Teacher taught me the- Grand Organizing Design.

The Fear of God

Throughout my spiritual quest, I encountered numerous people with a tremendous resistance to the Grand Organizing Design and religion. Compassionately, I understood. I could resonate with them because I have also felt this way at certain points in my life. It is interesting, however, that these were the times when I was feeling both powerless and helpless, and it was these feelings that engendered anger towards God.

Even today, I often meet people who express anger and fear at the very idea of God. The fear and anger they feel stem from feelings of helplessness, and from having the concept of God or religion forced upon them, either by well-meaning parents, or by an exuberant individual who had become reborn into a greater awareness of God's love and mercy. Meaning well and surely feeling liberated, many "born-again" individuals understandably want to share their newfound feelings of joy and faith with everyone they meet. Unfortunately, many people are too "turned off" by God and religion and are not yet ready to hear their message. Many people whom I have counseled have confided that their fear, anger, and resentment all came from being told that if they didn't surrender to this "loving God" or didn't obey His commandments, they would be damned. Feeling confused by such an apparent contradiction in how the nature of God was presented to them, they shut down.

Many of us, using a reasoning mind, were not willing to buy into a thought system that left us feeling guilty and damned. Undoubtedly we realized that if this thought system were valid, that would mean that we didn't have free will — that we could not act according to our wants and desires. At the first stage of our awakening, we often realize that fear is being used to manipulate us into believing in God, and that this tactic is similar to the coercion employed in a dictatorship. But could this thought system really be of God?

For many people, any discussion about God is very difficult, and they would rather avoid the subject entirely. As I began working with people in my practice, I became increasingly aware of this "fear of God." With this in mind, the primary goals of my counseling became:

1. To soften any fears that people had about becoming "religious," or about my attempting to convert them in such a direction.
2. To offer my clients an opportunity, through spiritual thinking, to experience, and therefore to know, God.

If, for a moment, people can agree that God is love, then they can start on a journey of examining the "fear" thought system in its proper perspective. This process results in enhanced clarity and in a full understanding of God and love, which indeed manifests a heightened perception for everyone, whether they consider themselves to be religious, spiritual, or atheist.

The Course Teachings

The foundation teachings of *A Course in Miracles* are love and forgiveness, and in the Introduction we are told:

This is a course in miracles. It is a required course. Only the time you take it is voluntary. Free will does not mean that you can establish the curriculum. It means only that you can elect what you want to take at a given time. The course does not aim at teaching the meaning of love, for that is beyond what can be taught. It does aim, however, at removing the blocks to the awareness of love's presence, which is your natural inheritance. The opposite of love is fear, but what is all encompassing can have no opposite.

This course can therefore be summed up very simply in this way:
Nothing real can be threatened.
Nothing unreal exists.
Herein lies the peace of God. (In -1,2)

What this is saying is that only love is real, because that is the will of God. Therefore, nothing but love really exists. When we fully accept this to be truth, we find peace. If we experience the opposite, or find ourselves pulling away from love, we act out of fear. It is the "splitting of reality" or of mind — the turning away from love or from God — that generates the experience of fear. From this split perspective, perception rather than knowledge becomes the filter of our experience. The Course teaches that will and thought are the same, and that when we think through love, we are creating, and therefore will experience, heaven. And when we think through fear, we are dreaming and will experience hell. We are, however, given free will, which allows us the freedom to decide whether we want to think through fear or to think through love. Whether or not we wish to experience Heaven on earth is therefore up to us.

The common goal of all spiritual seekers, faiths, and religions is, ultimately, love. Although it may not be possible to narrow down the world's many faiths to a single practice or religion, it is certainly possible for all people to have a single experience based on their discovery of miracles. Miracles are natural expressions of love that happen when people are willing to become a vehicle through which love can be expressed. We must consider that in our humanness, we are perceptual beings, and our past experiences will affect our current and future perceptions. In other words, we perceive new situations through the filter of our own desires or fears. Changing our perceptions from fear to love is, in my opinion, to prove the existence of God through experience.

As perceptual beings, we need to be consciously aware of differentiating between our own limiting personal perceptions and the all-encompassing universal truths that lie deeply within each of us, unadulterated. It is my deepest desire that, through considering and working with the ideas put forth in this book, the reader will receive help in understanding, integrating, and practicing the principles of Love (universal truths) explained in *A Course in Miracles*.

For me personally, living the Course teachings has profoundly magnified my natural intuitive abilities. The practice of love and compassion and the relinquishment of fear have significantly increased the clarity of guidance coming to me from non-physical dimensions. My promise to God to serve humanity through love, using whatever gifts He has inherently placed within me, has evolved the ability to do "readings." Essentially this means that I am a vehicle or voice accessible to God and Angelic guides to help others receive guidance. In a sense, I serve as a communication link. It is hard to describe in the context of the five senses what occurs at an extrasensory perceptual level of consciousness. For the most part I see pictures, spirits, angels, and hear guidance for another's life to help them experience a greater sense of peace and well-being.

Moreah Ragusa

Daily I demonstrate the Course teaching that, in reality, there is only one mind, that we are all facets of that one mind, and that all of us are able to access the unbounded information. The prerequisite for me in serving through this ability is non-judgment and the willingness to "be one". The Course teaches that we are responsible for *what we think and that our thoughts give rise to what we see; therefore, we are responsible for attaining Christ-sight — meaning the way in which we see the world.* My purpose is simply to show up and be the voice for God and the Holy Spirit. For the most part, the individual is not surprised by the guidance given, but the surprise comes from my sharing information that is often known only to the intimate people in their life. Tremendous healing results through the release of guilt and the acceptance of forgiveness of past mistakes. The practicing of the Course is without question an opportunity to access our boundless, infinite, loving, authentic self.

Why not just read *A Course in Miracles* and decide for yourself what it says? You could certainly do this, but it has been my experience that most people find it a challenge to understand and integrate its teachings. Not because it is difficult to do so, but rather because its teachings are so different from how we have been conditioned to think. For this reason, people often struggle with the principles put forth in the Course. This book is offered to assist those with little or no previous exposure to *A Course in Miracles* to understand the function of true love. For those who are already working with the Course, I offer this book as a reminder and a helpful tool for putting the principles into practice.

In my work as a psychotherapist[*] I have found that my clients are better able to work with the Course teachings when they have been given some background information. This can be obtained through reading books such as Marianne Williamson's *A Return to Love* or Kenneth Wapnick's *Forgiveness and Jesus: The Meeting Place of A Course in Miracles and Christianity.*

I have found that when individuals recognize that they are free from the false identities we are all conditioned to uphold, they become willing to surrender and experience their lives through love rather than fear. It is my hope that through sharing my own experience and knowledge, I can help the reader to release all fear of God and to surrender any judgment of all people and all religions. The ultimate goal is peace.

*(The term applied in the Course to someone who helps others through teaching its principles)

Someday, after we have mastered the winds, the waves, the tides, and gravity, we shall harness for God the energies of love. Then for the second time in the history of the world, humanity will have discovered fire.

Pierre Teilhard de Chardin.

Part One

Who Are We?

Part One - *Who Are We?*   27

    Spirituality   29
    Who is Satan?   33
    Organized Religion And Spiritual Organizations   35
    Free Will   37
    Spirituality And Karma   39
    The Idea of God   45
    Understanding the Son of God   47
    Understanding the Dynamics of Ego   49
    Each Soul is a Part of God   51
    The Christ Mind and The Dreaming Mind   53
    Atonement and Miracles   57
    Understanding Dilemmas   61
    Corrective Procedure of Atonement   62
    Atonement as Defense   65
    Love and Light   69
    What is Intimacy and Love?   73
    Fear   77
    What Is Sin?   79
    What Blocks Love?   81

Moreah Ragusa

Spirituality

People often misunderstand the difference between being spiritual and being religious. In the West, to be religious often means that one is practicing and following the rules and doctrines of a specific religion and that one is not as likely to be open to other thoughts and theories. Those who are interested in New Age philosophies or pursue metaphysical studies are commonly perceived as being more open to Eastern beliefs, such as reincarnation, that are often discouraged in some religious doctrines. In my experience, there are core issues in the beliefs of religious people and New Age thinkers that oppose each other and that are therefore often frowned upon within their respective groups. New Age people may believe themselves to be more open and non-judgmental, but I have encountered closed-minded individuals even among New Age folk. I have experienced that if you challenge their beliefs, they will often just as easily dismiss you from a gathering as any religious group might.

Kenneth Wapnick, Ph.D., a long-time friend of the now deceased Helen Schucman, and author of *Forgiveness and Jesus: The Meeting Place of A Course in Miracles and Christianity*, also writes on the desire to bridge the gap of understanding between the beliefs of mainstream religious groups and New Age thinkers. He writes:

> Those who begin the Course expecting to find — for better or for worse — the Christianity they had learned and practiced, or the Christianity that seemed to condone bigotry and persecution, will be

Rediscovering Your Authentic Self

very much surprised. They will find many of the words they were familiar with — atonement, salvation, forgiveness of sins, Christ, Son of God, etc. — but with different meanings or connotations. The crucifixion remains the central event in Jesus' life, yet the Course's interpretation is 180 degrees from the traditional teachings that Jesus suffered and died for our sins.

We can see A Course in Miracles as an extensive commentary on the Sermon on the Mount, perhaps the clearest distillation of what Jesus' teachings must have been, and whose principles of forgiveness are so perfectly exemplified in his own life. The Course helps us understand what these principles are, why Jesus made them the cornerstone of his gospel, and why he chose the crucifixion as the form in which he taught that our sins are forgiven. Before we can transcend the separatism of religion and know our oneness in God, the religions of the world must be purified of their errors. A Course in Miracles has been given to the world as one means of such purification." (Intro. Pg.10 Par. 2-4.)

Through the theories of fundamentalist and mainstream Christianity, we are taught that we are guilty because we disobeyed God when we ate the fruit of the forbidden tree, or, in the Course, we are taught that this was a time when we began to believe that we were separate from God. As we turned away from His will, we became defined as sinners, and were therefore required to earn our salvation. In the ancient writings of Patangali* sin is non-existent; there are only obstacles to one's union with God.

Patangali reminds us that the idea of sin promotes shame.

We must question if God could find His creation guilty. The Course reminds us that to sin means that we could alter our identity, which is perfect and innocent — to defile its original nature established by God. We are reminded that we make mistakes, but that those mistakes are correctible.

*A spiritual master whose Yoga Sutras or aphorisms intended to offer specific teachings and techniques of meditation. His writings are believed to be from the fourth century B.C. to the fourth century A.D.

Because only love is real, whatever we have thought through the mind of fear does not actually exist.

Moreah Ragusa

Who Is Satan?

The concept that Satan exists as a separate entity, and that he can embrace many disguises, is a fundamentalist belief that many Christians struggle with. According to this belief, Satan could be disguised as a New Age thinker, for instance, who appears to promote the Christian message, yet works under Satan's spell. The primary difference in the way in which fundamentalist Christians and New Age Christians think is that the New Age person has accepted the idea that her thoughts create her experience. Therefore, she has deduced that since thought is occurring within the mind, all things dwell within, not without. The idea of Satan lurking "out there" no longer makes sense, and the only place he could dwell is "in here"! Yikes! What a concept! What is the idea of Satan, then? For some, it is the idea of "a being," while others understand that Satan represents the belief we ourselves are able to alter our identity and act in discord with the way in which we were originally created, resulting in loveless actions.

The ego in its arrogance believes we can be something other than who we were created to be.

Moreah Ragusa

Organized Religion and
Spiritual Organizations

I believe that the primary reason why one chooses to belong to a particular religion is to feel safe, and to be part of a community of like-minded thinkers. Whether this community falls in the spiritual or in the religious category, its members will often receive a sense of security by adhering to the rules and doctrines that govern that specific group. They believe that compliance offers a better opportunity to achieve salvation. Sometimes, people feel compelled to question governing doctrines and rules that they feel may be limiting them in some way. I have witnessed, through my work, that these people fear being judged, frowned upon, or possibly even being excommunicated from their church as a result of such questioning. In my own experience with organized religion, any exploration of the experiences of others, or any attempts to understand how others perceived God, were discouraged. And, of course, I was cautioned of Satan's many guises. Personally, my biggest disappointment was to see that each of the different churches I attended believed that they, and only they, offered the one true way to God. Furthermore, I was led to believe that coming to know God through the direct guidance of clergy as either a priest, minister, pastor, or bishop in the church was crucial to my success.

Consider then, how much fear is built into this belief system! The bottom line appears to be that if a person doesn't believe as the church governs, they will not be accepted and assured salvation. So, once again, love and fear are merged and make for strange bedfellows. In my work, I have found that fear and guilt are the major reasons why people have become offended by this Christian approach. They conclude that, if they are told to believe in God because of their inherent guilt, and if the only way to absolve the guilt is to comply with doctrine, they're simply not interested. On some level, this approach leaves them feeling as though they have been manipulated. It's a live-or-die proposition, wholly devoid of love. How can that be God's will? The whole idea of God's unconditional love is turned upside down in the context of this approach. Does God love us only if we "behave" and adhere to certain rules? If so, we cannot avoid feeling manipulated as we recognize that this would defy God's own laws of free will and unconditional love.

F_{ree} W_{ill}

The law of free will means unrestricted free thought. In all spiritual texts, we are taught that we are permitted to think what we want; controversy only arises when we question if we can think whatever we want without God's condemnation. In the Course, we are taught that we can and should. The more important questions, we are told, are, what is thinking, and what is perceiving? In lesson 304, we read, *"Perception is a mirror, not a fact. And what I look on is my state of mind, reflected outward."* (W-p2.304.1:3) However, to accept responsibility for our thinking is crucial to our attaining authentic power, which equates with deliverance. Not because God will punish us, but rather because it is a "law of mind" that thoughts never leave the mind of the thinker, and that they become the filter of our experience.

Jesus taught, "As you think, so shall you be." In the Course, this law is expounded on and its meaning clarified. When we think through love, we will experience Heaven on earth, while thinking through fear will engender the experience of hell on earth. God does not banish us to hell; it is through our own ignorance that we experience it, while seeking to blame God or others for what is happening to us. The Course talks about how many of us secretly harbor hatred towards God for not upholding His law of free will, when in fact He upholds it perfectly. The real question is, do *we*? Do we accept responsibility for what we think and consequently experience? We must recognize that the love is in the mind of the thinker. We must look into what we've been taught to believe, questioning if it's possible that not to surrender to God or love will cause us to experience eternal damnation. Will it, or do we only think it will?

It is my deepest desire to bring clarity to the opposing thought systems between the Eastern, Western, and metaphysical religions. My hope is that they might be unified and more deeply understood. I have discovered that people who choose to operate from within the boundaries of a specific religion are usually people who operate most efficiently when governed by rules. They are people who function more effectively within a group setting, and flourish from within the disciplines of their particular faith. These people deeply believe that their way is the right way, and for them, that is true. Because discovering God is a lifelong journey, we each need to be given the opportunity to find God. We need to be able to do so without fear, and through reading and listening to others and their views on understanding and experiencing God. More important, we come to know God through a feeling of innocence, and therefore of feeling safe enough to go within, through contemplation, prayer, and meditation.

Spirituality and Karma

To define ourselves as spiritual means that we are affirming, to ourselves and to others, that we accept ourselves as being more than just a body — that there is an invisible part to our being that we want to include as we navigate through life. To be spiritual means we trust that we are living in a universe that loves and cares for us. It means that we believe that we are able to make mistakes, but that those mistakes do not alter our identity. To be spiritually minded means we believe that we can let karma rule. Karma is the cosmic law of a spiritual justice system of cause and effect. Scientifically, karma is reflected as the principle determining that for every action, there is an equal and opposite reaction. In both the universal and worldly courts of justice, we adhere to cosmic, rather than human, justice. We trust that what we put into life ultimately will come back to us. Life is a cul-de-sac, what goes in will eventually come out. Karma also means that we should not be so quick to determine what karmic experiences are being learned through the encounter of two souls in this lifetime. We trust that for every cause, there is an effect and that the effect experienced in this lifetime may have its cause in another.

Spiritual individuals understand that spirit is in a constant dance to seek balance. "An eye for an eye" is ultimately understood to mean that we must receive that which we have given. *"I have no neutral thoughts,"* (W-pI.16) is reflective of the fact that all thought creates form on some level of experience, and of the understanding that thought always precedes action. We trust that if a person makes

Rediscovering Your Authentic Self

the choice to take another's life, they will eventually have to go through the experience of having their life taken in order to balance their karmic debt or live a life filled with challenge. This law does not need to be governed by people because it is perfectly governed by laws that are inherent in Spirit.

Spiritual people absolutely trust that they are always in the right place at the right time and with the right people. *"There are no accidents in salvation."*(M-3-1:6) It means that we can relax in faith, knowing that we did, in fact, write our particular chapter within the collective Book of Life before we incarnated into a body. On each page in our book, there are opportunities geared to rouse us to our identity, in settings that include specific people. These people have the capacity to mirror and to jointly heal the wounds that we share.

There are within our chapter of such a symbolic book several paragraphs on each page, of which we must choose one. This one paragraph will be the determiner of the experience that has within it the potential to awaken us. The lowest or bottom paragraph experience is derived from a particular frame of thought most paralleling fear, while the top or highest paragraph is most paralleling love and forgiveness. The assortment in between reflects all possibilities of awareness. The highest or most God-reflective perspective is derived from the highest or most conscious loving thought that we are currently able to embrace. In this sense, then, truth is like water in that it seeks its own level. Yet it is important to realize that the destination of all paragraphs, so to speak, is the same, only the perception of self, and the road traveled, differ.

In other words, I can go to the neighboring city taking back roads or the most common route. I can drive in a worn-out 1990 Honda Civic, a 2001 E-Class Mercedes Benz, or anything in between. Each choice will provide a very different ride and experience. However, regardless of the choice I make, I will ultimately end up in the destination city. In this same way, our level of awareness gives rise to our thoughts, which in turn give birth not only to our experiences, but also to how we view them. To clarify, here are some examples of the differing levels of awareness that can determine how we will experience life:

Moreah Ragusa
Levels of Consciousness Through Which We View the World

Level Seven — Christ Consciousness — I am the Holy Child of God, one with the Creator. I have accepted that my nature is one of self-referral, and that all things are lessons that God would have me learn. I respond to every situation from a place of love. I am awake and observe, rather than judge, all things. Spirit comes before matter. I have awakened to find that the mind, body, and spirit are unified and are experienced as dimensions of the totality of what I am. My desires are met effortlessly in the instant that I become aware of them. At this level, my desires generally seek to reflect love, and love's presence.

Six — I am a reflection of my Creator. I am innocent and still as God created me, but sometimes I forget that I am the creator of my experience. For the most part, I have clarity of mind, and my needs are met both spiritually and physically. The relationship between my desires and the experience of those desires is almost instant. I drift between dreaming and wakeful consciousness. My experiences reflect both.

Five — I have recognized that miracles are both natural and possible and have begun calling on a power higher than myself to guide my life. I have begun to love myself because I am learning to release the belief that I am guilty. I regularly pray or meditate and have begun to recognize that both my will and God's will are one. My desires are accomplished through synchronicities. Through authentic identity, I have begun to bend the rules of time and space. Forgiveness has become a way of life.

Four — I believe in a power greater than myself, but have not found it to be constant and reliable because I confuse the roles of cause and effect. I feel guilty for past mistakes and therefore still have a tendency to judge and get angry. I still view God as a spirit or intelligence outside and apart from myself. I project my faults and feelings of guilt onto others. I am beginning to understand that forgiveness is a source of healing, yet am still afraid to look like a doormat for practicing it.

Three — For the most part, I feel as though I am always responding to the unkind actions of others. I feel that I am a good person most of the time, but life does not reflect my goodness. I try diligently to adhere to the rules of the family and social dictates, in order to feel safe. I am often judging others to feel better inside. I am

Rediscovering Your Authentic Self

afraid of God, or do not believe in Him because He has abandoned me. I do not correlate my thoughts with my experience and with the fact that my thinking creates my reality; in fact, I have not even paid attention to what I think about. I have a hidden victim-consciousness that propels me to seek safety from the ego. My desires are attained only through "hard work."

Two — I believe myself to be a sinner. I am not worthy of a creator's love, if in fact there is a creator. I have a cynical outlook, and I believe only in what I can experience with my five senses. I have a rational mind that does not leave room for the unknown; in fact, the unknown terrifies me so much that I deny being afraid by equating the unknown with the absurd. I am highly judgmental and believe that my happiness comes from others' conforming to my will. I am ignorant about the relationship of thought and experience; therefore, I completely confuse the levels of cause and effect. I am only able to attain my desires through aggressively "taking the bull by the horns," and to some degree believe that what one person attains is then no longer available to others.

One — I am a master of denial. I identify with my ego. I may or may not believe in God and if I do, I will not believe in a loving God but rather in a God of vengeance. In fact, I find the idea of God to be a good tool with which to manipulate others. What I perceive in myself to be negative characteristics is what I project onto God, and through this action, I feel justified to take actions into my own hands. I am still reliving my past and feel exonerated in judging and attacking others based on that past pain. I am almost totally ego-driven and use chemical or pharmaceutical substances to avoid having to deal with my deep yet unconscious feelings of guilt. I anger easily and try to escape my own pain by attacking others. I am almost capable of acting cruelly without conscience. Because of my own antagonistic nature, I assume that others are going to attack me, so I continually seek protection from the ego.

If part of my soul's journey towards enlightenment includes the experience of being arrested for a crime I did not commit, then each of these levels of thought will provoke very different responses to that same experience.

At Level Seven, I will trust that this incident is to experience and demonstrate my understanding of the power of love. I will not in any way perceive myself as a victim of the accuser.

At Level Six, I will see this incident as a final step towards my awakening. I will trust that I have a karmic agreement with the souls involved, and that the event is meant to test and reveal my faith in God. Forgiveness will be immediate as I recognize that only love is real.

At Level Five, the recognition that forgiveness is required in order to find peace will be entertained and embraced. The strength to forgive will come from calling on a power higher than myself.

At Level Four, the arrest for a crime I did not commit will be perceived as an assault on my identity. I will, at first, be overrun by fear, but then will begin to consider another way to deal with the situation, such as prayer and meditation for achieving clarity of mind. I will begin to assess areas in my life where I have falsely accused another, which will open the way to my practicing forgiveness someday.

At Level Three, I will feel tormented and believe that I am a victim of circumstance. I will look to blame others for the incident. I will find it extremely difficult to forgive. I will think that it is natural for me to respond to the incident. I will not entertain the idea that there might be reasons why this is happening to me because I fear facing the partial responsibility that I may have.

At Level Two of consciousness, I will respond with outrage. I will completely deny that there is a God. I will therefore not have a place to turn to for a deeper understanding. The situation will trigger the memory of all previous incidents and situations in which I have been a victim, and I will feel justified in seeking revenge in almost any form. Finally, at **Level One**, this incident will be seen as just another kick in the teeth! I will believe myself to be justified in my rage. I will continually seek to find a person other than myself to attack, in order to cope with my deep feelings of inadequacy and powerlessness. I will tend to be violent, and feel justified in being so, because life has dealt me such a bad hand! I am a total victim of life, reversing cause and effect.

Within each of these levels of awareness, we can find ourselves. We will have enacted all of them in differing experiences. Our goal, however, is to eventually remain in the top three levels depicted here.

These foundational levels of awareness engender specific experiences so that the soul may become aware of its thinking. The

Rediscovering Your Authentic Self

Course teaches that the purpose of the world is to reflect our thoughts back to us. From this premise, we are permitted to become the active participant and witness of the challenging events in our life, rather than being the helpless sleeping actor, who would otherwise have perceived the event to be both random and painful. Through spiritual thinking, we allow our faith to begin navigating us through particular life experiences that will increase our understanding of who we are, and ultimately of where our power lies. It means we understand that we are the conscious actors in the play called life, fulfilling our part. Consequently, we come to trust that our higher self is the director.

    Spiritually minded people use their five senses to interact with their perceptual reality, but they also use intuitive senses to define and experience their authentic reality. These intuitive abilities are intrinsic in all of us — natural extensions of our authentic self with which we were created. Living spiritually means we have discovered that there is both an inner and an outer world in which we interact. Through prayer and meditation, we explore and discover that the inner world is more reliable in truth than the outer. This applies because we are not so reliant on what our physical senses report as reality. We recognize that the outer is reflective of the inner and that therefore the cause is within. We learn to trust our gut feeling and our heart's wisdom. We confidently move forward, absolute in our ability to affect our world as we act through love.

    To trust this inner world takes faith and confidence in one's identity as a spiritual being. When we are spiritual, we do not necessarily operate by the laws of time and space — instead, we become free to bend the rules that no longer seem to make moral sense. We recognize that, to some degree, we have become collectively hypnotized by social expectations and rules, but that escape is always an option. Escape then becomes defined as leading our lives only by the cosmic laws of love. To live our lives spiritually means that we have accepted and established that Mind, Spirit, Love, and Light are interchangeable words, all describing who we truly are.

The Idea of God

God is an idea, and an idea is creative mental energy. For me it was particularly refreshing to think of God as an idea, because for the first time, I was allowed to mold and shape my understanding of this Creator. I soon discovered that as I grew in my understanding of an authentic self, I also grew in my understanding of God. It was in the book *A Course in Miracles* that I first came across the concept of God as being an idea. The Course suggests that any resistance we may have to God being an idea comes from our resistance to believe that each of us is also an idea.

It is crucial to understand the teaching, *"Ideas leave not their source, and their effects but seem to be apart from them."* (T-26.VII.4:7) This is a fundamental rule that must be borne in mind throughout the study of the Course text. Consider then that there is nothing about an idea that ever has to end; in fact, we are soon able to conclude that an idea is extended and expanded through sharing. When we share ownership of a physical object, then the individual ownership is lessened. But when we share an idea, it is increased because no part of it is lost in the sharing. *"If you share a physical possession, you do divide its ownership. If you share an idea, however, you do not lessen it. All of it is still yours although all of it has been given away."* (T-5.I.1:10-12) In fact, the idea is now greater than before the sharing occurred.

Author, lecturer, and spiritual leader Dr. Deepak Chopra teaches the principles of ancient Indian *Ayurveda* — "the science of life." In Ayurveda, God is defined as energy and as information that is self-referring. This self-referring quality, in addition to energy and information, is what identifies intelligence. When we stop and think of this self-referring quality in our own thinking-learning-evolving pattern, we see that it is true. We seem to curve back into ourselves in order to experience ourselves. This is congruent with the Course teachings that thought is the origin of experience, which in turn leads to another thought. The container of the thoughts is the Soul, and within it are its desires and memories since the beginning of time. The Course teaches that an idea can be forgotten, but it can never be lost. Therefore, if God is an idea and we are, too, then both can expand and extend through sharing, eternally.

My idea of God is one in which he is the divinely supreme intelligence of a loving parental Spirit. God is the creative energy of love. God is passion, compassion, playfulness, humor, integrity, wisdom, mercy, grace, endurance, and patience. In keeping with the teachings of ACIM, namely that God is an idea and that God is perfect, reason would tell us that God would have had to create the Son of God from Himself and that therefore we, too, are perfect.

Jesus, the man, using his Christ Mind, came upon the earth to atone and to prove through demonstration that only love is real. To atone means to allow the mistakes of the fear-ridden mind to be brought to truth.

A Course in Miracles tells us that the Christ Mind began to fall asleep to its identity. The false identity that arose to take its place was the ego. The symbolic "Fall from Grace" was an outrageous belief that we could oppose God's Will —meaning that we could think apart from love. As will be explored at length, we are taught that when we think apart from love, we are, in fact, no longer thinking, but rather are dreaming or hallucinating.

The "Fall from Grace" refers to the process whereby a mind that was aware of its oneness with all things, beings, plants, and animals began to conceive of the idea that it was now separate from them. Heaven is a state of mind that is in Love, and the natural home of the Christ Mind. The first coming of Christ, we are taught, was the creation of the Christ Mind, while the Second Coming is the collective awakening of that Mind to Its reality.

Moreah Ragusa

Understanding the Son of God

Paralleling the Course teachings, in this book I am referring to the Son of God as Christ, being the name of the mind that was duplicated from the Source.

Jesus incarnated so that He might experience human consciousness to transcend the belief in fear. He walked upon the earth, understanding the perceptual human mind and its evolutionary process and condition, while maintaining an awakened Christ Mind or consciousness. He understood the lower or human mind, but did not succumb to its fear-engendered perceptions. We are told in *A Course in Miracles* that Jesus does not have anything that we do not have, reminding that the capacity within us is the same capacity that was within Him. In the Bible, there is a statement reflecting this, in which Jesus says that even the least among us could do all that He did and even more. Within the Course, Jesus acknowledges that we are to see and treat Him as an equal yet elder brother. He is an appropriate guardian because He demonstrated that He did not have any excuse not to love, while we still judge and evaluate whether or not someone is worthy of our love. Jesus, among other enlightened beings, was a demonstrator of a fully actualized human being, embracing and living through the Christ Mind. Living through this Mind, we recognize our oneness, and we relinquish all desire to attack one another. I believe that as souls, this is what we all seek to achieve.

The Christ Mind is within each and every one of us, awaiting our acceptance. Because of the law of free will we are not forced to

Rediscovering Your Authentic Self

live from this Christ Mind. We are given the choice to experience the world through thoughts from the Christ Mind or from the lower, split, ego-originated thought system.

Understanding the Dynamics of Ego

    Ego is defined as the part of our being that we perceive as separate from each other and from God. It is our self-image that has been shaped and molded by others, in both a positive and a negative way. It contains within it all memories, including memories of not receiving the perfect love and nurture that are necessary for total personal and spiritual development. Our parents, who also suffered from unmet needs in their own childhood, often project their painful scars onto their children, thus perpetuating the cycle. Ultimately, we recognize that the healing of the ego can only come from a source outside the world that arose from it.

    Because guilt is the cornerstone of the ego-based thought system, the belief in the justification of punishment is unavoidable from the perspective of the ego. Therefore, it is imperative to understand that the origin of all fear lies in the guilt over our separation from the mind of God. Certain that we have attacked God in opposing His will; we feel that He is justified in attacking us in return.

    It is interesting to note that, on some level, the ego believes that we should receive that which we have given and which, it whispers, should make us terrified of God. This fear of God then causes us to seek a "savior" that is different from God. To this, the ego responds, "*I* will save you." The ego virtually projects its twisted approach to revenge onto God, so that we might not turn within and find God's constant and abiding love.

Rediscovering Your Authentic Self

Consequently, the ego is an identity that sees itself in constant danger of retribution, and it is therefore extremely defensive. The ego ultimately resolves this dilemma by secretly suggesting that we are guilty, but that it can protect us from our guilt.

> The thought of separation from God, states in the clearest form possible, that the mind which believes it has a separate will that can oppose the Will of God, also believes it can succeed. That this can hardly be a fact is obvious. Yet that it can be believed as fact, is equally obvious. Herein lies the birthplace of guilt.(M-17.5:3-9)

A Course in Miracles teaches that, although we believe during the waking hours that we are awake, we are, on one level, still dreaming. The mind that identifies itself as being apart from its Source is not awake. In reality, we are still connected, wholly innocent, and living within the mind of God. It is revealed to be mankind's mission to collectively awaken from the belief that we are separate from each other and from God. Within each one of us is a whole and perfect spirit born from, and reflecting, a unique personality of God.

Each Soul is a Part of God

One day while meditating, my higher self shared this example: Let's say that within God, there is one hundred percent grace, one hundred percent compassion, one hundred percent humility, one hundred percent wisdom, one hundred percent forgiveness, and so on. Each soul has the opportunity to be created from a unique percentage of each of these qualities, or attributes, that are God. So I may be seventy percent compassion and thirty percent humility, while my neighbor might be two percent humility, three percent wisdom, ninety percent grace, and five percent compassion.

Each soul originates from the totality that is God, yet is given a specific composite of qualities proportionately arranged to manifest a part, yet containing the whole. Each soul has the capacity to achieve the awareness of its own perfection.

The sum total of each of the souls completes the manifestation of the Son of God — known as Christ. We can liken this concept to the idea of a diamond within which all facets are coming together as a whole, yet each individual facet refracts light uniquely and differently, thus contributing to the manifestation of the total brilliance of a diamond. Without even one of these facets, the diamond is incomplete.

Imagine a single sheet of glass — smashing and allowing it to shatter in order to experience its vastness. Each single piece still contains all the intelligence, information, and material from which it originated, yet it can uniquely mirror the whole. Provided that not a single piece of glass is lost, the whole remains complete. Likewise

Rediscovering Your Authentic Self

we can ask, is the wave separate from the ocean or just an individualized aspect of it? In this sense, the soul is the wave, Spirit the ocean, and the sum total of both is God. No two snowflakes are alike and yet the elements that create snowflakes are identical.

The Course insists that we are still as God created us; therefore, we are perfect and innocent.

> *This is God's final judgment: "You are still My holy Son, forever innocent, forever loving and forever loved, as limitless as your Creator, and completely changeless and forever pure. Therefore awaken and return to Me. I am your Father and you are My Son.* (W-PII-C-10.5:1-3)

From this, we can recognize that it is our mission to accept the identity that God created for us, and not to create a new one, namely the ego.

We are reminded that not to accept our divine identity is in fact egocentric. The Course consistently makes reference to this belief as our "authority" problem. It implies that we believe we could do a better job than God! The ego does, in fact, believe this to be true.

Moreah Ragusa

The Christ Mind and The Dreaming Mind

The Course teaches that the Son of God is recognized to be much larger than one person. The Son of God is a Sonship and without exception, each and every soul is a part of the Sonship. Because only love is real, whatever we have thought through the mind of fear does not actually exist. The Course explains that whatever this "split-off, fear-engendered mind" thinks will be experienced, but that it is more properly identified as illusion or hallucination. Of course, we recognize that the purpose of a dream, illusion, or hallucination is to offer us the opportunity to see something we desire, but this does not mean that it actually exists outside of our mind.

There is a popular story of a person walking aimlessly in the desert while being scorched by the blazing sun. Desperately thirsty, he succumbs to the illusion of a mirage reflecting what looks like an oasis of water. However, the unfortunate reality of the situation is revealed when he is later found face down, sucking the desert sand.

ACIM teaches that the world does not actually exist outside of the mind that created it. The story of the thirsty man in the desert is a clear example of the hell we experience when we feel powerless to the desperate desire of a tortured mind. Thus, for us to see heaven means that we must see the world through the mind filtered by forgiveness, and that the message of forgiveness is then simultaneously witnessed by the eyes.

Rediscovering Your Authentic Self

This is possible through a mind that trusts that God is in attendance, in the present moment, in all situations and in all people. The Christ Mind lives and experiences its thoughts in the present, while the separated dreaming mind frantically races between past memory and future expectation. What this means is that all of our fearful thoughts originate in, and are based on, the powerless past ideas or experiences that we bring to a new experience. In so doing, we contaminate the present experience by not allowing it to remain untouched and innocent. Reality, being born in a loving mind, always expresses itself in the present.

Being a miracle worker means that we understand that we are the light that shall be brought to darkness where situations reflecting anger and suffering are prevalent. In those situations we simply ask the Holy Spirit, which is like a phone line between God and ourselves, to use us as an instrument. In so doing, we accept the atonement for ourselves, meaning that we own our innocence and offer all that obstructs that innocence to the correction of the Holy Spirit. We then call forth a miracle, which is to call for a loving perception of what is going on.

In Part II of the lesson book, we find the clarification of the term, "What is the world?"

1. 1. *The world is false perception. It is born of error, and it has not left its source. It will remain no longer than the thought that gave it birth is cherished. When the thought of separation has been changed to one of true forgiveness, will the world be seen in quite another light; and one which leads to truth, where the entire world must disappear and all its error vanish. Now its source has gone, and its effects are gone as well.*

A certain mind is a mind that dwells in its identity as it was originally created. The fact that we have become perceptual reflects that we have moved away from knowledge and into a desire to learn rather than to know. A perfect mind does not need to learn, as it is already flawless. Consider when we dream — how we become all the characters within our dream. Incredibly, we are able to sustain our own identity while at the same time taking on certain personality qualities of other persons within the dream.

Moreah Ragusa

Also, the mind has the ability to become a floor, ceiling, table, as well as any buildings or natural settings that also support the dream setting. It is fascinating to note that we are able to do all these things while maintaining our own unique identity. In a dream, we are able to effortlessly become interactive with all the aspects of our own being, both with the aspects that we like and with those that we are afraid of, and yet we somehow manage to keep them separate. But are we separate? Of course not, because we are the dreamer.

Also consider that while we are dreaming, we absolutely believe that our dream is real. Our heart rate increases, our blood pressure can rise or fall, and the body's sweat glands all respond to the dream pictures within your mind. What we are being shown is that we cannot deem our reality to be based on an experience that we are going through. In the case of a dream, the reality is that we are safely lying in our bed.

Our reality is that we are holy, innocent, and perfect in the eyes of God because God is not dreaming. We have, in reality, never separated from His holy will for us — we only think that we have. The Course teaches that all our joy comes from doing God's will because that is our natural state. Once again, our free will comes into play, and if we choose to live our lives feeling separate and alone, we are given the freedom to do so. We will learn, however, that such a state of mind is so far removed from who we really are that it would naturally make our life very painful. We have been told throughout our lives that to live a life absent from God will cause suffering. The truth is that when we live our lives absent from God and from love, then the conditions we create for ourselves are indeed like a "hell" that nurtures fear and pain. Not by God's will, but by our choice. Instead, we are invited to make a conscious choice to lead our lives through the perception of love, and in so doing, co-create Heaven on earth.

As spiritually grounded parents, we trust that our children have chosen both sets of parents for specific learning opportunities.

Moreah Ragusa

Atonement and Miracles

Atonement can be defined as the "reinstatement of truth." Whenever we feel fear or guilt it is because we are not living in the moment. Fear is derived from the belief that in the future, we could experience anyone or anything that is separated from love. Guilt is the belief that we had separated from love in the past. Because both are actually impossible, since only love is real, and it encompasses all things, this awareness returns us to right-mindedness. In any given instant that we return our awareness to the fact that all things are in accordance with and a part of love, we are experiencing the now, or the holy instant. This action from fear and guilt to the awareness of love is the process of the atonement.

Consequently, the acceptance of the Holy Spirit within our minds is the receiving of the atonement. In *A Course in Miracles*, we are taught that Jesus is the proof of the atonement. He was and is a perfect embodiment of this principle. His life on earth was a demonstration of the power of the Holy Spirit. The Holy Spirit's purpose is to enter into the dream world and guide us home. It reminds us of the truth. Its function is judgment, but not in the way we understand judgment to be. Judgment, in the terms of the Course, is left to Him who knows.

The Holy Spirit's function within our mind is to heal us on a causal or thought level. The Holy Spirit would not be helping us by changing our results. To do so would be to diminish the power of our mind, and this would violate an inherent property of mind — the law of cause and effect. The Holy Spirit does, however, heal our perception at a causal or thought level, which by nature changes our results and experiences.

Shame and guilt are powerful agents that disrupt our lives and undermine our health. A client came into my office one day hoping to find some clarity about a number of difficulties that were interfering with his work and his life. He had been contending with severe back pain that would flare up under stress. At times, the pain was so severe that he was completely immobilized and unable to work.

In the reading that I did for him, I noticed a small child appear, asking if he could pass on the message that "it was okay." He understood why his father had done what he had done, and that he had never been meant to incarnate. It seemed that there was an agreement between them, and that the child would be waiting for his father on the other side. My client broke down in tears. He was overwhelmed in sorrow and shame, and for the first time confessed his guilt in demanding an abortion several years ago. He explained that the pregnancy took place at an extremely difficult time in his life, and that he just knew in his heart that he would not be able to provide for a child.

My client was completely taken by surprise by this child's message, as no one, except the child's mother and he, knew of the abortion. He had literally carried the guilt and shame on his back for several years. In my office that day, we prayed that he might be able to shed this burden. We called on the Holy Spirit to undo the pain of this past decision. As my client allowed himself to be forgiven, his back pain disappeared, never to return.

To accept the atonement is to accept God. It means we accept that we are perfect because we are created that way. In accepting the atonement, we also humbly accept our identity as Sons of God, individually and on behalf of the whole Sonship. To accept our perfection and innocence means that we must be willing to release our guilt. Since the ego was formed on the belief that the Son of God is guilty, it is deeply committed to suppressing our innocence. The ego is a great liar. Within the frame of its foolish reasoning, the ego defends the lie that we must harbor guilt. If we are innocent, the ego can't exist. Therefore, to call upon the Holy Spirit simply means that we ask for our sanity to be restored and our minds to be awakened. We ask that our perceptions might be healed so that we will be motivated by love rather than by fear.

Miracles are natural expressions of love. To ask for a miracle means we ask that the blocks to our awareness of love's presence be removed. It is further a request to change our perception from fear to love. We ask the Holy Spirit to restore truth to our awareness. In ACIM, the Holy Spirit is referred to as the great transformer of fearful thought, or illusion. Again, we must remember that when we are thinking through fear, which is always an act of separation, we are not actually thinking. We are, in Course terms, hallucinating. Hence, the thoughts that we have through fear can have a temporal experience or effect as long as we allow them to remain in fear. Like water that seeks its own level, thought seeks its experience. An effect can only have power over us as long as we continue to mirror in thought that which gave rise to the experience. Only the thoughts we think through love are real and can affect us eternally. Therefore, in order to receive a miracle, we must be willing to raise our thinking to a level of love, which always precedes understanding. At times, this might feel impossible to do on one's own, particularly when it requires forgiveness at a deep level. Therefore, we are taught that, in joining with others, we can accomplish miracles that we are unable to manifest by ourselves.

> *The miracle is much like the body in that both are learning aids for facilitating a state in which they become unnecessary. When spirit's original state of direct communication is reached, neither the body nor the miracle serves any purpose. While you believe you are in a body, however, you can choose between loveless and miraculous channels of expression.* (T-1.V.1:1-3)

Rediscovering Your Authentic Self

As we awaken to who we are, we become more accepting of the strengths, weaknesses, and undeveloped parts of ourselves and others.

Moreah Ragusa

Understanding Dilemmas

The Course emphasizes that the Holy Spirit is able to use all events, illnesses, and encounters as opportunities to fulfill Its part in our awakening. One of the qualities that make us awake is that we are conscious of our ability to communicate not only verbally but also through mind. The body is said to result from the desire to avoid communication — "to be fenced off," apart from God. Thus, there can be many forms in which the effect or "dilemma" appears, representing our wish to be alone. All of these forms, however, reflect the same mistake.

Such dilemmas could manifest as an illness, an accident, a disagreement, or as depression or poverty, but these details are not important to the Holy Spirit. It can take all situations that were made to hurt and separate, and use them to heal and join. *"They become but means in which you can communicate in ways the world can understand, but which you recognize is not the unity where true communication can be found."* (W-pI.184.9:5.)

We do experience the effects of the level of thought which gave rise to the outcome. For this reason, medication works for those who believe themselves to be bodies, but does not appeal to those who understand that illness is created on the mental level. When we connect with the Holy Spirit, we reconnect with our identity as spirit or mind, reflecting reality. Any error of identity is referred to as a "level confusion." By restoring the awareness that we are spirit, we are able to correct the error at its source — the belief that we are a body rather than spirit or Mind.

If we want to receive a miracle, we must first acknowledge that we are responsible for what we think. This is a crucial first step in atonement because our minds are so powerful. Second, we must ask for restoration of the peace that was given to us in our creation. Then, as we return our minds to the time the error was made, we ask the Holy Spirit to undo all the consequences and the effects of our mistaken thoughts, for ourselves as well as for God and the Sonship. This allows our atoning to not only heal our own lives but also the whole Sonship. At this point, we surrender our guilt as we once again accept our innocence.

The Corrective Procedure of Atonement

Decision cannot be difficult. This is obvious, if you realize that you must already have decided not to be wholly joyous if that is how you feel. Therefore the first step in the undoing is to recognize that you actively decided wrongly, but can as actively decide otherwise. Be very firm with yourself in this, and keep yourself fully aware that the undoing process, which does not come from you, is nevertheless within you because God placed it there. Your part is merely to return your thinking to the point at which the error was made, and give it over to the Atonement in peace. Say this to yourself as sincerely as you can, remembering that the Holy Spirit will respond fully to your slightest invitation:

I must have decided wrongly, because I am not at peace.
I made the decision myself, but can also decide otherwise.
I want to decide otherwise, because I want to be at peace.
I do not feel guilty, because the Holy Spirit will undo all the consequences of my wrong decision if I will let Him.
I choose to let Him, by allowing Him to decide for God for me.
(T-5.VII.6:1-11)

In faith, we trust that our prayer was heard and answered. We recognize that our request for a miracle was answered through a shift in our perception, as we take a new look at a situation that initially appeared frightening or painful. Once again, what we are really asking for is that love's presence returns to our awareness.

Since our perception from an ego personality was not real, it is absolutely within the Holy Spirit's ability to undo whatever was experienced. It is through healing the cause that the outcome is changed, not through undoing the effects. When we think through love, we are actually co-creating with God. When we think through fear, we are projecting, and thus experiencing, an ego-based dream reality.

The Course reminds us that we can liken this situation to the experience of a nightmare. We identify with the feeling of fear and believe that we are in danger, but then someone turns on the lights and awakens us to our reality. Initially, we may even perceive the light in the room to be part of our nightmare. But with the continual, gentle beaming of light and a softly calling voice, we awaken. When this occurs, we do not generally believe that a miracle has happened, although on a mind level, the same principle is occurring. The truth or miracle of our being safely in our bed never changed, even though we were experiencing a nightmare.

Rediscovering Your Authentic Self

Thus, when we do not defend, we "prove through demonstration" that we are able to accept our inherent innocence and authentic reality.

Moreah Ragusa

Atonement as Defense

In *A Course in Miracles*, we are taught to use the atonement as a defense. Because we are wholly innocent and nothing can alter that reality, we do not need to defend our positions. In fact, to defend our position implies that we do not yet have total ownership of our innocent identity. To illustrate this principle, let's imagine how I would react if someone came into the room and either implied or told me that I was a man. I would not reply by defending my womanhood because I *know* that I am a woman. Another person's unawareness of my womanhood can in no way change my reality. Therefore, if an individual were to challenge my gender, I would probably simply smile within, roll my eyes, and bless them on their way.

However, if I struggled with my sexuality, I would feel a desperate need to defend my position because on some level, I would believe the challenge to be based on truth. In fact, I might feel and express outrage because I cannot believe that this individual has the audacity to speak out loud what I have worked so hard to avoid facing.

Thus, when we do not defend, we "prove through demonstration" that we are able to accept our inherent innocence and authentic reality. I believe this to have been the main message of the life of Jesus. Consider what little effort is required towards defending what you are certain of. For this reason, we are taught that to defend is, in fact, to attack. The attack is on the identity of the Sonship as a whole because the souls that make up the Sonship are one in reality. Therefore, they all share the claim to innocence.

Rediscovering Your Authentic Self

We are taught to use the atonement as a defense because when we are in contact with our innocence, we actually project that innocence outward, not only through our words, but also through our energy and action. When we choose defenselessness, we can expect either of two responses from our aggressor: One is a mirrored surrender from our aggressor in response to our claiming our natural identity. The other — and this can come as quite a surprise — is an even more intense and aggressive attack. This heightened aggression is the direct ego response to defenseless, because the ego equates defenselessness with powerlessness. This is, of course, diametrically opposed to the Course teachings.

So what do we do when we are being attacked emotionally, energetically, or psychologically? First, we need to pray that we might be able to see the situation from the perception of love. Second, we need to move away from a victim approach to seek strength and trust that the Holy Spirit will respond fully to our slightest invitation. Next, we choose to open our heart and begin to communicate our position, so that all parties are heard and understood. Finally, we ask for a miracle and trust in the Holy Spirit's response, while staying unattached to the outcome.

Our ability to practice the power of defenselessness increases with experience. Through the unfolding of miracles, we learn that it is truly the only powerful answer. We become better at asking the Holy Spirit why such aggressive people are in our lives, and we trust that they offer us opportunities to use our Course principles. Once again, it is our ability to embrace our innocence, and that of our brother or sister, that restores peace.

We easily recognize that not all souls act from this innate innocence. However, it is our mission here on earth to work towards the goal that all souls will eventually become aware of that innocence. It is up to us at which point we decide to learn this.

> *"The power to work miracles belongs to you. I will provide the opportunities to do them, but you must be ready and willing. Doing them will bring conviction in the ability, because conviction comes through accomplishment. The ability is the potential, the achievement is its expression, and the Atonement, which is the natural profession of the children of God, is the purpose."* (T-1.III.1:7-10)

When we embrace our real identity, we become a part of the solution rather than being part of the problem.

"Projection makes perception." All people are the Sons of God and therefore are right even when they speak insanely. When someone who is disconnected from their authentic source speaks or acts, they are not always likely to be kind. If we respond to their loss of identity, we exacerbate the problem.

The Course points out that when a person speaks from their ego personality, they are so removed from reality that on one level they are insane. This means that any person who acts from their ego personality is so far removed from their authentic identity that what they say is a reflection of that mind state. Freud's definition of neurosis is the separation from oneself. This is in agreement with the Course teachings. To defend your position with a person that is in such a state of mind is to enforce their illusion because your reaction validates their illusion and makes it real.

Through this principle, we understand the profound words and demonstration of Jesus, "to turn the other cheek." To do so is to demonstrate that you are not at the effect of unkindness. Contrary to what you might think, this is not a statement of spiritual martyrdom; it is a statement coming from an awakened soul. To turn the other cheek means that you are fully awake and not under the spell, or at the effect, of fear. You subsequently send the message that you do not wish for the other person to remain under the spell of fear, either. *"As you teach so shall you learn."* (T-6.1.6:1)

The Course reiterates that love is always the perfect response. To love means that we leave our hearts open, even in the presence of someone who has closed theirs. In accordance with the Course teaching, "we are one," and we will eventually learn that what we give to each other is what we will also receive. This is true because of the reality that there is a single mind that we share. Thus, what is given increases in the mind of the giver, but can only have an effect on the receiver if the receiver responds. Therefore, to turn the other cheek is to practice the atonement and dismantle fear; it is wisely the practice of defenselessness.

The practice of this principle may, at first, engender fears of being a doormat. However, this is really impossible unless we have given up our true identity. In my own life, the experience of "turning

Rediscovering Your Authentic Self

the other cheek" has always been very liberating. If, individually, more people would "turn the other cheek" in the name of peace, our society would be greatly blessed by a heightened collective ability to do so.

The principle of not responding to illusion reminds me of Soviet President Mikhail Gorbachev's statement to former President Reagan, that he was going to perform a "ghastly deed" in that he was going to deprive the United States of an enemy. We ask, then, who truly had the power? Was it not Gorbachev in his defenselessness? Or was it President Reagan, whose country had spent billions of dollars each year to defend against a country that was no longer considered an enemy?

Moreah Ragusa

Love and Light

> Love is always patient and kind; it is never jealous; love is never boastful or conceited; it is never rude or selfish; it does not take offense, and is not resentful. Love takes no pleasure in other people's sins but delights in truth; it is always ready to excuse, to trust, to hope, and to endure whatever comes. Love does not come to an end. (1 Corinthians 13:4-8)

My understanding of love has evolved as I have come to better understand the examples set by the spiritual masters of the ages. There are truths that these masters lived by. A Course in Miracles teaches that, in reality, love is all there is, and that love is everywhere. Reality is defined as what is eternal and changeless. It emphasizes that the opposite of love is fear, but that, in actual fact, love, which is all encompassing, has no opposite. We only think it does. All that really exists is love, it manifests as light. Remember that love is naturally identifiable as unification, while opposing or denying the parts of love employs the perception of separation that gives rise to fear.

Love and Light are Universal and governed identically; they are both under the same laws. A quantum light wave is composed of positive (positron) and negative (electron) phases. Positrons and electrons are inseparable and they each influence the other. If one spins right and I change the spin left the other does the opposite simultaneously. Light appears when two opposites in equal proportions are unified. Each individual wave/particle collapses and Light appears.

Rediscovering Your Authentic Self

We have and are composed of positive (positrons) and negative (electrons) emotions too. Consequently, we have highs and lows in consciousness; we have a dark and light side.

Our values- or what we feel is good or bad determines each side. Since different people have different values, the reality is that there is nothing either good or bad. The judgment is made by who is asking. For instance, some say that it is good to be nice however, too much nice gets irritating and can facilitate dependence and weakness rather than independence and strength. Alternately too much meanness can shut people down while a little will get us going, or make us more aware of what we are doing or putting into the world. This is true of all qualities and traits.

Emotions come from perceptions. Perceptions are often half-truths, because we have not been conditioned to see both sides of anything or anyone. When we do see both sides however our heart magically opens, and gratitude and grace take the place of fluctuating emotions.

Values and beliefs give rise to perceptions, and that is ok. What causes pain for others and us is projecting our values onto others, or trying to live up to another's values rather than our own. Values vary from person to person, culture to culture and so on. The differing values are balancing out globally, because there is balance. Balance is the nature of love and light.

Love is the convergence and synthesis of all traits. Like a magnet, which has two sides or charges, so does love and light. You can't perceive love or light without being aware that both sides are present, so start looking.

To clarify — love that moves naturally towards itself is defined as extension, while love that appears to be separate or having something missing, is called projection. This, then, gives rise to perception. The experience of a illusory pulling away, or missing ness is felt as fear. This statement might seem somewhat contradictory until we come to understand light. Light is the manifestation of love, and love is energy and is experienced through mind. On a quantum, or subatomic, level, love is the intention, and mind is the expression of that love. Attention, or awareness, is the part of love that seems happy to remain unmanifest, while another part is intention, which by nature desires to manifest and is seen as light.

Moreah Ragusa

We know that energy cannot be created or destroyed; all that can happen to energy is that it is altered in its form. If a room is lit, the light fills the room in its entirety. If you put your hand up in front of the light, your hand will block out the light and cast a shadow. The light, however, is still fully present; it is only your hand that blocks its permeation. This is how we are taught to understand love and fear, truth and illusion. The light represents truth, while the shadow represents illusion. We are given a choice to either accept the light or to block it, which creates shadow figures that we can falsely perceive as being real. Blocking the light does not obliterate it. From this, we can conclude that light and love are ever present. We cannot create this light, for it is from this light that we were created. We are to receive and express this light and love. As the light bulb is the vessel for the electricity, so are we the vessels for God to move through.

This is an inseparable relationship — God, the un-manifest, is manifesting through us. We cannot experience the effects of electricity until we have a light bulb through which it can pass. We can, however, obstruct that light to our awareness and instead interact with the shadows that we cast. Because love is ever present, all that is needed for us to become aware of its presence is for us to remove whatever blocks love, and accept it instead. Our fear to accept love comes from the ego-based lie that we have betrayed God. We often feel as if we were afraid of fear, but what we are truly afraid of is the love that is God.

ACIM reminds us that we associate hatred with strength, and love with weakness. I believe that one of the reasons why this is true in our society is because we also associate love with sacrifice.

I have come to comprehend the true meaning and power of love through experience, by transcending any type of fear-based situation through it. If we have transcended fear, we have experienced love's power.

We are afraid to accept love or God because we believe that to do so would mean the loss of our identity. We believe that to return to love means that we lose ourselves. Not so.

When we return to love, we discover that we lose our separated selves as we regain our true identity. The only part of ourselves that we lose is that which identifies with fear. We transcend the pseudo-soul known as the ego. We do not lose our

Rediscovering Your Authentic Self

God-given personality. Instead, we gain a heightened awareness of our own totality.

What Is Intimacy and Love?

Individually and collectively, we are in constant pursuit of love and wisdom. Beneath each and every one of our desires, there is a longing for freedom, happiness, peace, and to truly know ourselves.

Trillions of dollars are spent each year by advertisers to convince us that if we have their product, we will attain the love and happiness that we are seeking. But we need not seek outside ourselves for love and happiness. In fact, seeking happiness outside ourselves is a futile and depressing venture. Most of us have spent years seeking that special something that will fill the perceived void we feel within us. The void that we perceive is nothing other than a belief in separation, which, we have discovered, is the idea that we are apart from love.

To fully explore this concept, we must first recognize that we are, on some level, terrified of finding that which we seek. What we seek is love, ultimately revealed as an interactive, intimate, and wholly dependent relationship with our Creator. Consequently, we must realize the importance of changing our mind about God and Love. We cannot turn to either until our idea of both shifts from one of fear, fluctuation and retribution to one of inclusion and understanding.

Now we know that love is the synthesis of two opposites. All pairs; kind and cruel, mean and nice, happy and sad, up and down and dark and light come together. All traits or states come with their opposite, they are inseparable 'bedfellows.' It is only when we see half the pair that either pain or pleasure is experienced.

For instance, let us say that love is a coin, then in order to have the coin means we need to take both sides of it. If we want only heads or only tails we can't have the coin at all. Intimacy occurs at moments that we see and appreciate both sides of each other; it is also why such intimacy can occur during and following a good fight!

Intimacy is born out of loving and wholly committed communication. It is the melting of our protective boundaries. It means that we are letting down our guards, that we are allowing ourselves to be openly exposed and vulnerable. Vulnerability is not a weakness — it is a spiritual strength. It occurs when we are willing to show both sides of our total nature, both the 'saint' and 'sinner'. Subsequently, Vulnerability has no opponent! It is the reflection of the atonement principle, which is founded on the principle that only love is real- therefore I am real. It means that we understand fully that our all-encompassing, innocent Christ Mind is the creator of our life's experience. Spiritually speaking, intimacy means the acceptance of oneself and of all people and all experiences that are coming into one's life.

What empowers the spiritual seeker to live from this position is love, and the surrender of the belief in fear and guilt. When we truly love, we trust. When we are aware of love, we are patient. When we extend love, we are on purpose. When we accept love, we are living in grace.

Love and intimacy are often misunderstood to be a feeling or sentiment. They are neither. Love is a choice; it is a decision that we make. The misconception that love is a feeling stems from the difference in feelings that can arise depending on whom we are with, and which memories are aroused when we become aware of love's presence. Our past memories of experiencing love — or the lack of it — shape our feeling-response.

A mother's love for her child is continuously present, but when her child approaches her with open arms, she becomes more aware of this love as it streams from her heart. The idea of love in reference to her children will produce feelings of protectiveness, nurturing, adoration, gentleness, and caring. When her husband arrives home from work, she will once again become aware of the idea of love and experience love's presence rising into her awareness. This time, the feelings will be different than they were with her child. With her husband, she might feel beautiful, wanted, feminine, important, or possibly even helpless and defensive if on some level she has perceived him as being unkind. It is important to understand that, in this case, the helpless, defensive feelings are not obliterating the love that is always present. Her value system is. The defensiveness and helplessness are reflective of her beliefs thus operating like the hand that blocks the light, which reflects her fear, and blocking the acceptance of love's presence.

Love does not change as it is offered to friends, family, lovers, and co-workers. What changes is the level of acceptance to love's presence when we are interacting with others. We appreciate those that support our values and beliefs while we resent and dislike those that do not. When we learn to appreciate both those that support and challenge our values we live intimately with life and each other. These boundaries of how much love is appropriate and acceptable in a particular situation come from values, standards and beliefs set by religion, society, and family. In the Course, we are taught that there is in reality only one type of love, and it is to be equally given to, and received by, all of the Sonship.

In fact, the belief or "idea" that there is a "special love" is not in accord with the Course teachings. We are asked to commit one hundred percent to each of our relationships so that love can be experienced in all of them. (This will be explored at length in Part Three — *Relationships*.) Commitment means that we are willing to communicate honestly and lovingly what we're thinking, and to allow any subsequent feelings of fear to be surrendered, thus transformed by love.

What becomes illuminated is that fear, of itself, has no power; the power that fear needs in order to be validated comes from us, when we join with it.

Moreah Ragusa

Fear

The idea of fear comes from the perception of separation, or being alone. Sin, then, can be equated with fear. Fear arises only when we perceive a situation that appears to be threatening to our physical, psychological, or emotional safety. There is a wonderful line in *A Course in Miracles* that states that the separation occurred because the Son of God forgot to laugh.

> *Let us return the dream he gave away unto the dreamer who perceives the dream as separate from himself and done to him. Into eternity, where all is one, there crept a tiny, mad idea, at which the Son of God remembered not to laugh. In his forgetting did the thought become a serious idea, and possible of both accomplishment and real effects. Together, we can laugh them both away, and understand that time cannot intrude upon eternity."* (T-27.VIII.6:1-4)

We are made aware through this line that we often perceive situations from a state of self-consciousness, rather than whole consciousness — "all is one." It implies that if we trust in our God-given identity, the situations we encounter will be perceived differently. Remember that the foundation of the Course teachings is that only love is real and that it is all encompassing. It also states that the opposite of love is fear. What becomes illuminated is that fear, of itself, has no power; the power that fear needs in order to be validated comes from us, when we join with it.

Rediscovering Your Authentic Self

From the study of the Course, we learn that love is truth, and that perception that gives rise to fear is illusion. It is illusion because the projection that simultaneously gives rise to perception stems from guilt.

In the Course, we are asked to examine, based on the inherent principles of love, whether an experience equates reality. It does not, of course, due to the way the mind works, with thought and experience being inseparable. We are once again reminded of what happens when we dream at night, and when we absolutely believe that we are awake and that the dream is reality, even though it is not. We are shown that fear is dreaming, and that it only appears to block love. In *A Course in Miracles,* fear and the idea of separation are said to be the proper definition and understanding of sin.

Moreah Ragusa

What Is Sin?

If we remember that love is ever present and all that there is, we will begin to truly recognize its presence. From the recognition of love's presence comes appreciation, provided we don't let fear overpower our decision. Be aware that fear is the seed from which many other blocks to love manifest. Other manifestations are guilt, judgment, anger, jealousy, control, manipulation, selfishness, and dishonesty. Fear, which stems from a belief in separation, is the foundation of the ego's thought system, while guilt is the cornerstone that sustains it, and that is why it is so psychologically and emotionally unsound. We are a unified being; therefore, using a thought system that is based on separation is, by its very nature, incompatible with who we really are. Remember, we were created with love; it is in us and available to us.

The paradoxical story that is presented in the Course states that we believe that the price of our existing as an individual was paid for by annihilating God. We went from being the one to being the many. The unseen to the seen, light into matter. The ego states thus, "You are eternally guilty and dammed to die. The only one who can save you now is I." It then proceeds by stating that, "Your mind is evil so forget you have one and turn to me to save you. I can offer you a divorce from your sin by seeing it in other rather than in yourself. " In the lower sleeping mind is the ancient memory (based on guilt) that individuality became forever wedded to us a Sinners. Truthfully, anytime we see only one half of a situation or person we

Rediscovering Your Authentic Self

are by definition, seeing half the coin- or making a mistake. Since the ego can't conceive of grace or pardon it also can't conceive of making a mistake it chooses instead to call half-truths sin.

Like all things outside of love, fear can be used to bless or to harm. For example, fire - in the positive, can be used to bring warmth, while in the negative can burn down our houses. In the positive, water can quench our thirst, while in the negative it can drown us. Likewise, a mother's womb carefully protects, nurtures, and feeds an evolving embryo into a baby. However, there will be a critical point in time when the baby is fully developed and must exit the womb. If, on the other hand, this natural expulsion is prevented in some way, then that same cocooning womb becomes a toxic and suffocating death trap.

Because fear causes us to move to the fight-or-flight response, defenses arise that can save our lives in life-threatening times. When fear is blocking love, it is a powerful deterrent to moving forward. A positive aspect of fear is that it is a powerful force that may actually protect us from sustaining injury in situations of physical, emotional, or psychological danger. In earlier stages of human development and consciousness, fear was a protector. Through the powerful fight-or-flight mechanism, humans survived and evolved. Fear did have a place in our evolution. But now, it need not control each decision we make. There are times and points, therefore, where fear is no longer a protector, but a dangerous ally. For this reason, discretion is necessary.

For the most part, at our present level of consciousness, fear is the first reaction at times of powerlessness — but we need not stay in a fearful frame of mind. Empowered and encouraged by the love of God and His Angels, we can immediately move on to love as the next reaction, and thus transcend fear. As we awaken, we strengthen our conscious ability to deal with, and overlook, fear. Although we may still recognize the presence of fear in a person, place, or situation, we no longer need to be its hostage. Fear will eventually banished from the mind as a response mechanism. When this happens to us individually, it ultimately affects us all collectively.

Moreah Ragusa

What Blocks Love?

Fear blocks love, and it is generally linked to our need for power. We seem to be afraid of surrendering to our innocence and to the innocence of others. This is so because to maintain innocence surrenders guilt and that is insane to the ego. *"Thoughts of God [innocence] are unacceptable to the ego, because they clearly point to the nonexistence of the ego itself."* (T-4.V.2:2; parentheses added)

When we are afraid, we feel powerless and put up defenses as a protective shield. We do so in the hope that this will take away our fear. Of course, it doesn't work because *"all defenses do what they defend."* (T-17.IV.7:1) The goal behind a defense is two-fold: first it is to prove our innocence, and second, to establish that since we are innocent, the other isn't. *"Ideas leave not their source."* (T-26.VII.4:7) This maintains the idea of separation through proclamation of the other's guilt, which is key in establishing the life of the ego.

Remember that to defend something means that it is at risk of being taken. If it can be taken, it is not real. And that is why defenses don't protect truth, as they seem to. Instead, they are the arsenals that the ego uses to sustain guilt. Of course, the ego proclaims that this is the only way to maintain our innocence. Consequently, there is no alternative but to navigate through life assessing who is worthy of our love and who is trustworthy enough to allow us to lower our defenses. Naturally, we will be in a continuing search for that "special someone" who is safe enough to love. Yet, since we are afraid to love on the deepest level, and

Rediscovering Your Authentic Self

because we associate love with a melting in of who we are, our heart and lower mind are in constant conflict.

The ego is quick to respond to this conflict by dictating that it is only safe for us to love if we follow the ego's rules. As a result, we ultimately feel as if it were our duty to police the Universe, and to make sure that all is governed according to our individual rules. We then proceed to do this with our families, our peers, our businesses, and ourselves. And we project onto others the rules that we set for ourselves. These rule projections, such as helplessness and defensiveness, are what blocks love. To make this concept easier to understand, I would like to share the following story:

One day, I offered to loan my new car to a friend of mine. Immediately after making the offer, I felt a twinge in my gut. I asked for guidance and, through it, was assured that my car would not be seriously damaged. What was clear to me was that I was about to undergo a lesson in love. In my recent New Year's resolution, I had just asked for some learning experiences to help me live with an open heart, to make me aware of any of the blocks within my mind to love's presence. This lesson was the answer to my prayer.

My friend not only needed to borrow my car, but she also had to find someone to watch her two-year-old son while she met with a friend for lunch to celebrate her birthday. So, in addition to my car, I offered that my daughter would baby-sit.

When my friend returned three hours later, she asked me if I had gotten a new car. I proudly smiled yes, and told her that I had thought it would be a wonderful surprise for her to drive in my new luxury car. She then announced that a large rock had hit and severely cracked my windshield. I stood silenced, not sure of what I should say. She commented that "these things always happen" and that it was unfortunate it happened when she was driving my car. I explained that I did not have windshield coverage and that it would cost about seven hundred dollars to replace the windshield. Just then, one of my clients arrived. My friend quickly left, and nothing further was said about the cracked windshield.

I was quite shaken and confused as to what I should do, so I turned within and asked for guidance. The inner voice of the Holy Spirit asked me to write down the reasons why I was upset with my friend. In doing so, I realized that I was troubled because she had failed to thank me for lending her the car. She hadn't offered to pay for the replacement of the windshield — not even to *share* the cost. She failed to treat me as I felt a friend should treat another friend.

Then the Holy Spirit asked me if I had ever done any of these things. I had to reply with an honest yes; in some form or another, I had done them all. I remembered borrowing a book, accidentally tearing the page and not replacing the book, although I felt it would have been right to do so. I remembered times that friends made me a cup of tea, and I left their home having failed to say thank you — although I was grateful. And I remembered feeling too afraid to share pertinent information with a friend — information that she deserved to know — for fear that she would be angry with me. Then the Holy Spirit asked me if I felt that I had been forgiven for these mistakes. Yes, was my reply once again. The Holy Spirit then asked if I felt that my friend should be forgiven. Yes, I replied, but my concern was coming from the belief that it was my place, as a spiritual friend, to share with her my upset. I wanted to do this so that we could correct the situation.

I had often advised my clients to give the information that was needed to the person they were upset with. Yet, somehow I felt that this was not what this particular lesson was about. The following day, I awoke and again began to pray for guidance. I recognized that there was tremendous power in choosing to pardon. I realized that I was being given the opportunity to leave my heart open during an upset, rather than close it due to my opinions about how the situation should have been handled.

A line from *A Course in Miracles* spoke softly in my mind, "Do I want to be right, or do I want to have peace?" Peace is what I wanted. I decided that it was not my duty to project my beliefs about how a friend should treat a friend. Those were my beliefs, and I should live by them, but I had no right to expect the same from my friend. I decided that my worth was not in my friendship, and that I could not be made to feel that I was a doormat without my own permission. I decided rather to hold fast to my God-given identity as love.

Because my identity includes my friend, it also included our combined innocence. I had taught my children, my family, my friends, and my clients, that we are not what we do, and I realized that it was time for me to walk, rather than talk, that truth. My friend called a few days later, and as I recognized her voice on the phone, my heart filled with love for her like it had never done before. She made no reference to the windshield crack, and I no longer needed her to do so. I paid to replace the windshield and expected that to be the end of the matter.

Three weeks later, however, on the advice of my husband, I called my insurance company to see if, by chance, windshield coverage had been placed on my car. My agent immediately responded that he was certain that I hadn't included that coverage in my policy, but that he would pull up the file, just to be sure, and let me know. To both his and my surprise, the coverage was in place. He told me to submit my bill for reimbursement.

What blocks our awareness of love's presence is our fear of being unified; unified with God, and with everything else in the Universe. Most of all, we are terrified to be unified with each other. To recognize the innocence that God has placed in others is terrifying, because it reflects our own innocence. The ego's belief in our guilt fuels an absolute need to judge situations, as well as each other. When we buy into the ego's belief, it triggers a common defense mechanism within us — judgment. The ego commands that when we judge others, our own guilt is diminished, and therefore we can temporarily become innocent. Thus the underlying idea, engendered by society, is "give to get rid of." Through this approach, of getting rid of our feelings of guilt through projection, we satisfy the ego for the moment. Feelings of guilt and judgment will sustain this belief while we are separated (from God, from all things in the Universe, and from each other), which ultimately sustains the ego's life.

If this thought system seems insane to you, you are absolutely right. The ego fears the unity that love provides. This fear, held out by the ego, encourages us to feel powerless. There is no strength in being alone, yet that's exactly how the ego wants us to feel, so that it might play the role of savior.

Another block to our awareness of love's presence is the belief that there is always some excuse not to love. As we awaken to our identities, we will remember our part in God's plan. We will come together and once again accept our function as miracle workers. We will finally accept the atonement for ourselves, which in turn joins us to each person we meet. In the East, they have a word symbolizing this joining; it is *Namaste*. It means, "I celebrate the place within me where we are one."

Rediscovering Your Authentic Self

The choices we make are reflective of who we think we are.

Moreah Ragusa

Part Two

The Power of Choice

Part Two - *The Power of Choice*   87

- Choice   89
- Inauthentic and Authentic Power   93
- Relationship Levels   97
- Transcending Defense Mechanisms   101
- Cause and Effect   107
- Reflection and Projection   111
- Heaven or Hell?   117
- Creating Heaven on Earth   119
- To Live in the Moment   127
- Solving Time Conflicts   133
- Miracles   135
- The Mind's Role in Illness   137

Moreah Ragusa

Choice

As human beings, we are destined to make choices. Each day, we are expected to make a myriad of decisions, some of which are unconscious, while others are conscious. We must decide what to wear, what to make for lunch and dinner, and what route to take to work. These are the smaller decisions that we must make on a daily basis, and generally they will not leave us feeling stressed. However, most of us are apprehensive about making decisions that will propel life changes. What initiates this fear are the beliefs that we should know the outcome and that there is a right and a wrong choice. Because not knowing is an insult to our ego, it responds promptly.
The physical world is in constant change, and so we are prone to feel insecure. The world's changing nature is due to the fact that it is itself an "out-picturing" of a mind split off from its reality as a knower. The learning mind is therefore mirrored in the physical experience. There is no question that our minds possess great power. Stop and consider that the entire phenomenal world is the direct product of our thought of separation. From this contemplation, we can truly appreciate the mind's power.

> *No one who understands what you have learned, how carefully you learned it, and the pains to which you went to practice and repeat the lessons endlessly, in every form you could conceive of them, could ever doubt the power of your learning skill.*

Rediscovering Your Authentic Self

There is no greater power in the world. The world was made by it, and even now depends on nothing else. (T-31.I.3:1-3)

Because our minds made this world through the idea of separation, the mind can also change or modify it. For this reason, it is up to us, decision by decision, to allow the lower, fear-ridden mind to react or the higher mind that emanates love. The choices we make as individuals, moment by moment, will change our individual experience and eventually the world as a collective experience.

The lower (ego) mind strives for solidity and control as it seeks out security. It believes that security comes from governing, planning, and organizing the people and events in our lives. Our lower mind sets up ideals and measures everything against those ideals. We have an image of what an ideal parent, child, or sibling should act like, what an ideal job is, and how an ideal partnership with our mate should be. I remember watching *Little House on the Prairie* on television and dreaming of having a family unit that would be as loving, safe, and solid, as this one appeared to be. The character played by Michael Landon was the ideal father, and I measured all fathers against that ideal. Similarly, one of my ideals of external power was formed at age seventeen from watching the TV program *Dallas*.

We have been conditioned to feel as though neither our lives nor ourselves measure up. The constant bombardment of external ideals presented through movies, television, books, and fantasies makes us feel inadequate — we fear that we're not good enough. But when the mind begins to heal and subsequently to remember and awaken, fear no longer operates as its foundation. Consequently, the fear of making a decision diminishes as we feel more secure, and we trust in our universe.

In *A Course in Miracles,* we are taught to let the Holy Spirit decide for us, on behalf of our true identity. We have trust in Its decision because It is aware of who we are, and knows all the unforeseen aspects and people that are involved in the decision we are about to make.

"Let go — let God," is a common phrase that I live by. Most peoples' fear around this phrase is that God does not fully understand all of the details within the decision they have to make. Or that He will forget about our file or its importance. We further believe that

what God wants us to do is something we don't want to do — a direct reflection of our belief that a relationship with God entails the sacrifice of our desires. On some level, we believe that God is out of accord with where our soul's ability and experience lie. We forget that we received those very qualities from our source in the first place and that it is our right to employ our God-given talents. God understands — it is we who do not.

We are only ever asked to make one decision, and that decision is whether we want to perceive a situation or person through the eyes of love, or through the eyes of fear. Daily we choose to experience ourselves as the child of God or the child of the ego. In the end, it is our *perception* that will guide our action. Since perception is not always an accurate out-picturing of the truth, we are really asking the One who knows to decide for us. This decision allows our minds to return to peace, to once again operate through faith and trust, rather than through the ego's fear, control, and manipulation.

One of my clients is just learning and living by the principles of *A Course in Miracles*. In the following story, I would like to share her direct experience of the liberating power of choice.

Nancy is the owner/operator of an outfitting business that owns rental property. One bright Monday morning, she received a call from a staff member, alerting her to severe damage found in a basement suite that had just been vacated. The caller urged Nancy to go and look at the damage, but instead, Nancy responded: "You know what? — I'm having a great day, so I'm not going to go and look."

The next day, she received another call, and this time she was informed that, at the request of her business partner, the police had been called in and were filing a report. Again, she was urged to come down right away. "You know — I'm having another great day and I choose not to come down," was her response.

Her staff were amazed because this was not how they had expected their boss to respond, based on reactions they had seen from her in the past. On the third day, Nancy received another call requesting her to view the property, and again she responded with, "I know you're not going to believe this, but I'm having another great day. Please just ask one of the repairmen to do the repairs."

Rediscovering Your Authentic Self

The following week, Nancy's insistent employee handed her a stack of pictures with the top one exposed. "Wow!" said Nancy, "They certainly were serious about wrecking the place, but you know — I'm having a great day." She handed the pictures back to the employee without viewing them.

Happiness is a decision we make. Nancy and I had discussed this at great length. She now understands this concept perfectly and has learned to apply it in her life.

Moreah Ragusa

Inauthentic and Authentic Power

We live in a world of relationships. We have relationships with people, with our jobs, our cars, our environment, our money, our God, and ourselves. We are continually searching for power. What we are actually seeking, however, is our inherent innocence, which is reflective of our security, and we intrinsically know that power is security. *True power comes from owning one's identity, while inauthentic power or force comes from one's search for that identity.* A person who has true power does not seek to control others. The desire to control comes from an inner feeling of guilt and powerlessness. When we have true power, we are kind, generous, compassionate, gentle, caring, and forgiving to those who are temporarily feeling powerless. Knowledge is power, because it does not need to defend its position, it simply knows and is confident. Knowledge comes from identity and, like love, it awaits our invitation.

In order to obtain authentic power, we must be willing to surrender our defenses. To defend is to attack. To attack is to divide, and to divide is to engender powerlessness. Authentic power comes from a sense of unity as it accepts all people and all conditions within itself. Authentic power recognizes that powerlessness comes from fear and therefore is not real.

> *Defenses are not unintentional, nor are they made without awareness. They are secret, magic wands you wave when truth appears to threaten what you would believe. They seem to be unconscious but*

Rediscovering Your Authentic Self

because of the rapidity with which you choose to use them. In that second, even less in which the choice is made, you recognize exactly what you would attempt to do, and then proceed to think that it is done. But afterwards, your plan requires that you must forget you made it, so it seems to be external to your own intent; a happening beyond your state of mind, an outcome with a real effect on you, instead of one effected by yourself. (W-pI.136.3;4:3)

In this way the ego seeks to "resolve" its problems, not at their source, but where they were not made. And thus it seeks to guarantee there will be no solution. (T-17.III.6:1-2)

When we feel powerless within our relationships, we are apt to recoil within ourselves. Then we move into "defend—attack—manipulate" mode. We turn to specific defense tactics that we learned from our parents, from other role models, and from society as a whole. In order to harness our true power, we must take ownership of, and responsibility for, all aspects of our life.

In this perfectly and infinitely organized universe we must trust that there are no mistakes and no coincidences. In light of this, have you ever stopped to consider that, as an eternal soul traveling in time, you *chose* your birth parents? Why do you think you chose *them*? We chose our birth parents in order to experience which personality traits work as blocks to our giving or receiving love. Our parents were indeed carefully chosen by our souls before we incarnated, because our souls knew that they would be able to demonstrate to us the defense tactics that our souls wished to transcend or to overcome. For example, your soul may have seen a need to transcend its feelings of powerlessness and helplessness in relationship to the defense tactics within its family dynamics. Consequently, parents become the primary actors in our play, as they are the most important soul relationships we have as we evolve.

Let's suggest that some of the specific defense tactics within my particular family were control, manipulation, and perfectionism. During my childhood, I would have watched either one or both parents enact these defenses in their twisted hope that by doing so they would regain their individual power. As a child, I would have watched one of my parents appear more powerful, while at the same time watching the other fall into powerlessness as a result. We can see this every day! Through my observations, I would have learned what appeared to be the proper rules of response in my world. I would also have learned that inducing guilt was a powerful weapon to use in order to take back lost power.

Let's further say that my soul's mission would include being prepared to resist and hold its power in place while in the proximity of someone acting out these specific defenses that I had witnessed. Naturally, at first, I might try to repeat my parents' drama, to make my partner feel guilty in order to stop him from controlling me. However, I will eventually come to learn that this is not the way to reclaim power honestly. Authentic power is attained and sustained by *not* responding to another's defense tactics. Choosing to be defenseless is a powerful way to regain power from a belief system that we no longer wish to be imprisoned by. Society has programmed us to associate defenselessness with powerlessness, but we must learn to escape this misaligned perception. When we own our defenselessness, we own our innocence, and thereby regain authentic power. Try this the next time you feel the urge to attack in response to someone else's defense tactics.

Since I did indeed have a very manipulative, controlling mother, I learned to "act" perfectly. I was afraid of her anger and, in turn, did my very best to always please her. I learned that if I was perfect, I could keep her intimidating and controlling defenses at bay. I also learned that through my own manipulating, I could effectively keep peace and order in all areas of my life. As a result of this childhood scenario, my soul has repeatedly attracted me to marriages with men who were intimidators via control. I now know that it is my soul's mission to transcend the programmed "I must be perfect" role. That role, having come from a feeling of helplessness, produced within me feelings of disempowerment and, at its extreme, rage. Therefore, my defenseless strategy was not authentic as it stemmed from an inauthentic me. My sense of being inadequate fostered rage because I was in effect manipulating my true feelings. The misguided message I was getting was, *"I am what I do, and if I don't do anything, I am useless."* In my first marriage, my husband controlled me through intimidation, and this was easily seen by others. Through his intimidation, I experienced gross verbal

Rediscovering Your Authentic Self

unkindness. My learned passive-aggressive behavior tempted me into submission. As I healed, I learned to hold on to my power, with the result that my sense of self-worth increased.

In my second marriage, the drama of intimidation by control actually increased in intensity, but from my new perspective, it appeared to have lessened on some levels. My second husband was an alcoholic. Because my father suffered from alcoholism, my choice to attract a partner who had this illness was made to nurture my healing. Once again, I was offered the drama of intimidation, this time being acted out by a husband experiencing alcoholism. This, in turn, resulted in a barrage of tearing verbal attacks. Since my self-worth had increased, it now took more intimidation than in the previous marriage to get me to surrender my power. With time, I was once again able to increase my self-worth enough to end that marriage. My sense of self continued to increase, and I made a decision to simply accept my husband as he was and where he was on his journey. His values and mine had become very different, the needed effort to sustain both became work that I was no longer willing to do. As a result of that realization, I began to feel a sense of closure from the task for which our souls had been brought together. Within months we Separated- then lovingly divorced.

Relationship Levels

ACIM teaches us that there are three levels on which relationships come together, and we will explore these at length in Part Three, which addresses relationships. On the first of the three levels, there is the casual, or what we might consider to be the "chance" or coincidental meeting, but which, we are taught, is no accident. Then there is a more in-depth level of relationships where two souls are given an opportunity to heal their minds and learn to love unconditionally. These relations appear in the form of co-workers, spouses, friendships, and love relationships. And lastly, there are the life partners, where two people have a lifelong relationship in which *a perfect balance* of growing and healing is afforded *both souls*. We've all tried to understand the dynamics that gave rise to the break-up of a relationship. We've heard the familiar phrases that people "grew apart," or that they "just didn't see eye to eye anymore." In my case, both had become true. However, with my acceptance of my husband's character came an understanding that even my second marriage was a success, in that it had afforded many opportunities to increase forgiveness, self-awareness, authentic identity, and self-love for both of us. It is what I chose to do with my heightened awareness that ultimately determined my future in that couple relationship. Although my second marriage ended, my relationship with my second husband did not. Because we share parenting responsibilities for our two sons, the lessons that were presented in the marriage continue, although my reaction to those triggers has changed. In fact, the lessons that were afforded me

Rediscovering Your Authentic Self

during this marriage continue through a mutual desire with my ex-husband to lovingly raise our sons. For me, acceptance has remained my key to peace beyond the marriage.

This may appear to be a dichotomy, but in my third marriage, the intimidator archetype via control is the greatest of all three marriages! An archetype is a universal pattern or picture that is associated with a word, such as "hero," or "mother." The picture or association that is reflected by such a word is defined as the archetype. The deeper I went inside my mind, the more concentrated became the core issues that I had to heal. Consequently, my ability to transcend this situation is now possible only through my improved self-love and because my authentic power has so greatly increased. To transcend this archetype means that I am able to maintain an open and loving heart, no matter what is presented. My authentic identity is becoming so prominent that acceptance of my husband is *natural*. I am no longer threatened by his drama of intimidation, which, if unchecked, would again trigger my defensiveness and misdirected need to vie for power in the relationship.

Let me give you an illustration of what this means. Let's say that I'm an Ivy plant breaking through the soil. At first, the rupturing of the soil above me might look catastrophic. However, if someone is watching, they will soon see my tender green sprout emerging. Let's further say that the place that I have chosen to break ground in is next to a very high brick wall. I have within me an intelligence that urges me upward to find the sun. The wall is so tall that I must climb and climb and climb. When I finally reach the top of the wall, the sun's rays nurture me. As I look down, I stand in awe of the distance I have grown. I realize in wonder and amazement that it was really the *wall* that supported my climb.

People often believe that as they are transcending another's defense mechanism such as control, their own control is decreasing as they increase in power. This is not true. By nature, my sense of power increases as I increase my awareness and my sense of self. Power and the opposition to that power are always proportionate in polarity, so we are continually offered the opportunity to grow through them. Initially, it might seem as if the archetype you are facing were a big gray monster, but through your transcendence, that monster will decrease in its ability to strike you, and ultimately in its intensity.

Moreah Ragusa

For instance, if I am attracting people that have control issues, I must recognize and take ownership of the fact that I am attracting them to me so that I might heal through seeing my own internal issues around control. The more internal control I possess from owning my authentic identity, the less a controlling person can pull me off center. The more centered I become; the bigger the control issue must appear to be in order to test my current level of power and stability. This cycle will continue until my mind is healed of the belief in external power. At such a time that my mind is healed, I will begin demonstrating that power as seen in the life and teachings of Lord Jesus, Lord Buddha, and Lord Krishna. The way we can know that we have transcended one of these archetypal patterns is when we are in the presence of a person who is enacting them, and we no longer feel any discomfort within our bodies or allow our hearts to constrict while in their presence. What essentially happens is that in reflection of our accepted identity, we are finally ready to accept others exactly as they are, and not as they appear.

Rediscovering Your Authentic Self

It is not our responsibility to remove our character defects, but rather it is through the acceptance of our reality that those defects fall away.

Moreah Ragusa

Transcending Defense Mechanisms

To authentically transcend defense mechanisms such as control, manipulation, dishonesty, or victimization, we need to increase our willpower *not* to respond. We can do this through our heightened awareness that fear is the perpetrator. In order for us to have enough strength within us to not feel threatened, we must nurture a powerful sense of self, which ultimately gives rise to an increased amount of willpower.

During Jesus' sovereignty upon the earth, He was greatly tempted by these archetypal patterns until eventually they had no power to seduce Him. For instance, His guidance to "turn the other cheek" was offered because He, too, experienced unkindness. His decision not to respond in a loveless manner gave Him power over unkindness. In His decision to enter the desert and go for forty days and forty nights without food, He was given the opportunity to meet, among others, the archetype of the saboteur. In honoring His decision, He triumphed over this archetype.

Jesus shares the Christ Mind with us, and consequently the belief systems that we are also working to transcend. For this reason, He also needed to be tempted. As He was able to transcend all archetypal patterns, which vie for power, He achieved His dominion not only for Himself but also for all of mankind. In this sense, He delivered us from the evil, which we now define as fear. Because of Jesus' clarity of identity, temptations did not overcome Him in His life. In His accomplishment was our accomplishment also done, because we share one mind. It is our resistance to accept our perfection that keeps us journeying on our path to personal awakening. When we trust that His message is that *only love is real*, we are able to embrace that we are innocent, free, and delivered.

Our attempt to transcend the control drama does not mean that we must deny our feelings to respond if they are there! We are told to bring these feelings of resentment and disempowerment to the Holy Spirit that It might heal our minds. Our personality defects are not a part of our authentic identity, so we must bring them to the Holy Spirit that knows who we are. It is not our responsibility to remove our character defects, but rather it is through the acceptance of our reality that those defects fall away. It is our *willingness* to bring our thoughts of fear and frustration to the Holy Spirit that liberates us. In doing so, *we discover that it is our feelings of separation from God that are healed. Consequently, as our self-love increases, any urges to strike back at others subsides. In addition our protective defense mechanisms begin to diminish and ultimately disappear.* Over my three marriages, my sense of self increased in direct proportion to the intimidator control defense mechanism that I was (and *am!*) transcending at a given time.

The bigger the temptation becomes to get sucked into another's defense mechanism drama, the more power can be attained by *not* getting sucked in. The greater the soul becomes, the greater the defense obstacle can appear, until finally it is no longer a belief and simply disappears. Consider some of the enlightened beings who have demonstrated this: Mother Theresa, through unconditional love and acceptance, demonstrated her faith that God's perfection was in India amongst the ill and impoverished. Gandhi demonstrated his conviction towards maintaining peace. The Dalai Lama has perfectly defined defenselessness. Why do you suppose each of these souls has had to overcome such adversity? Because they were aware that they had the power to transcend such suffering. On some level, they also needed the experience of overcoming such suffering through the application of that power — *the power of love.*

Through psychological study and exploration, I have discovered that we each have twelve of these archetypal defense mechanisms. There are four that are shared by all of us; they are: saboteur, child, prostitute, and victim. The other eight are unique to our individual families. The family unit as a whole works on the same defense archetypes. The easiest way to identify what your family's archetypes are is to call to mind the strengths and the weaknesses in the personalities of your mother and father. You will find defense issues such as abandonment, judgment, and denial, and roles such as controller, intimidator, manipulator, perfectionist, liar, and deceiver. Specific traits define archetypal roles such as rescuer, hero, matriarch, and ruler. The roles that we embody can be used in either constructive or destructive ways. We must learn to use these archetypal patterns in positive rather than negative ways.

For instance, the *saboteur* archetype reflects a lack of willpower and can tempt us into putting aside goals that we have set for ourselves. If this archetype is unsuccessful and, instead of succumbing to its influence, we exercise our power to react positively, we will actually *gain* willpower. By remaining persistent in the pursuit of our goals, we continually strengthen our willpower.

The *child* archetype encourages us to relinquish responsibility for what we create, but on the positive side, it has the capability of welcoming us to act responsibly. In the negative, this same archetype prompts us to react without love when another has acted that way. "Well, he started it!" is a statement typical of this archetype. In the positive, the *child* pattern affords us the opportunity to overlook and forgive fear in its many forms. Being responsible for what we think encourages us to understand that we are the master of our life.

The *prostitute* archetype will tempt us into ignoring our inner guidance and move away from an unhealthy situation. We ignore this guidance because we believe that a change in the direction, and thus the unknown, may hold more fear than the present unhealthy situation. For instance, I may have a conflict of opinion with my landlord, and my guidance might suggest a discussion to find an amicable solution for both. The *prostitute* archetype will raise thoughts of conflict and possible eviction. The thought of a potential eviction might trigger feelings of abandonment and the deep feelings of inadequacy that I have been suppressing. The whole idea of initiating communication with the landlord will then be discarded as it is being associated with greater loss than gain. On the positive side, however, the *prostitute* archetype teaches us that when we move forward facing our hidden beliefs and fears, we are able to transcend them as we plug into the laws of love that embrace faith and trust.

Rediscovering Your Authentic Self

Some of the strengths that you may identify in your parents' personalities are kindness, understanding, honesty, forgiveness, compassion, generosity, and affection. The strengths and weaknesses that you discover in your parents' personalities are also yours. As discussed earlier, you will have chosen your parents based on karmic debt and soul agreements. The determiners of those agreements are soul-engendered by the types of "dramas" that you have both given and received in interactions with these souls. In addition, karma is built by the issues that have predominantly been the focus of your mental activity since the falling asleep to your identity began. You can access these archetypal patterns through deep introspection and meditation. In doing so, you may discover that your soul wanted and needed to learn about self-reliance. The parents you have chosen will have agreed to afford you such opportunities through the archetypes that are also part of their learning experience. Prior to your incarnation, you will have decided that these particular strengths and weaknesses had the greatest capacity for helping you to attain your goal of awakening. Your soul's mission is to be in the proximity of the weaknesses it needs to transcend, while not losing its (your) sense of self and the authentic power that embraces you.

All of your relationships will contain the strengths and weaknesses of your parents. The people that you will like will be those who mirror your own strengths. The people that you will dislike will be those who mirror back your own weaknesses, which are actually the archetypal patterns that tempt you into feeling weak. You may have had an intimidating and controlling parent, but that does not necessarily mean that you will control others in the same fashion you were controlled. Instead of trying to control others, you may make desperate attempts to control yourself to please others.

Trying to control self is a coping mechanism that I have also used. In my case, my wound was coming from the belief that others were controlling me; therefore, what was being mirrored is that, unconsciously, I felt out of control. On some level, I was getting in touch with feelings of not being able to take on responsibility. This, of course, is an outrage to the ego. The ego's response was, therefore, a subdued feeling of powerlessness, which consistently resulted in my "trying at all costs" to be perfect in order to diminish the pain of my feelings of inadequacy. By burying the real issues, I was able to control others via the "model of perfection" — a role that I would resent my husbands for inducing!

The madness of this cycle was unending until I finally recognized and owned my part in the sustaining of the control drama. The option to not respond to a controlling person had never been modeled to me in my childhood — I made a conscious choice to learn not to respond with my own fear. I ultimately realized that my need to feel safe, which engendered my need to control others through behavior, was being mirrored as the same need that each husband had. My ability to forgive myself enabled me to be willing to forgive them also. Once again, I had experienced the principle emphasized in the Course, that *I am free to save myself by saving others*. I had recognized that the people in my life had, in fact, the same core wounds as I did, and that through the intercession of the Holy Spirit, our relationship could be healed.

In my ability to forgive is the gift that I, too, might be forgiven.

Moreah Ragusa

Cause and Effect

We each have an individual and highly unique relationship with the world. We are the master creators of our world as it appears. *A Course in Miracles* continuously reminds us that the world is within our minds. *"I am responsible for what I see. I choose the feelings I experience, and I decide upon the goal I would achieve. And everything that seems to happen to me I ask for, and receive as I have asked."* (T-21.II.2:3-5)

Although it is true that on one level, we are all affected by the world around us, it is also emphasized that we are responsible for our reaction to it. In addition, we are reminded that we are also responsible for what happens to us. Therefore, a stepping-stone towards achieving mastery is to know that expectation is, in fact, a determiner of experience.

Likewise, authentic power is harnessed through accepting that we outwardly project, through the filter of our beliefs, the inner world that we interact with. In this sense, we are both the directors and the actors of the play and everything else we experience, including the people in our lives, and the surrounding props. Our props, so to speak, represent our fears and beliefs, and so they will be reflected back to us. In understanding this, we become more aware that the decision of how to create our life is driven by our understanding of who we are, and subsequently what our purpose is. If we believe this to be true, then our world is both a reflection and the effect of what we think.

Rediscovering Your Authentic Self

We are taught that there are no coincidences, and that each person we meet and every situation we are in is drawn into our experience by a karmic law of cause and effect. ACIM is a course in cause, meaning its aim is to teach us about what we think and how that thought creates our experience. Through the power of the Holy Spirit, and the use of the atonement principle, we are then able to heal the unwanted effects in our life. It is important to remember that we are asked to take responsibility for our life.

We are taught that the people in our lives are our guests. They are actors fulfilling their role within our part of the universal play. They have been given a particular role in order that we might interact with them to better understand our own core beliefs. Let's say that, for instance, my soul had a great desire to practice forgiveness in this lifetime. I might write into my script a person who would abduct and harm my child, and thus would require my forgiveness. This may seem absurd, but try to stay with the principle here as it relates to the developing and transcending nature of the soul. The soul that will be chosen to play the role of the abductor in my script will be one with whom my child and I have a karmic agreement — one we both wish to transcend. "An eye for an eye," or "As I give, so shall I receive." For instance, in another congruent lifetime, *I* may have been the abductor of *their* child. Or possibly my child played the role of abductor, and the perpetrator in this scenario was the forgiving parent in another. The goal of my own soul will be to forgive this person through knowing and accepting that the karmic law of cause and effect will balance out our debt.

In my ability to forgive is the gift that I, too, might be forgiven. Although I will not have a conscious memory of creating this script, I can have faith that the Universe records all events that transpire between souls and, therefore, there is no soul in a relationship to another soul that has not been drawn to that soul by karmic law. The karmic law of "an eye for an eye," and "a tooth for a tooth," does not refer to human justice, it refers to universal justice, which means that we must receive that which we have given. It also means that we are not equipped to judge the agreement between two souls, because we simply do not have enough karmic information about what agreements are between them. *The way that all karmic debts are healed between people is through the conscious act of forgiveness.*

Moreah Ragusa

A few years ago, people in North America were deeply touched by headlines reflecting a couple's tragic loss of their child. We heard the story of the minister who had to endure the horrific pain of the loss of his son. A drunk driver had caused the death. The reason that this minister touched the hearts of many was that he almost immediately forgave the driver. Because of the minister's ability to forgive, and his trust that it was his child's time to return to his natural soul state, a karmic debt between his soul and that of the assailant was ended. This minister made the decision to forgive instead of condemn, and to trust and heal rather than doubt and be angry. From this individual's choices, the world saw that such an act of faith and unconditional love was possible. In his ability to forgive was it demonstrated to the world that through love, fear is abolished. Within this minister was perfect faith in God and his soul's plan for ascension.

Cause is thought, and effect is experience. The relationship between cause and effect is indivisible as well as interdependent. A cause without an effect is impossibility, as is the reverse is true —an effect cannot happen without a cause. In Heaven, God is first Cause and His Son is His effect. In order for God to be a Father, He needed a Son. God does not, however, need us to be His creation in order to exist. God's existence is. His Fatherhood is, however, established through us. *"...the Father is a Father by His Son."* (T-28.II.1:2)

It is important to understand that if something is shown to have no effect, it cannot have a cause, according to universal law, and therefore it does not exist. The law of cause and effect functions both in Heaven and on earth. Cause is equated to mind or thinking, and effect is equated to action and form. Cause that is created through love, or by a mind connected to God will have eternal effects. In a parallel manner, a thought that is generated by a fearful mind will have a temporal effect versus the eternal. This law of cause and effect cannot be broken, but it can be explored to see if, in fact, the thought that was generated came from love or fear. The Holy Spirit's function then is to demonstrate that the ego that generates these false beliefs has no effect over the spirit that God created us to be.

What has no effect does not exist, and to the Holy Spirit the effects of error are nonexistent. By steadily and consistently canceling out all its effects,

Rediscovering Your Authentic Self

everywhere and in all respects, He teaches that the ego does not exist and proves it. (T-9.IV.5:5-6)

We are taught two primary principles in this regard. One is that cause, or thought, always creates form on some level, and another is that a thought never leaves the mind of the thinker.

Because of these facts, we are taught to heal our minds, which will result in thoughts that are used for love's purposes only. When we use our minds inappropriately, by perceiving through fear, we draw into our life experience that which reflects the thought. If I believe myself to be a victim, I will draw into my experience people who will victimize me in some fashion to help me fulfill my role. I remember in my earlier years believing that to be a martyr was to be holy. This belief was repeatedly reflected to me in painful experiences. During my childhood, children on the playground would continually tease me and throw stones at me, and in my teenage and early adult years, the condescending words, "Oh, you're just too nice!" reverberated painfully upon my ears and heart. What these children were teaching me is that if I wanted or needed to be a martyr, they were not going to be my friend. I suppose my role as a martyr engendered guilt within them, and they simply weren't interested in such a relationship. My prayer to God would be to release me from always feeling not good enough, abandoned, and unimportant. Meanwhile, I self-sabotaged my progress through the belief that being a martyr made me spiritually important.

Because we are not aware of the power of our beliefs, we often feel as if our prayers for help go unheard. In reality, however, our prayers are being answered perfectly in accordance with our belief system. I have come to learn that *the most powerful prayer that we can utter is that we might know ourselves as God knows us.* Thankfully, God *does* know us and is never mistaken in who we are. In His perfect trust and understanding of our power, He allows us to learn *life's greatest lesson — as you think, so shall you be.*

Moreah Ragusa

Reflection and Projection

The Course reminds us that the only purpose the world has is to show us our thoughts. The development of projection, which stems from perception, is a basic law of mind: we discover that, what we see within determines what we see without. For most, this seems frightening at first, because of what we believe ourselves to be, and also because of the apparent level of responsibility it places on us to keep conscious of what we believe, and thus think.

This is reflected in one of Jesus' primary teachings — "As it is within, so shall it be without." This teaching perfectly verifies this law. "**The world but demonstrates an ancient truth; you will believe that others do to you exactly what you think you did to them. But once deluded into blaming them you will not see the cause of what they do, because you want the guilt to rest on them. How childish is the petulant device to keep your innocence by pushing guilt outside yourself, but never letting go!**" (T-27.VIII.8:1-3)

By its nature, this process will determine how we view the world and, consequently, how we react to it. The steps that the mind follows are to first look within and then project out into the world that which we have seen within. We cannot avoid projecting, because this is the way the mind functions. The results, however, will greatly depend on how we choose to use the mind. The Course distinguishes between two different types of projection. The first one, "the correct use," is defined as "*extension,*" which is the natural out-picturing of the love that is accepted within. The second one is, as stated in ACIM, that an *"inappropriate use of extension, or projection, occurs when you believe that some emptiness or lack exists in you, and that you can fill it with your own ideas instead of truth."* (T-2.I.1.:7) Hence, what becomes apparent is the significance of learning of our unadulterated perfection and also accepting it.

The ego's goal, being contrary to the goal of the Spirit, is to always distort the "present" reality of a person or situation, in order to project what it views in us, namely guilt or lack. Then it places the lack or guilt onto the situation, and consequently feels "justified" in its attack. In keeping with the ego's purpose, which is always to maintain guilt (and which, of course, is in orientation to the past), the ego insists that we overlook the present. It does so in order to maintain our sins, and this, as we have seen, is what maintains the ego. Viscously then, the ego holds these sins against us in reference to the past, so that it can avoid the place of correction, which is always in the present. We can now see how projection so contaminates our relationships — both with our selves and with others.

As we have been shown, we are an idea within God's mind. Therefore, there is no separation between the idea and the mind that extended it to us. *"Ideas leave not their source, and their effects but seem to be apart from them."* (T-26.VII.4:7) We are the perfect reflection of God. As cause and effect means thought and experience, God is able to experience Himself as cause through experiencing us, as we are also able to experience our true self by accepting our cause. We, too, are able to experience ourselves as cause, through owning and experiencing what we think. *What we observe with love is known to be our creation, and what we observe with fear is known to be our hallucination.* This is the founding idea behind reflection. We will ultimately see ourselves in each other. The parts of ourselves that we see in others that we like, will remind us of our greatness. Conversely, the parts of ourselves that we see in others and that we despise, will reflect our powerlessness, guilt, and lack.

From this understanding, we might conclude that we are afraid of finding darkness in others or in ourselves, but this is not so, for in reality we are terrified of finding our light. Since light is properly understood by the ego as an aspect of God, the search for it is instilled as being dangerous. Because we have been nurtured to feel guilty and thus afraid of God, we in turn are terrified to seek the light in either others or ourselves. This is true because if we see it in others, we will on some level see it in ourselves, and this would be destructive to the ego. In the same way, light and darkness cannot co-exist, and neither can spirit and ego identities co-exist. For this reason, we are taught that we cannot serve two masters. We will ultimately either be host to God or hostage to the ego.

The Course emphasizes the ego's arrogance, as it first denies and then expels our true identities as the sons and daughters of God. Further, the madness continues as our perceived self-image, meaning the image that the ego has of us and which we accept as true, distorts what we seek to find. Because of the guilt that we are convinced is within us, we seek desperately to get rid of it. We become helplessly trapped within the way the mind operates and cannot be freed unless we find something that is within us but not of us (the Holy Spirit) to correct what we believe ourselves to be. Until we accept that identity as our only reality, we will remain terrified to see the light within.

Because we believe that we are sinners, we expect some form of punishment, which terrifies us of God and of love. For this reason, what we are truly afraid of is our brightness. I often remark to people that not nearly as much is expected from us as human beings, as would be expected of us as spiritual beings. As a "God-ling," we would live embracing patience, kindness, trust, humility, honor, and compassion. We would embrace the love that continuously surrounds us and we would accept it eternally. Recognizing that it is every soul's mission to regain its created identity, it is through mirroring these God-like traits that we attain our goal.

Everything in our experience is a reflection of our thoughts. The car we drive, the clothes we wear, the friends we choose, and the words we speak reflect our current belief of who we are. What our thinking also reflects is how worthy we feel we are to receive great things. Worthiness is intimately linked to our acceptance of abundance, and we'll address this in greater detail in the next chapter.

In light of these truths, we must learn to ask greater questions when we find ourselves in situations or experiences that we would like to alter. One of the great questions to ask is, "What is this situation reflecting back to me about a current belief that I'm holding?" or, "Why do I feel it necessary to receive that unkind

Rediscovering Your Authentic Self

remark or innuendo from my partner? Are my thoughts about myself abusive, and is my partner therefore mirroring them back to me?" Remembering that we always have a choice to change what we think will once again prove to be effective in restoring our authentic power.

When an action or event is being played out in your life, it is doing so to help you better understand what you are doing with your thinking. Rather than taking the victim role in your play, choose instead to once again be the director! Your higher Christ-self does not ask you to blindly receive a script and then follow it. It encourages you to remember that you are given the choice to direct your actions in accordance with who you truly are.

One of my clients has returned a great sense of peace to his mind through using what he defines as the "hot knife principle." Working in sales, he is at times met with slanted comments that attract his ego response. When someone offers him an opportunity to "bite" and thus get burned by another's ego — which, he has learned, will ultimately prompt his own ego to respond — he chooses to pass instead. He refers to this opportunity as the "hot knife offer." Repeatedly, his willpower and self-love have been strengthened through the choice to say, "No thanks, I no longer need to go there."

Oftentimes, we mistakenly hold a belief or perception about another person, situation, or issue. *Projection* occurs when that perception or belief has its foundation in one of our *own* currently held beliefs, not the other's belief or reality. In effect, the other person's reality and our own may be two totally different things. This is illustrated in this story taken from my file of personal recollections:

On a bright Sunday morning, approximately a year after my daughter had moved in after having lived with her father and stepmother for a while, she walked out of her room with a cautious look on her face. I was feeling overwhelmed by the amount of housework that seemed to be piling up around me, and I began assessing within my mind a belief that lately she simply wasn't doing enough around the house. I didn't say anything to her, but the look on my face and the energy leaving my body must have spoken louder than words. The blood in her face began to fade as fear embraced her body. I immediately began asking for her to do her part in the Sunday housecleaning event that was about to occur.

"Sure," she replied, seeming somewhat relieved. Seconds later she asked, "You're not mad?"

"Mad about what?" I questioned.

"You're not upset that I didn't come home last night until 5:30 in the morning?"

"I didn't know that you came home at 5:30 in the morning."

Her face began to sink once again. She told me how sorry she was and explained that she had fallen asleep on her boyfriend's couch. She then promised to be more careful in the future. She shared with my husband and me how frightened she had been of the consequences that she anticipated. She shared with us how different this situation would have been for her if she had still been living with her father and stepmother. She was truly terrified of what our reaction would be, based on her past experiences with her father. In the past, it had been demonstrated to her that, to some degree, she was what she did and that she was not trustworthy. I compassionately listened, and then told her that being more careful in the future would be fine. She continued speaking about how frightened she was of our finding out what time she had gotten home. My husband and I both understood and again articulated that we trusted her in her account of what had happened.

What occurred for both my daughter and myself was projection. For her, the thoughts of being in trouble for coming home so late caused her to believe that the gloomy look on my face was related to her lateness. Her past experience with her father and stepmother was now being projected onto myself and my husband in this situation. For me, her sheepishness seemed to confirm my belief that I needed to tell her that she had not been pulling her weight around the house. Neither projection was true, as both stemmed from past experiences, which caused each person to make assumptions without actually communicating them. Projection is the source of the majority of the conflicts that we experience. We can easily avoid these conflicts by simply living in the moment, listening carefully, and communicating clearly. It is when we have expectations and make assumptions that we get into trouble. You probably won't have to look back too far to see this in your own life.

Love is the way we walk in gratitude.

Moreah Ragusa

Heaven or **H**ell?

Throughout the Course we're taught that Heaven and hell are both a state of mind. Because everything is mind, spirit, or love, we can quickly realize that when we think through love, we experience Heaven, and when we think through fear, we experience hell. *We are taught very firmly in ACIM that neither Heaven nor hell are separate locations. They are levels of mind that extend thought, which gives birth to experiences.* From this we can reason out and understand that it is our choice whether we experience Heaven or hell in our lives. We are told that at the time of our physical death, we awaken and remember who we are. Many religious people believe that if a person has not lived according to the ten commandments, they will suffer in hell. This is true only to the extent that if we do not lead our lives through the principles of love and do unto others as we would have them do unto us, we experience the effects of fear that engender a state of mind known as hell.

A Course in Miracles is passionately aimed at releasing guilt and fear. Do you think for a moment that this could be accomplished by teaching people that their failure to live in accordance with God's laws will result in eternal punishment? When you truly understand the power of love, you will see that God does not manipulate his children through fear. God *is* love, and judgment which stems from fear is nowhere within that love. Judgment, in Course terms, is "as you think, so shall you experience."

As far as our individual ideas of God are concerned, we project our own ego identifications onto Him. If we remember that

Rediscovering Your Authentic Self

what we perceive in ourselves is what we will perceive in others, then our idea of what God is and how He works is directly related to who we perceive ourselves to be, and what we deem to be an appropriate response to a particular action. Therefore, our individual understanding of God changes as we better learn to understand who we truly are. We can see from this perspective that as we humans perceive and judge one another, we believe that God, too, would judge us in that same way.

To the ego, this kind of thinking makes perfect sense, but to love, it is insanity. Take suffering, for example. When we do not live in accordance with the laws of love, which were created to offer us eternal peace and joy, we suffer. This suffering stems from living by rules that were not created for God's holy sons and daughters. They are rules that were created to establish that we are separate entities in need of constant protection. When we suffer, it is not by God's will, nor by His hand, for His will for us is to live in perfect joy. *When we suffer, it is by our own decision.*

So this begs the question, why would anyone choose to suffer? The answer simply comes from the ego's belief that we are guilty and we deserve it.

Moreah Ragusa

Creating Heaven on Earth

To awaken to our identity is to realize that we can create Heaven on earth. When we live our life through the perception that "all is one," our peace and calm returns. To live in Heaven simply means that we recognize each other to be our brother and our savior. Our brothers and sisters are our saviors because it is through accepting them as they are that we are given the opportunity to heal our feelings of lack, which in turn unveil our deepest fears and help us to awaken to our identity.

An experience I once had demonstrated to me how the Holy Spirit can use all situations for Its purpose, which is always intended for the healing of our mind. We had a problem with the electrical wiring in the first location of the Angels Answers centre. The ensuing conflict with the landlord, which I could see coming and therefore wanted to run from at all costs, was an opportunity for healing, as far as the Holy Spirit was concerned. The problem had to do with insufficient power and circuits to maintain reasonable use of electricity, and repairs were required. I felt that the cost of these repairs was the responsibility of the landlord, because the space was being rented to us as being suitable for business occupancy. In the opinion of the electrician, however, it was unsuitable for both residential and commercial use. Reluctantly, I approached the landlord with this information. From the perspective of the Holy Spirit, this situation was offering me an opportunity to deal with conflict lovingly, when in the past, I would have just caved in, suppressing my feelings in order to avoid confrontation.

Rediscovering Your Authentic Self

I told the landlord that because our centre had non-profit status, I would be able to get the repairs done at a significantly lower cost, and that I was also willing to share in one-third of the repair costs. He was outraged at the idea that he should pay at all, and the matter was dropped. Day by day, the problem grew worse until one day, there was not even enough electricity to turn on the lights in the centre. I had no choice but to call the landlord back and again approach the situation. Again he insisted that it would be my responsibility to pay for the repair.

Deadlocked in these opposing views, I did two things: one was that I prayed and requested a miracle, and the second was that I followed my inner guidance and called a lawyer. The lawyer reviewed the lease terms, which appeared to be in the landlord's favor. However, the lawyer also suggested that the issue would really be between the landlord and the town if the electrical wiring was not up to code standard, considering that a license had been issued based on the assumption that the wiring was adequate. For me, finding out that such a code existed was the first of several miracles that would follow in connection with this situation. I have found that when I boldly move ahead in areas that I have been afraid to embrace, there are miracles that occur along the way to encourage me to keep going.

Once again, I picked up the phone and called the landlord. In the conversation that followed, he sidetracked from the electrical problem and raised a number of issues related to my tenancy that had been bothering him for some time. He did so regardless of the fact that all of these issues had already been dealt with and settled between myself and his wife, the other occupant in the building. For at least twenty minutes, he vented his anger and I defended my position. I pointed out to him that I had been an exceptional tenant because I had put in at least six thousand dollars in improvements, in addition to purchasing from his wife all the furnishings and decor for the centre. However, this argument was completely ignored, because the ego tends to overlook the positive in a situation or person. The call ended abruptly with the landlord saying that he would check into the situation himself.

Through the process of this telephone call, I met and overcame my fear of dealing with anyone, especially an intimidating male business figure, in a position of authority. From using my voice to share, not attack, I learned that I could speak honestly and still hold on to my identity as a child of God.

Ninety minutes passed before I received a call back from the landlord. He had indeed investigated the facts that I had presented and now realized just how sweet a deal it was. He was now happy to pay his part of the costs. He said that he was sorry for interfering in matters that had already been agreed on between his wife and myself and that he would butt out in the future. Further, he was hoping I would forgive his brashness. "Of course," I replied, fully conscious that we had both been given a new start, an opportunity to begin again.

When people are treating us unkindly, it is within our power to choose to pardon them and make the conscious decision to love them anyway. Initially, this may feel unnatural and even difficult. However, we are encouraged to be willing to accomplish our goal through atoning, and in so doing, join in the Holy Spirit's plan for salvation. The Holy Spirit teaches us that willingness is all that is necessary for the other person to fulfill his or her part in the atonement. We can offer love instead of hate to each person that we scripted into our play. This brings us nearer to the awakening of the whole Sonship. *It is easy to love someone who acts loving towards us; it is powerful to love someone who does not.*

The following story reflects another lesson in the power of trust and love in healing relationships:

My son Dustin came home from school one day, and I quickly recognized that he had been in a fight. He offered details about a boy named Lewis, of whom he had been afraid for the past three years. The two boys had attended the same elementary school and had quarreled with each other early in their relationship. Since that first fight, my now thirteen-year-old son lived in fear of ever again coming face to face with his assailant. Apparently, the day had come for Dustin to meet his fear and, once again, these boys met face to face. A few intimidating remarks from Lewis tempted my son to agree to settle the argument physically. The two boys fought for a long time — it felt like hours to Dustin. Exhausted, he called a cease to the fighting and spent the rest of the afternoon in the sick room, humbled, angry, and pretending to be ill.

After much discussion on the topic of fear, which also prompted me to get in touch with my own pain from similar

Rediscovering Your Authentic Self

childhood events, Dustin and I decided that he would return to school without giving further attention to the matter. I prayed for a miracle and asked that the angels protect him. Dustin was very much afraid that if I became involved in the situation, it would only escalate.

Everyone in our family thought that my son's assailant, being two years his senior, would have felt satisfied in Dustin's defeat. We were wrong. On the second day, Dustin returned even more battered and bruised than the day before. My heart sank as I looked into his bruised face, and I felt his feelings of powerlessness and pain. Once again, I was prompted to get in touch with my own childhood experiences that were reflected in the confrontation experienced by my son. We discussed karma and the law of cause and effect as I assured him that he was on some level, bringing on this experience. As part of the healing, both he and I relished in the possibility of getting back at his assailant. I was very hurt and angry and not about to pretend about how I felt. I knew that it was not psychologically healthy or "spiritual" to try and move my son into a state of forgiveness too soon. I knew that this would be a *process* for both him and me.

I told Dustin that I would have to intervene, as the attacks were otherwise likely to continue. He agreed, but said that he no longer wanted to attend that school. I promised him that he would be safe from now on because I was going to look into the situation. He was terrified, and I was angry. I knew that very soon I would begin my own process of forgiveness of both his assailant and those that had assailed me in the past. I immediately recognized that through my son I was given an opportunity to address an area of my own life that I had not yet healed.

Viewing the situation as if it were a motion picture, we talked about what might be the reason that he had given his assailant this role. He told me that he didn't know why but, shockingly, he did say that he now understood the Columbine incident and how children become so enraged that they enter schools and begin shooting. A powerful lesson in understanding was unfolding for him through his bruised level of empowerment. To be certain that he would be safe, he asked me if I would do an Angel reading for him, and I agreed.

I then asked the Holy Spirit to be a medium through which information could be passed. I joined my mind to Dustin's mind and began to receive impressions and information. (*In an Angel reading, I go to the place where all is one. In so doing, I am able to effortlessly see into the lives of others. I am able to communicate with non-physical beings at a level of mind that reflects unity consciousness.*) From this reading, we received confirmation of our belief that a boy who is this angry must have a reason. We were also told that Dustin's assailant was himself the victim of assault. His perpetrator was his own father, and he was filled with rage and fear and simply needed someone on whom to release these feelings.

    The following morning, Dustin and I headed to school to see what could be done to resolve the situation. That morning, the school's administrative staff was attending a meeting in a neighboring town. I spoke briefly with my son's teacher to bring him into the picture and to ensure that Dustin would be protected, of which the teacher assured us both. The following morning, I was unable to accompany Dustin to school because I was expecting a client from out of town. However, I promised Dustin that I would call and speak with the teacher to once again ensure his safety. I called repeatedly, but each time the phone was answered by the secretary's voice-mail, and all that I could do was leave a message. Ultimately, for me, this turned out to be a time of perfect faith and trust because I had asked God, His angels, and the Holy Spirit to ensure my child's safety.

    It wasn't until one o'clock that afternoon that my call was finally returned and I was assured of Dustin's safety. Through this experience, and by having to let go of communication that day, I was forced to feel my own vulnerability, and in that state, I completely trusted that God had heard my prayer. This experience allowed me to understand that defenselessness by choice is a powerful salve to heal our feelings of powerlessness.

    We eventually had a meeting at the school with the principal, both children, and parents. At this meeting, it was verified that Dustin's assailant was terrified of his own father. This news came as no surprise to Dustin or myself, and it brought forth compassion in both our hearts. I already knew that this child must have been suffering greatly within his mind to demonstrate such violence towards my son. My decision was now to become part of the solution.

Rediscovering Your Authentic Self

For Dustin, his lesson was that when you fight, there is never a winner. In our group meeting, I made both children aware that no matter who wins today, there will always be a tomorrow that the loser might want to use to even the score. I explained to both children that, because Lewis was not very tall and Dustin was likely to grow considerably taller than Lewis, if Dustin's anger was not healed, he may in the future pursue Lewis, no longer having size as a barrier. I felt that this explanation and our discussion would serve to resolve the situation.

My son learned from this that when a person feels powerless, they can become very dangerous. Through this experience, Dustin was finally able to meet and transcend his three-year-old fear of meeting up with the other boy. He also learned about the power of choice, and about the inner power that was gained by forgiving someone who had attacked him. For both my son and myself, our sense of peace and understanding returned as a result of our willingness to continue to see the innocence within Lewis.

To live in a state of Heaven implies that we accept *all things* into our experience. It means that we remember who we are and that all things that come into our experience are opportunities for our growth. The truth about free will is that we are given the choice to perceive the world through the eyes of love or through the eyes of fear. Our perception will manifest our experience of either Heaven or hell. *Because our outer world is an outward projection of the inner belief systems we hold, we are told not to try to change the world, but rather to change the way we think about the world.* The result of a healed mind is a peaceful mind, and by individually contributing to the whole Sonship, we can collectively bring peace to our world. For this reason, the best place to begin accomplishing world peace is within ourselves.

It is a fair question to ask what we should do about the war, hunger, and violence that appear to be ravaging our planet, as this is truly an "out-picturing" of hell. We do not need to die to experience hell. Many of us have experienced some form of living hell while here on earth. In *A Course in Miracles,* we are repeatedly told that the hell we perceive is not real because the thought system that gives birth to our hell is our dreaming mind, which extends hallucinations. This does not, however, give us permission to live a life of denial. Instead, we are asked to continually fill our minds with peaceful and loving thoughts, and passionately transfer that love and peace to those in need. We are asked to forgive each other and ourselves for the guilt that is, as is repeatedly mentioned, the cornerstone of the ego-based thought system.

It is our mission as people on earth to allow ourselves to experience the Heaven that is ever present and awaits our invitation. We do not need to create love and peace as much as we need simply to allow it to be restored to our minds. There is no quicker route to peace than the absolute acceptance of the teaching that only love is real.

In accordance with *Course* principles, we are asked to keep our attention on loving each other and on restoring Heaven to our experience. Heaven on earth is defined as the peace within our minds. We are asked to apply love and forgiveness whenever necessary in our individual lives, in our communities, countries, and, ultimately, the world. World peace is possible because it needs only to be accepted, not created.

Through faith, we trust that all things, both joyful and horrific, serve to bring us closer to God.

Moreah Ragusa

To Live in the Moment

We are taught in the Course that time does not exist. Scientists say that time cannot be proven. The Course teaches that both future and past thoughts are coping mechanisms that the mind uses to feel safe. We have made an agreement as people to measure change through a tool called time. On an atomic level, the material world that appears to be constant is in continual change. Even in our bodies, cells are continually dying and being born so that we can experience a solid form. Our bodies are, in the terms used by Dr. Deepak Chopra, "a river of energy and information."

This is not the real world. In the real world, we are eternal because we were created that way. The mind was created in a state of Heaven. It has never left that state and will continue to remain there eternally. The physical world of change was made so that we might experience our thoughts through location, time, space, and change, but it is not necessary for our eternal mind to become victim to them. We are taught that, in order to free ourselves, we must practice the principle of living in the moment. In Course terms, this is referred to as the "holy instant." We are continuously reminded that eternity happens in every instant, that all our suffering comes from thoughts that pertain to either the past or future. It is also emphasized that perfection exists within each instant. And we can experience it only when we leave this moment unclouded by the past or the anticipated future. *If we allow each moment to be untouched by either the past or the future, we can restore our peace.*

Rediscovering Your Authentic Self

To live in the moment is a powerful teaching that has repeatedly ended conflicts in my current marriage. Ignoring this principle can escalate a situation from bad to worse. When I was making plans to open our centre, my husband and I discussed the financial responsibilities. He is a natural businessman and has been extremely successful in achieving his desired outcomes. His style is to maintain rigid control throughout the planning and organizing process. Because he believes that control is a good way to operate, it becomes true in his experience. I, on the other hand, do not operate in this way. I make plans in the present moment, but do not try to plan or take preventative measures for something that may or may not happen in the future. *"A healed mind does not plan. It carries out the plans that it receives through listening to Wisdom that is not its own."* (W-pI.135.11:1-6)

So this concept is where my husband and I always get into trouble as a couple. It is okay for me to live my life in accordance with my rules. It is also okay for him to live his life in accordance with his own rules. What ultimately presents conflict is when we proceed in a joint venture using our different thought systems. In planning my new business, I was willing to estimate the costs that I would incur, but was also willing to receive miracles for some possible situations in the future. My approach was driving my husband crazy. The result of this conflict was, as it usually is, a period of silence. I frequently push his buttons when applying my "let go — let God" approach.

To my husband, a planner and organizer, my approach is an invitation to crash. Because he loves me, he is afraid to see that happen. In the past, our differing belief systems caused both of us to become frustrated with each other's unwillingness to bend. Over the years, I have learned that, rather than arguing, I should pray. In this particular case, that's exactly what I did. I asked the Holy Spirit to intervene in our conflict so that we might lovingly resolve it. I asked for a miracle. A miracle is to experience that instant of time that is unaffected by past memories or future projections. My miracle simply allowed the moment to be. The immediate result for me was peace, followed by a greater understanding of my husband's concern for my well-being.

The morning following our disagreement, my husband's silence revealed that the conflict was still present. When he left for work, he didn't kiss me goodbye as he usually did. I chose to sustain my peace, knowing that a miracle was on the way. At about 11:30 that morning, I received a call from him. His voice was gentle with kindness as he questioned me about another matter. In that moment, I had to make a choice. I could hold on to past feelings of resentment, or I could choose to accept this moment and the love that was being offered in it. I chose to live in the moment. Love and understanding filled my heart and mind, and I thanked him for his concern for my success. He replied by sharing his frustration over his own endeavor of building a new dealership. He shared with me the unforeseen problems that appeared to be leading to a budget overrun. I simply listened, told him that I loved him, and appreciated my miracle as I hung up the phone.

Our peace was restored because of our willingness to let the moment be untouched by future projections, past memories, or by second-guessing what the other was thinking. When we ask for a miracle, we ask for reality to be expressed in a present-time experience.

The only way we can retrieve the past is through our memory. We are taught in the Course to use our memories wisely by retrieving only love, since nothing else exists. We are only to retrieve the love we have given and love we have received. Once again, this is based on the principle that *only love is real*, and that means that anything in our past that originated from fear does not exist. Does this law sound like a form of denial? Absolutely! In order for us to retain peace, we are asked to identify and turn over any fear within us that translates into illusion. In surrendering our fear to the atonement, we deny fear's power. Thus, it becomes "effect-less," meaning without cause, or nonexistent. We are asked to do this for the reinstatement of our own peace of mind.

> *True denial is a powerful protective device. You can and should deny any belief that error can hurt you. This kind of denial is not concealment but a correction. Your right mind depends on it. Denial of error is a strong defense of truth, but denial of truth results in miscreation, the projections of the ego. In the service of the right mind the denial of errors frees the mind, and re-establishes the freedom of*

Rediscovering Your Authentic Self

the will. When the will is really free it cannot miscreate, because it recognizes only truth.
(T-2.II.2:1-7)

Fear jumbles up our thinking and taints every thought, event, and situation it touches. Our distortions in thought always come from the entrapment of either the fearful past, or fear of a disempowered future. Our free will, being grounded in our authentic identity, always seeks to deny errors and consequently finds love.

The opposition to the law that *only love is real* comes through the human desire to bring justice to people. In our society, people are accountable for their actions. And so, too, are they in Heaven. If we did not hold people accountable for their sins, we feel they would be "getting off" or getting away with something. What we need to remember is that if a person's action comes as a result of fear, it is an illusion. Through their errors — the out-picturing of fear — we are afforded the opportunity to love and heal instead of judge. Remember, we can only make illusions real in our experience by responding to them.

Does this mean that the terrorist attacks against The World Trade Center and the Pentagon should be ignored? Of course not! But we must remember the founding rule in the Course that all people either act lovingly or are desperately calling for love. It means that in the face of such a loveless act, we must turn to the power of love to repair the horrendous suffering. We must remember that we can choose the way in which we want to be affected. We can still choose peace. Through faith, we trust that all things, both joyful and horrific, serve to bring us closer to God. We must allow ourselves some time and love to heal our wounds, so as not to respond from a consciousness of retaliation that will inflate the error.

We must seek understanding of terrorism, considering that it is fear at its grossest level. It is bred by a deep feeling of powerlessness. It is nurtured by pride and self-righteousness, and the only salve for such an infected wound is love. We must honestly look within and weed out any feelings of hate and anger that we harbor against any people. We must return our minds to the errors in thought that have stemmed from fear, and turn them over to the atonement in peace.

For the war-torn desecrated countries and people, we must pray — pray that they might share in freedom and consciously act towards that goal. We must stop separating ourselves from one another. We are taught through the Course that we can pardon mistakes within the world of illusion, so that we may also be pardoned. Because the law of mind operates effectively at all times, policing is not our concern. As we think, karma will take care of the situation.

The next concern we may have is that if we do not react to a person's loveless action, we may become something of a doormat, individually or as a society. *The truth is that when we do react to a person's loveless action, we become a doormat to fear.* What we give to others we truly give to ourselves, because ultimately we recognize that there's only one of us here. If I go deep enough into your mind and you go deep enough into mine, we discover that it is the same mind. This is what I demonstrate by doing Angel readings for people. I accept our unity and then I am able to "see" the thought manifestations and experiences of another person. What I'm really doing is seeing into the identity we share. To free ourselves, we are given each other, and as we learn to live in the moment, we begin to recognize this interconnectedness. The action required to restore our peace, therefore, is to forgive the past mistakes that we, and others have made.

To live in the moment means that there is no need for us to hold fast to the planned events in our life.

A healed mind does not plan. It carries out plans that it receives through listening to Wisdom [Holy Spirit] that is not its own. It waits until it has been taught what should be done, and then proceeds to do it. It does not depend upon itself for anything except its adequacy to fulfill the plan assigned to it. It is secure in certainty that obstacles cannot impede its progress to accomplishment of any goal that serves the greater plan established for the good of everyone.

> *A healed mind is relieved of the belief that it must plan, although it cannot know the outcome which is best, the means by which it is achieved, nor how to recognize the problem that the plan is made to solve.* (W-pI.135.11-12:1)

The Course reminds us that we are to live in the moment and that we should not attempt to plan our lives around all the possible unforeseen events in our future.

When we are afraid, we feel powerless and put up defenses as a protective shield.

Moreah Ragusa

Solving Time Conflicts

There are countless times I have watched miracles appear in the timing of my office appointments, which, I'm sure, are carefully arranged by "receptionist angels." To illustrate this, I would like to recount the synchronicities involved in the following story: Some time ago, I had a distressing dream of having several people show up at the same time for one appointment. In the dream, I handled the situation quite well, trusting that it was all part of God's plan. Two days after I had this dream, we received a record amount of snow. I had begun booking that day's appointments approximately five weeks earlier, but because these appointments had not yet been confirmed, I had later made other bookings for those time slots.

The first call I received that morning was from a woman who had booked morning reading appointments on that day for herself and two friends. She informed me that because of the weather, the three of them were now unable to come. Since these particular appointments had never been confirmed, I had rebooked their times. When the woman called to say that they would not be able to come, I said nothing about her forgetting to confirm the appointments; I simply rebooked her times as I smiled and uttered a silent thank-you to my angels for "un-creating" this apparent mix-up.

Three days earlier, another person had cancelled their appointment for this same period, leaving a vacant spot. A few hours following that cancellation, someone called who was in crisis, and I was able to give her the vacant spot. Two days later, she cancelled because her child was ill. I was definitely experiencing what most people would think to be a "cancellation crisis"! An hour following this latest cancellation, yet another person called to cancel their afternoon appointment. Then the tide turned. I received a call from another person believing that their appointment was that morning, while it actually was for the next day.

Later that day, I received a call from my husband informing me that the hot tub in our house needed immediate repair. He asked for a time slot in which the repairman could work on the hot tub without disturbing the privacy of a session, since at that time, I was seeing clients in my home office. Privacy is an issue because the hot tub room is adjacent to the room I worked in and it was only separated by a set of glass French doors. In light of the previous train of re-bookings and cancellations, I was able to provide the repairman with the vacant time slot that was now available. I had to sit in absolute wonder of all of the synchronicities that had to transpire in order for me to see such a miraculous dance of events.

That morning, I had also made arrangements to meet with a group of people regarding an upcoming walk for world peace. It, too, was canceled because of the weather. Due to an oversight, I had double-booked and was saved again! What became evident to me once more is that my life is lovingly and directly guided by my Father's will for me, which is always joy.

I was multi-tasking during the writing of this book. I was opening a new office within the Angels Answers centre, while continuing to see clients on a full-time basis. I had been questioning myself on how I would find enough time to do it all. The angels answered my question.

This is one of many stories of such happenings in my life. Cancellations are a fact of life for people in many professions. In my work, it frequently happens that someone will cancel an appointment, and then, within minutes, another person in crisis is given the opportunity to see me immediately. If I were attached to the appointments in my calendar as if they were absolute, never changing from the way I had written them in, I would feel powerless and frustrated. I have chosen instead to become the *observer* of the events in my life, and therefore I am never disappointed. For me each day is somewhat like Christmas, or fishing — I never quite know what will take hold in the next moment.

I have long since decided that my limited perceptual plans don't work, but God's do.

Moreah Ragusa

Miracles

We can experience all types of miracles throughout our lifetime, and I know that I have been blessed by many of them. I have experienced relocation, the manifesting of wanted objects, the collapsing of time and distance, spontaneous healings, and truly hundreds of incidences where my perception was changed to recognize love's presence, which ultimately results in a miracle.

One might ask why it is that I have received so many miracles. The answer is simply because I have asked. In my childhood, I knew without a doubt that I was being guided through some very difficult and emotionally traumatic years. At a very young age, I knew I could overcome anything because of the miracles that continually reminded me of God's love. Miracles have deeply touched my life, and so for me they are more than just sporadic events, they are common daily experiences that I embrace.

There are fifty miracle principles in *A Course in Miracles*. It is through studying and putting into practice the teachings of the Course that I have learned to practice these miracle principles. This book is dedicated to helping you better understand and apply miracle principles. When we think of miracles, we often think of spontaneous healings of cancer or other terminal illnesses, or perhaps of a mother that is suddenly able to free her child from the underpinnings of a vehicle. Another miracle may be where a person is able to defy the rules of nature in the face of a natural disaster.

These miracles are demonstrations of the principles that we have been discussing in this book. A miracle is a change in

Rediscovering Your Authentic Self

perception, which enables the thinker to recognize and experience reality, instead of experiencing events that extend from their fear-ridden, separated mind. A miracle is the expression of love, which is reality. The foundation of a miracle, therefore, is based on the fact that only love is real and nothing else exists. All miracles extend as expressions of that truth.

One of my favorite Course principles is the first, which says, *"There is no order of difficulty in miracles. One is not 'harder' or 'bigger' than another. They are all the same. All expressions of love are maximal."* (T-1.I.1:1-4) That is to say that there are no larger or smaller, more or less difficult problems to overcome. Curing cancer is not a greater miracle than curing the common cold. The reason that this is true is because both the common cold and the cancer are expressions born from fear, stemming from a mistaken identity. It is our idea of what cancer is, and the collective belief in its power over the child of God, that needs to be healed.

Our peace comes from understanding that all blocks to love and the expression of that love are viewed equally. In keeping with our learning that miracles are maximal expressions of love, we are taught that they are equally and effortlessly accomplished. Miracles occur in the moment. Miracles are not bound by the rules of time and space as they adhere to the cosmic laws of love. The purpose of miracles is to reverse, and therefore to transcend, the rules of time and space in order to remind you of who you are. To paraphrase the Course, both miracles and the body are learning tools. When the learning is accomplished, these tools are no longer necessary. Learning is accomplished through our remembering that we are Spirit, unbounded, eternal, and at the effect of only love.

Moreah Ragusa

The Mind's Role in Illness

I remember the time when I started to truly understand this principle. Everyone in my family had come down with colds and flu. I carefully cared for each one of them as I nursed them back to health. During the week that everyone was ill, I did not become ill myself, but approximately two days after their recovery, I began to feel a scratching in my throat. I immediately searched my mind for past situations in which I may have used my mind inappropriately. The only thing I could think of was the slight pride I felt at not becoming ill while the rest of my family had. I knew that this thought, in creating a separation between my family and myself, was enough to begin the process of my own potential illness.

A miracle was what I needed. I had recently been reading in *A Course in Miracles* that people are not always able to receive spontaneous healings. For people with a fear-ridden mind, there is a danger that an immediate miracle might induce more fear, which would, in fact, exacerbate the current experience. This is possible because we are programmed to live by certain rules within the physical plane, and the breaking out of those rules can cause an even greater sense of strain and fear within the mind.

I understood this while I atoned. I prayed to be ready for a miracle to eradicate my cold symptoms. I returned my mind to the error which I believed was my belief in separation between me and my family, the pride in being slightly more spiritual, and to some degree the feeling that I would be justified if I got sick after caring for everyone else for so long. As a result of following the steps in atonement, my inner guidance clearly suggested that I should just take a vitamin. I knew that the vitamin was not required as far as the Holy Spirit was concerned, but that it must have been intended to enable me to receive the miracle without fear. I then felt the need to ask the Holy Spirit to heal my mind from my eroding belief of being spirit. I began to pray, and a bright light appeared in my mind. I was in awe of the peace that began to fill my being. Following the prayer, I swallowed to see if the healing of my mind had immediately healed my throat. I found that the scratchy soreness persisted.

My ego relished through thoughts that the Holy Spirit had failed me. I didn't respond to the idea, but instead made a decision to trust that the healing had occurred, and my mind needed only time to accept it. I pondered the great peace that had just enveloped me, and recognized it as a reward that surpasses all understanding. Within minutes, I had simply forgotten to pay any attention to the soreness! It wasn't until a few hours later that I realized my throat was healed.

Sometimes, at this point, the fear factor can sabotage everything. While a part of me was thrilled, the other part was somewhat afraid of my own God-given mind power. However, following the recognition of my fear came the inner voice that reminded me of God's constant abiding love. I then remembered that the power was not *of* me but placed *within* me, which then eliminated my fear. My lesson was that the healing of my throat occurred when the Holy Spirit restored my mind's identity.

As difficult to accept as this may be for those who are hurting or have loved ones who are also in pain, the Course reminds us that all illness stems from a fear of awakening, a fear of love, or a hidden desire to make someone who has hurt us "pay." A kind of "look what you did to me," retribution that is the ego's fuel for survival. Notice that all of these fears are directly related to the belief that we are bodies. This is, as has been demonstrated, an established belief of the ego. For this reason, a miracle does not heal the body — this would validate the error — it heals the mind.

It is always the mind of the thinker that is guided by Spirit that does the healing. Conflict within the mind comes from the belief that mind can attack. Mind cannot attack because it is all encompassing, and there is nothing outside of mind to attack. Its *disillusioned* belief that it can attack is demonstrated by attacking the body. There is no creative ability in matter, and the body cannot do anything of itself — it is simply an extension and a learning device for the mind. If the mind is in conflict, the body will outwardly project that conflict.

The body itself is neutral and is animated through instruction from the mind. When the mind is very angry, it can use the body to act out its wishes of attack upon another person's body. Mind does this in order to escape from the powerlessness that it is feeling. This is a vicious, endless cycle of internal attack, which always ends in suffering. The end of suffering occurs when we allow our mind to be healed through the Holy Spirit, which results in health.

How and what we think will always affect our bodies. Keeping our thoughts in present time keeps our bodies well, because energy follows attention. It is vital to our well-being to keep our attention on what is real. Holding memories of past pain and harboring resentment towards people in our past costs us our precious life force energy, which results in the deterioration of our health. The restoration of our health comes from living in present time and accepting both the past and present circumstances of life. In doing so, our health is restored because ownership and acceptance is power.

If we perceive a situation to be difficult, we are asked to call for a miracle to heal our perception that we might see it through love. A miraculous healing is not so mystical to understand because it happens in the eternal present. When the mind attacks, it does so in either past or future reference. However, neither past nor future actually exist, so in reality, neither does the illness. An ill body is the outward projection of an ill mind seeking health. When we are experiencing illness, we must remember that God is present with us even through this experience. We need to ask different questions at this critical time, rather than questions that are often victim-oriented. For example, we can ask for understanding of how our soul can transcend the illness that is presenting itself. We can trust that although illness stems from the previously mentioned fears, it is still possible for the Holy Spirit to use the illness as a path towards awakening.

In my own case, I have found it to be a powerful tool in the midst of illness to question both my body and the illness for the purpose of the illness. Usually the answers are related to a belief that I'm currently holding which renders me either helpless to the past or powerless in this moment. From feelings of powerlessness comes fear and thus separation. My experience has been that through the process of seeking understanding, my health returns

In the study of ACIM, we are taught that the world does not actually exist. This statement might sound outrageous at first, but consider again that the outer world is a reflection of the dreaming mind that is controlled by either past memory or future expectation thinking. Therefore, it is an out-picturing dream of the mind that has fallen asleep. There are particular rules that govern the sleeping mind which do not apply to the awakened mind, which lives in accordance to the cosmic laws of love. The laws of the awakened mind are governed by love, which is knowledge, truth, and timelessness. Miracles attest to the awakened mind, and to Him who knows that he is the Son of God. Awakened masters and sages have always been able to defy the rules of time and space because they are awake. This does not mean that we are unable to offer and experience miracles until we are fully awake. It does mean that the Holy Spirit, which is always within our mind, is awake and therefore extends miracles through us on our behalf.

To be a miracle-minded person, one needs to continually offer miracles to others as well. We need to constantly remind ourselves that there is no greater gift that we could give. What we are truly offering when we offer a miracle to someone else is the conscious awareness of love's continuing presence. By asking for a miracle, we are inviting love's presence to be restored to the person to whom we are offering the miracle. To be a miracle worker means that we live a life that overlooks and pardons fear, guilt, judgment, and condemnation. "Miracle-mindedness" means that we empower one another in our shared identity.

In understanding miracles, it is important to remember that energy follows attention, and action follows thought. We live in an eternal "now," which means that in the instant we decide to do so, we can be reborn to our innocence and our perfection. What Jesus demonstrated for us was that we are born to be the creators of our lives, and in the acceptance of this, we become co-creators with God. *In any moment that we allow neither the past nor future thoughts to prevail, a miracle can happen.*

Part Three

Relationships

Part Three - *Relationships*   141

   The Holy vs. Special Relationships   143
   The Separated Dreaming Mind   145
   Three Levels of Relationships   149
   The Special Hate Relationship   155
   The Special Love Relationship   161
   Transcending Our Fears   165
   The Dynamics of Special Love
      And Hate Relationships   169
   The Dynamics of Attraction   171
   Healing Our Wounds and Filling the Void   175
   Transcending the Ego   177
   Summary of the Special Relationship   181
   Finding Our Inner Power   183
   Our Relationship to God   187
   Our Relationship to Our Parents   189
   Transcending Archetypal Patterns   193
   When Is It Time to Leave a Relationship?   197
   Our Relationship to Spouse and Children   203
   Healing Archetypal Defense Mechanisms   205
   Nurturing Our Children's Self Esteem   209
   The Holy Role of the Stepparent   211
   Love Asks No Reward   215
   Nurturing Our Relationships   219
   Surrendering Feelings of Guilt   221
   Love In Abundance   223
   Our Relationship to Outer Relationships   227
   Remembering Our True Identity   231
   Our Relationship to Prosperity   233
   Creating Abundance   237
   The Unhealed Healer   239

The Holy vs. the Special Relationship

A Course in Miracles teaches that there are two foundations on which relationships are built: guilt, or love and forgiveness. One type of relationship is referred to as the *special relationship*, which is sustained by guilt, and the other is the *holy relationship*, sustained by love and forgiveness. Because guilt has such a strong influence on ego dynamics, this topic deserves to be fully explored. Our earliest memories include feelings of guilt. Most psychologists agree that guilt is the central life issue that confronts most people. Guilt-ridden memories begin in childhood and progressively accumulate throughout our lives. For many of us, they include cheating in school exams, stealing from the candy store, getting caught smoking, lying about mistakes we have made, and picking on a sibling or a younger, more helpless, child. We continue to feel this guilt through adolescence and adulthood, when we feel guilty for losing our tempers, ignoring the beggar on the street, skipping church services, failing to perform spiritual ritual acts, lying to our employers, avoiding taxes, and for harboring sexual feelings, forbidden by values of morality, towards certain people. The list is endless, and the guilt goes on and on, unless a correction is found and accepted.

For those unaware of a possible spiritual solution to the overwhelming and deeply seated guilt, the ego's plan for salvation is secured. The reasons we can remember for feeling guilty are just the tip of the iceberg. Beneath the surface lies a greater belief so powerful that it is able to divide the conscious from the unconscious mind. It is a belief so deeply rooted that we feel it is impossible to

Rediscovering Your Authentic Self

correct. On some level, we believe that not even God is able — or willing — to free us from this permanent feeling of guilt.

The Course explains for us where this feeling of guilt comes from. Guilt arises from sin, which, we are taught, is a lack of love — the post-separation condition. Sin is the belief that we can separate, and have indeed separated, ourselves from our Creator, who is Love. It is the belief that this separation actually occurred that gives rise to the idea of a false self — the self that opposes the authentic self that God created. Guilt tells us that we have sinned, and in doing so, it establishes sin's reality. Consequently, the ego, which arises from the belief in a separated self, emerges. The ego then protects itself by projecting or placing upon another this original thought of separation. From this act, the world of form arises, which seems — impossibly — to exist apart from the split mind that created it through thought.

> *You do not realize the magnitude of that one error. It was so vast and so completely incredible, that from it a world of total unreality had to emerge. What else could come of it? That was the first projection of error outward. The world arose to hide it, [the error of separation] and became the screen on which it was projected and drawn between you and the truth.* (T-18.I.5:2-4;6:1-2)

Moreah Ragusa

The Separated Dreaming Mind

As will be explored in detail in the section on healing the body in Part Four, we are taught that the world of separation is a world of bodies which became the literal embodiments of the ego, and which symbolize the sin of separation, or the attack on God's will. It is this perceived attack for which we feel so corruptibly guilty. For this reason, we are taught that the material world is as inherently illusory as the separated thought that gave rise to it. Because ideas leave not their source, the idea of the world exists only in our separated dreaming mind. Thus, the world, being born of fear, is a world of past and future, conflict, scarcity, suffering, and death. Our world is therefore recognized as being the upside-down and backwards reflection of God's world, which is a world that exists in the present and offers abundance, peace, and eternal life. The Course elaborates:

> The world you see is the delusional system of those made mad by guilt. Look carefully at this world, and you will realize that this is so. For this world is the symbol of punishment, and all the laws that seem to govern it are the laws of death. Children are born into it through pain and in pain. Their growth is attended by suffering, and they learn of sorrow and separation and death. Their minds seem to be trapped in their brain, and its powers to decline if their bodies are hurt. They seem to love yet they desert and are deserted. They appear to lose what

Rediscovering Your Authentic Self

they love, perhaps the most insane belief of all. And their bodies wither and gasp and are laid in the ground, and are no more. Not one of them but has thought that God is cruel. (T-13.In.2:2-110)

The cruelty of such a world resides not in God's Mind, but rather in ours. We are taught that the separated self makes idols such as cars, relationships, houses, jewels, padded bank accounts, and every other thing we look toward to make us happy. *"Seek not outside yourself. For it will fail, and you will weep each time an idol falls."* (T-29.VII.1:1-2) In reality, what we are doing is trying to suppress our pain, and we believe that this will allow us to be happy. The greatest of all the idols that the separated self engendered is the body. What we seek as a source of pleasure is not as it seems. *"While you believe it [the body] can give you pleasure, you will also believe it can bring you pain."* (T-19.IV-A.17:11)

We are taught that idols or objects will bring us pain for two principal reasons: first, that once we have become attached and dependent upon them, their absence will be experienced as painful; and second, that pain naturally results every time we expect anything outside of love to be a source of pleasure, as this implies that the idol's presence is essential to our joy and well-being. Guilt is being nurtured in both instances because we are giving up the truth — the true source of our power. Instead, we are placing our power in idols, thus denying the real power that God and His Spirit do have. Once again, we are reminded that all our real joy comes from doing God's will.

When we understand the distorted perspective with which the underlying guilt stains our minds, we can continue to explore the reasons why the ego seeks relationships. We can now clearly identify the distorted and tainted uses that the ego has for any relationship.

> *The ego always tries to preserve conflict [guilt]. It is very ingenious in devising ways that seem to diminish conflict, because it does not want you to find conflict so intolerable that you will insist on giving it up. The ego therefore tries to persuade you that it can free you of conflict, lest you give the ego up and free yourself.* (T-7.VIII.2:2-4)

Moreah Ragusa

The holy relationship occurs when we invite the Holy Spirit to enter into our union, to eradicate sin (guilt), and to operate at the foundation of the relationship. To the ego, this is intolerable because its existence relies on our willingness to see sin in another. Through seeing sin in another, the ego is able to maintain itself, being the embodiment of sin. Being based on guilt and fear, the ego then "proves" the sin of separation. For this reason, it is committed to keeping us away from our own guilt. When this happens, we are not apt to question the validity of our guilt and ultimately refuse its reality. *"Thoughts of God are unacceptable to the ego, because they clearly point to the nonexistence of the ego [guilt] itself."* (T-4.V.2:2) Remember that, to the ego, a relationship is a way of maintaining the guilt of another person. Their guilt, therefore, appears to us as the "hero" or "savior" of our own innocence. However, the reality is that when we project our feelings of guilt onto another person, we are silently enforcing them within the mind we share but perceive as our own — "as we give, so shall we receive." Therefore, in seeing the problem outside of ourselves, we are rendering ourselves powerless in the relationship.

Denial and projection are the foundational bricks on which the special relationship is built. What the ego is keeping secret is that the fear that gave rise to the guilt is its own. In approaching the guilt, we are revealing the one who stands behind it, and it is this Divine Self that the ego fears.

In Kenneth Wapnick's book *Forgiveness and Jesus*, we read his brilliant dissertation of the ego's tactics:

> Yet there must be some solution of this problem of guilt, otherwise the fear and anxieties it generates would be too overwhelming for us to bear. And the ego does provide us with an answer. Despite its dependence on guilt for its existence, the ego offers us a means whereby we seem to be free of it and protected from the terror it induces in us. If the ego did not provide us with this assurance, we would never give it our allegiance. In the midst of the terror over expected retaliation for our sins reinforced by overwhelming guilt, the ego calls to us, saying: "Turn to me and I will free you from this terrible burden of your guilty self. Your fear will disappear and you will find safety and peace." Since the ego has already

Rediscovering Your Authentic Self

excluded God from the role of savior by virtue of our fear of Him, in desperation we have no recourse except to turn to the ego for help and to accept its version of salvation. To help us deal with the overwhelming experience of our guilt, the ego employs two basic dynamics: denial or repression, and projection. These dynamics are what Freud called defense mechanisms — the psychological devices we use to defend against the dangers we perceive — and is perhaps the area where he made his greatest contribution. (T-1.p1.2-4)

Through the study of the ego and its use of defense mechanisms, which are glorified extensions of the "fight-or-flight" survival response, we can more clearly understand the ego and see how it works. Therefore, we become consciously able to choose again. Projection and denial are then easily identifiable as the "cell bars" that are used to imprison us through the dynamics of guilt.

Moreah Ragusa

Three Levels of Relationships

We are taught in the Course that there are three levels of relationships through which the Holy Spirit can function to heal, and thus awaken our minds. The first level of relationship is the casual encounter, such as a meeting in an elevator, or passing an individual while walking down the street — perhaps even a misdialed telephone number that briefly connects us with an unknown caller. The second level is slightly more intense in its nature, and could include relationships between friends, co-workers, and neighbors. Third-level relationships are parent/child and sibling relationships, as well as marriages and friendships that last a lifetime.

The Holy Spirit can use all three levels, from casual to lifelong; to help us heal and uncover what blocks us from the fullest expression of love.

The special relationship is the favorite of the ego's ploys to maintain its existence. It is also the fertile ground on which the Holy Spirit is able to plant the seeds of corrective thoughts. In the special relationship, cause and effect are reversed. The ego desperately hides the joy that is a natural picturing out of our authentic identity. The Holy Spirit's recognition of this turns idols into reflections of a healed mind. This means that the new clothes, new car, new house, better job, or new partner are now recognized as effects or expressions of a person who is in touch with who they are, as innocent and abundant.

When this correction has been made, a person is no longer looking to those idols as a cause of their happiness. Instead, the objects that were once idols are now seen as things. These things, then, are effects, reflective of the cause, which is within us, rather than the idols that we look to in our search for the cause. Through the Holy Spirit, the idols (meaning a protector of guilt) which were sought for pleasure (meaning to avoid our own feelings of guilt) and which were being used to remain apart from love, and even to avoid it, are then transformed to become natural reflections of our real identity. The joy that naturally stems from our identity, which is love and is therefore innocent, is properly seen as the effect.

In a holy relationship, anything that blocks love's presence within each individual will be offered to the Holy Spirit for transformation. Although our individual wounds (defense mechanisms) will be brought forth, the healing of these wounds is not to be perceived as a threat to the relationship. Instead, it is recognized that the revealing and consequent healing of our wounds is to be seen as the liberation of the relationship.

Relationships at all three levels are meant to be "holy encounters" between the sons of God. The amount of time it takes to heal a relationship issue between two souls is not as important as achieving the goal set for them by the Holy Spirit. In the Course, we are taught that the Holy Spirit operates like a matchmaking computer. It knows exactly which souls have a karmic agreement to join together in order to heal their respective wounded personalities and to ultimately facilitate their joint awakening. We are taught that God brings each and every person into our life in order that we may give and receive his or her love. We are reminded that there are no coincidences. *"There are no accidents in salvation."*(M-3.1:6) Even the small child that bumps into the leg of an adult while he runs down the street is part of the experience that brings an opportunity for healing.

In the first level of relationship, two souls interact in a brief moment in time. These encounters can be as simple as riding in an elevator together, passing each other on the street, or signaling while in rush hour traffic in hope of entering another person's lane.

The second level of relationship is when two souls come together for a longer period of time to accomplish a specific learning opportunity, and then are released. This level of relationship can take the form of a dating couple, two peers, co-workers, neighbors, friends, and even marriage.

Moreah Ragusa

The third level of relationship, which is the least common, is the active relationship with a soul that will last a lifetime, such as a parent/child relationship, a sibling relationship, or a marriage. What has occurred on the third level is a perfect balance of learning and teaching between two souls that is ongoing throughout their lives. The Course emphasizes, however, that all relationships begin as "special," with the goal being to make them holy. For this reason, the "Eyes of the Universe" are continually observing how we treat each other at all three levels of encounter.

On the first level, we are exploring how we treat others, and how others with whom we share fleeting moments affect us. Some find it easy to love in these often superficial relationships, while others experience emotional absence stemming from fear or judgment. What is being observed is how we view and treat each other when we think we will not necessarily be held accountable for our actions.

On the second level, which is found in the majority of the relationships we encounter, the learning/teaching balance becomes unequal, defined as the commonly stated, "We outgrew each other; our paths grew apart." In addition to this scenario, we flee relationships due to our susceptibility to the ego's demands to just "find another" who will better serve the perceived undeveloped parts of our personality! This imbalance, or the unwillingness to heal these core issues, is what drives us from relationship to relationship. The ego signals us that a different learning partner is required at this time. Our solace eventually comes from the recognition that, while a relationship may end on a physical level, the love and forgiveness that the relationship gave birth to, and that we experienced, will continue eternally on an emotional and psychological level.

We are also reminded that the end of a relationship does not mean that the relationship was a failure. On the contrary, the Course emphasizes that a goal was set between the two souls involved, that the goal was accomplished, and that therefore the relationship was, in Heaven's eyes, a success. In the acceptance of this success, guilt is abolished and peace restored. Subsequently, there is tremendous freedom to be gained for individuals who feel they have been wronged, abandoned, or betrayed by another person. Equally liberated is the person who feels that they have wronged or betrayed another. Both need to recognize that their souls made the karmic

Rediscovering Your Authentic Self

agreement, fulfilled the agreement, and therefore agreed to move on for more learning. The ultimate success of all relationships, including sibling, parental, romantic, and casual, is determined by the ability of the respective partners to forgive both themselves and each other. Remember that the Course emphasizes that those things which we are able to forgive in another — meaning we no longer want to be at the effect of those things — is what we will be forgiven for also.

Finally, the goal of all three levels of relationships is that we accept, invoke healing for, and love all people as they are, in all situations. For this reason, we are exposed to people for different lengths of time, and placed in a myriad of dynamic scenarios, to see if guilt is still perceived on any of the levels.

When the goal of two souls who came together is accomplished, a real sense of completion will start to pulse in one or both of the souls. Their inner guidance will begin to send out messages that the relationship has fulfilled its function towards the salvation of both souls. By our worldly standards or rules, a relationship that ends on a physical level is judged as the failure of the individuals. This, however, is of no concern to the Holy Spirit. Since love is eternal, the love and forgiveness that was shared between these souls is also eternal. The learning and love that each individual soul gave and accepted during the relationship will be carried into subsequent relationships for the rest of their lives.

To recap, when a relationship comes to a close, it is either that the goal between the two souls was accomplished, or that there was a recurrence of severe psychological or emotional violation that tore down the self-love and self-worth of one or both souls. When this happens in a conspicuous way, such as, for instance, in verbal or emotional violence toward a spouse, then the Holy Spirit, the angels, nonphysical guides and teachers, all begin supporting the release of the abusive, psychologically dysfunctional relationship. Although within almost all of our love relationships, there are some elements of dysfunction, abuse, and pain, our heavenly teachers do not condone or support gross levels of unkindness.

What occurs between two struggling souls is an unconscious, yet karmically influenced attack. Prior to their incarnation, two souls may have set up such a learning opportunity, fully believing that they were capable of loving and forgiving whatever painful soul memories they shared from the past or from a previous life. In keeping with the understanding that the spirit always seeks balance, these two souls will come together again. Whether or not balance is accomplished now or later is determined by their ability to turn a special relationship into a holy one through the practice of forgiveness and their willingness to allow love's presence to return to their awareness.

The Holy Spirit is not attached to the time it takes to accomplish our goals as much as It is interested in our achieving them. The Course introduction reveals:

> *"This is a course in miracles. It is a required course. Only the time you take it is voluntary. Free will does not mean that you can establish the curriculum. It means only that you can elect what you want to take at a given time."* (I-1: 1-6 italics omitted)

From this, we recognize that all relationships are used as opportunities to practice the Course teachings and that all people will eventually learn them. The time at which we choose to take these teachings is up to us. We are, however, encouraged to do so sooner rather than later, to help remedy the extreme levels of lovelessness that currently affect our physical survival.

To the ego, the purpose of our special relationship is to have a special love outside of the oneness that was created for us.

Moreah Ragusa

The Special Hate Relationship

The Course emphasizes that the foundation of the special relationship is not based on love; it is actually based on hate. In this relationship, the responsibility for our own happiness and the misery we feel is shifted onto another. The ego directs, "I am not responsible for, or the cause of, my unhappy situation. It is you who has done this to me." In addition, the ego whispers, "IF ONLY..." This victim orientation is used to establish a false sense of innocence that results in powerlessness. If only I had better parents, a more loving partner, or a more understanding employer. If only the government or church were more liberal (or conservative). If only something outside myself were different — then I would be happy. This ego strategy brilliantly places the solution outside of ourselves, where it cannot be solved. The Workbook states:

> *The ego's plan for salvation centers around holding grievances. It maintains that, if someone else spoke or acted differently, if some external circumstance or event were changed, you would be saved. Thus, the source of salvation is constantly perceived as outside yourself. Each grievance you hold is a declaration, and an assertion in which you believe, that says, "If this were different I would be saved."* (W-pI.71.2:1-4)

To the ego, the purpose of our special relationship is to have a special love outside of the oneness that was created for us. The goal of the special relationship is to find an object or form as an underground storehouse for the projection of anger that results from our continual feelings of guilt. The ego's defense against our undesired guilt, once it has become real in our minds, is a two-stage process: First, we deny that the problem is with us as we project it onto another, and then, seeing it in them rather than ourselves, we feel justified to condemn.

> "Anger always involves projection of separation, which must ultimately be accepted as one's own responsibility, rather than being blamed on others. Anger cannot occur unless you believe that you have been attacked, that your attack is justified in return, and that you are in no way responsible for it." (T-6.in.1:2-3)

In view of what we have learned of the ego's plan to maintain its belief in our guilt, thus freeing itself, we can clearly see the need for projection. There will be no holds barred, as projection reinforces the guilt in another. All evidence, real or imagined, will be used for this purpose. Anger will be totally justified in our minds for the constant attacks we perceive. The ego whispers constantly, "Look what you have done to me, you are the cause of all my pain. By your hand I have suffered. Now recognize your guilt, so that I can be freed of mine."

We all have experienced this scenario in one way or another. The frustrated employee who is reprimanded at work for his disorganization, and then returns home and yells at his teenage son for uncompleted homework; the procrastinator who is late for work and then rages as she races through traffic, blaming her tardiness on others' not driving fast enough; and the child who fails to study and then blames the teacher for his poor instruction. Even in the Bible, we encounter this denial of responsibility through the ego's ploy when God questions Adam and Eve about their mistake, and the blame is quickly transferred from Eve to the serpent. (Gn3:12-13)

The guiltier we feel, the greater will be our need to deny and project. The ego tells us that in order to get rid of our guilt, we must see it in another. Their defenses in response to our attack will then justify our anger. In this vicious, endless circle of suffering, the ego gets the last laugh. The more we attack, the guiltier we feel. The ego's plan for salvation then becomes magnified as it first tries to convince us that we are guilty, and then appears as the savior of our guilt. Strangely, we feel admonished of our guilt by seeing it in another. In this act of projection, guilt is certain to be maintained, and the ego is thus assured of its survival. In the Course, we read:

> *Yet projection will always hurt you. It reinforces your belief in your own split mind, and its only purpose is to keep the separation going. It is solely a device of the ego to make you feel different from your brothers and separated from them. (T-6.II.3:1-3)*

From this guilt/attack cycle, it becomes clear how fear must naturally follow guilt. Since on some level, we know that attacking is a mistake because it is an act of separation which breeds an "I vs. them" perception, we believe that in keeping with ego rationale, we should be punished for this sin. Having projected our guilt onto another, we then expect them to do the same in return.

Projection, being the fundamental cause in the special hate relationship, insists that we misuse the present. Accordingly, the hated person's past mistakes are seen as justification for our attack. Each and every fault is therefore marshaled to build our case against them. The ego will not overlook a single shred of evidence, which will be added to an arsenal that is then used to justify the verdict of "guilty" and subsequent attack. In these particular relationships, we have unconsciously chosen a certain partner because of suspected vulnerabilities. These vulnerabilities will be used so that our partner's past can be used to "justify" our need to project out, and unload the guilt we feel inside. The ego will certainly ignore the present reality of our partner's identity so that it can maintain a verdict of guilty upon them. In the Course, these souls are referred to as the "shadows of the past," which *"...represent the evil that you think was done to you. You bring them with you only that you may return evil for evil, hoping that their witness will enable you to think guilty of another and not harm yourself...The shadow figures always speak for vengeance...This is why...whatever reminds you of your past grievances attracts you, and seems to go by the name of love, no matter how distorted the associations by which you arrive at the connection may be."* (T-17.III.1:9-10;2:2,4-5)

Rediscovering Your Authentic Self

In contrast, in special love relationships, our own "sins of the past" are prevalent, and thus we seek someone outside of ourselves who is seen to be more holy than we see ourselves to be. In so doing, we seek to find absolution from the guilt we feel inside. The unfulfilled needs that have not been met in the past are dragged into the present and are placed at the feet of this "special someone." This person will be viewed as that special self that we perceive ourselves to be devoid of. Subsequently, we will attract a person who also has this need in the opposite position, which will then lay the foundation of the special love relationship. The agreement is that each has certain responsibilities that can be met by no other, which maintains the special love relationship.

For example, we have heard of women who are "in search of a father" instead of a husband. They are searching for someone who will meet the need for a father figure that remained unfulfilled in their childhood. Their idea and expectation of what an ideal father should be is now being transferred onto a special partner. Such a woman's choice of partner will be greatly influenced by what her particular societal image of the father role entails. Among other expectations, love and protection will be included if that is what she felt was missing in her childhood. She will therefore seek a man who desires, due to his own unfulfilled childhood needs, to fulfill this part. As long as both people agree to play their respective parts and meet each other's unfulfilled needs, the relationship will be sustained. However, if one or both parties negate their responsibilities, then the hate that is actually underlying the relationship will be exposed.

The ego's incredible need to reinforce and hold on to guilt is seen as the cliché of "self-fulfilling prophesy." Because of the inherent function of mind, our worst fears, stemming from our guilt, which we believe then justifies our need to attack and punish, are brought about through the fear we are so desperately trying to avoid. Unfortunately, we will remain unaware of the fact that we ourselves are the cause of that fear.

When we perceive the present in terms of the past, we become paralyzed and unable to see what is really happening in this moment. Because people have responded in particular ways in the past, we expect them to do so now. Through this expectation, we eliminate the opportunity for a different future. Likewise, when we have observed a situation that has evolved along a set path, we expect the same now. Once again, our expectations directly affect the outcome. Our behavior, which always extends from what we think and believe, becomes inseparably the cause of the outcome.

In the special love relationship, love means that there must be sacrifice.

Moreah Ragusa

The Special Love Relationship

In the special love relationship, there is a belief that to find someone special will mean salvation. This is the most insidious device the ego employs in its attempts to rid us of our guilt. In the special hate relationship, the pattern that maintains guilt is detectable once exposed. In the special love relationship, however, the hate is cleverly concealed. We have already learned that guilt is based on the premise that inside of us there is a void, an incompetence and incompleteness that must be filled.

Guilt tries to persuade us: "Within you, there is a void and what surrounds that empty space is also valueless. Therefore, not even God wants you, nor can He even fill this void." From this lie, a deep sense of despair arises to which the salvaging ego responds, "I can save you by finding outside of you an idol — a special love to save you from your hopelessness; to fill, or rather hide, that sinful gap."

The Course teaches:

> *The special [love] relationship has the most imposing and deceptive frame of all the defenses the ego uses. Its thought system is offered here, surrounded by a frame so heavy and so elaborate that the picture is almost obliterated by its imposing structure.* (T-17.IV.8:1-2)

Our acceptance of what the Course refers to as the "scarcity principle" is the relished moment the ego awaits. This belief is the

Rediscovering Your Authentic Self

perpetual impetus that calls forth for us to seek outside of ourselves a special someone to fill our inadequacies.

The ego responds to our sense of incompleteness and desperation, saying, "If this is how terrible you feel inside without hope of ever subduing your guilt-engendered being, I will seek out someone to complete you." ACIM states: *"No one who comes here but must still have hope, some lingering illusion, or some dream that there is something outside of himself that will bring happiness and peace to him."* (T-29.VII.2:1)

In compliance with the ego's pronouncement of our inadequacies, we embark on a search to find completion. This process has a particular formula that is followed: There are certain lacks and needs that are within my broken self that cannot be healed by myself or by God. Therefore, I must seek that special someone with those special characteristics and qualities that can fill my needs. In having you in my life, my special need will be met. I will finally find my completion in you. Because of your love and acceptance, I can then finally feel worthwhile and approve of myself.

The ego is not concerned about who is chosen, provided that they are willing to play their part in this hellish scheme. Those who are willing to fulfill their part are the people we love. We dismiss those who are unwilling to do so, and continue our search for the one who will. When we are, in turn, able to fulfill a role within the same formula for a special partner, we see the relationship as a "marriage made in Heaven." We have come to believe that the reciprocal of both partners filling the perceived lack they respectively feel is "real love." The Course refers to this as follows:

> *The "better" self the ego seeks is always one that is more special. And whoever seems to possess a special self is "loved" for what can be taken from him. Where both partners see this special self in each other, the ego sees "a union made in Heaven."* (T-16.V.8:1-3)

In the special love relationship, love means that there must be sacrifice. What is concealed is that in this particular set-up, hate is disguised as love, therefore, to love means the need for sacrifice. What seemed to be a union made in Heaven is revealed as truly being a union made in hell. The special love relationships are clearly not founded on love and sharing, but rather on sustaining each other's hopelessness and incompleteness. The sacrifice factor, born of a feeling of incompleteness, is continually enforced within our ego-driven mind. The ego promotes this thinking in order to keep our partner feeling guilty and, therefore, grateful for our presence in the relationship. As explored, both parties are required to fill the "special needs" or inadequacies that each perceives are within them. Then, a silent agreement is made that states: "Everything is fine, my special love, provided that you continue to meet my needs, so that I can avoid my own feelings of helplessness and guilt. In return, my love, I will fulfill your special needs so that you might also avoid the pain that you feel inside. But remember also that to stop fulfilling your part leaves me with no alternative but to punish you and possibly even to leave you." It is the last statement that finally unearths the hate in this special love relationship. "I love you *if*" is the condition that maintains it.

Remember that, in the ego's point of view, the value in others is proportionate to their ability to shield us from our guilt. Therefore, it becomes vital that our special someone maintains their part in this deceptive relationship. Consequently, any action or awakening to what is going on, which reveals a desire to stop filling that need, is met with swift yet certain guilt-driven manipulation. The slightest deviation from the arrangement is seen as an overwhelming threat that is fueled by an outburst of terror and anger that up to this point had been subdued. We are desperate to hide the self-loathing and hatred we feel. We will consequently stop at nothing in order to return our special someone to his or her original position of protector of our separated engendered fear.

In light of the extreme fear that is felt, the prime arsenal of the ego will now be revealed. Manipulation will be the tactic now employed as we make our partner feel hopelessly guilty of no longer caring for us. We will bombard them with tears, accusing them of being the real cause of all our pain and sorrow, and telling them that only their return to their role of savior from our feelings of guilt and helplessness can possibly stop our pain. We have brilliantly now made them the cause of the terror we feel and felt prior to their arrival, as we stand before the image of ourselves that we can't stand. Obviously, healing can only take place if we stop sobbing long enough to evaluate the validity of our guilt. But if our special love declines our invitation to continue acting as our savior, it is precisely at this point that the Holy Spirit can begin guiding us home to God. The sense of hopelessness, which we all feel at times, is also what brings us to a place of surrender. If we choose not to surrender, we will make an attempt to fill this void with yet another idol. In doing so, we once again block healing, rather than allowing love to heal the wounded parts of ourselves.

Moreah Ragusa

Transcending Our Fears

A personal experience illustrates how these dynamics can be played out. One of my greater fears is of traveling to unknown destinations without another adult by my side. In fact, one of the first fears that arise for me during an argument that entertains the possibility of a separation from my husband is this very fear. It doesn't matter if my unknown destination is downtown Calgary, or one of the neighboring towns.

My youngest son, an avid hockey player, creates through his passion an ongoing opportunity to travel to uncharted towns in search of a team to play hockey games with. Normally, my fears of traveling don't surface because my husband does the driving. This is an "unspoken agreement" between us! One crisp autumn day, however, the driving duty was unexpectedly turned over to me. The summer and fall had been especially busy for my husband and myself, and I was looking forward to spending the Sunday afternoon together watching our son's game. My husband, on the other hand, had spent the morning and early afternoon raking leaves and founded a different plan.

Just moments before we were to leave, he announced that I should go alone. I was furious. My feelings of rage were disproportionate to the change in plan that had been suggested. I was angry for what appeared at first to be a series of reasons but which, in reality, was only one. First, I was angry with him for not prioritizing what, or rather who, was more important. Second, I was upset that he had not alerted me sooner to this change in plan. Third,

Rediscovering Your Authentic Self

I was annoyed because I saw his move as a way of getting back at me for not setting aside my writing to help him on previous occasions.

Most of all, I was angry with him for failing to do his part in our agreement, namely driving! I was so mad and filled with pride that I didn't have the common sense to even ask him if my route to the northern town was correct. Instead, with all the force I could muster, I slammed the garage door in the hope that he might feel guilty and shamed for changing our plans.

I drove down the highway praying and asking for a miracle. I needed clarity in two ways: first, for the fastest route to the game, and, more importantly, for the deep sense of rage that I was feeling. The inner voice spoke clearly, telling me to first call home to confirm the driving route to avoid getting lost, and second, to change my perception. So I did. I was relieved to hear my daughter's voice on the other end of the line, which allowed me to save face, or so I thought. I was empowered to discover that, in fact, I did have the best way to get to the arena. While driving and internally dialoguing, I discovered that the best way for me to get in touch with my fear was to face it. I recognized that this fear was about getting lost and not finding my way home. It brought up feelings of vulnerability and helplessness that undoubtedly were reflections of all the areas in my life that I felt powerless in.

It also denied my faith in the ability of the angels to guide me, as they had done so many times in the past. I realized that for the past eight years, I had placed on my husband the responsibility for getting me to where we had to go. The fact that I had felt so unimportant because he did not fulfill my expectation forced me to get in touch with the realization of just how quickly my love could turn to hate! Even I was surprised at how quickly my gentle, loving nature could be flipped upside down when I was faced with a core issue in my life. I realized that my husband's not conforming to my fear, which was masked and justified, as a desire to "be together," was a gift of transformation if I wanted it to be. I decided that I truly did, and committed that from that day forward; I would embrace rather than reject any opportunity to go into the unknown.

A week later, I confessed to my husband the terrible fear I had of traveling to unknown places, and he was stunned. He had been unaware of my fear and the great anger that I had felt that fine autumn day. For me, a new level of power emerged, but even more important was the awe that I felt, once again, as I saw how the Holy Spirit was able to transcend my neurosis into enlightenment.

In *Forgiveness and Jesus*, Kenneth Wapnick gives a beautiful analogy of the special relationship:

> We can summarize the meaning of the special relationship in considering a glass jar, about one quarter filled with instant coffee granules. The jar represents our self-concept, or how the ego views us, while the coffee symbolizes our guilt, which the ego has convinced us is our fundamental reality. The ego teaches us to avoid this guilt at all costs, otherwise we would be overwhelmed and destroyed. Thus, we deny or repress our self-hatred, pushing the coffee to the jar's bottom which represents our unconscious. Once we have accepted the ego's idea as true, we are committed to keeping our guilt denied and at the bottom of the jar. What maintains the success of our denial is a secure lid, which now becomes the function of our special relationships. As long as we are in specialness, the guilt we project onto others is "safely" buried in our minds. The special partners - whether hate or love - remain our lid as long as they play the game of guilt. When they do not, the lid on our jar begins to unscrew. The guilt rises in our awareness and we panic as the ego has taught us to. Still within the ego's system we have no recourse but to have the lid screwed on tight once again, manipulating the special partner through guilt. If this fails, we must throw the lid away, finding another who can now fulfill that function for us.
> (T-1.p5.20:)

To the ego, our partner's guilt ensures the continuation of the relationship, while forgiveness is seen as the end of the relationship.

Moreah Ragusa

The Dynamics of Special Love and Hate Relationships

The role of the martyr is alive and well within the special relationship dynamics. To the ego, to give means individual loss, which indicates that it's payback time, and this continually reminds us of love's sacrifice. The ego invests highly in maintaining guilt within our partner, as this guilt is crucial to enabling the ego to maintain the special relationship. In the ego belief system, being in a relationship means that we are in need of those special qualities within our partner that are devoid in us. On some level, we recognize that we are somehow sacrificing something of ourselves in order to be with our partner. This tactic nurtures, enables, and feeds the ego entrapment that the special love relationship is founded on. Cleverly disguised and repressed, however, is our realization that, in order to remain a prisoner within this special love relationship, we must sacrifice the truth of our being whole and complete and without the sin that the ego demands.

To the ego, our partner's guilt ensures the continuation of the relationship, while forgiveness is seen as the end of the relationship. Claiming the absolute innocence of one's partner is preposterous to the ego, which "dictates" that the realization of their innocence would result in the end of the pact that the relationship was founded on. What the ego actually implies is that if our partner were "truly innocent," they would surely not want us. In addition, the ego is highly committed to seeking the guilt in others in order to give us a

Rediscovering Your Authentic Self

false sense of absolution. It continuously implies that our partner is the problem and that if they could only change, all would be okay. To acknowledge our partner's innocence is to acknowledge his or her identity, and to the ego that is like depriving fire of oxygen. In truth, to recognize our partner's inherent innocence means the transcending of our own ego, the result being the forming of bricks that will lay the foundation of the holy relationship.

An additional goal of the special relationship is to separate a partner and that particular relationship from the rest of the world, and to defend it against the rest of the world. The need for doing so is obvious in that this special person is the one who functions as savior to the exclusion of others. The familiar "three's a crowd" comes to mind. The unity of our being supports the law of "to give is to receive." However, the ego is threatened by this law and therefore defends the special love relationship at all our cost. This thinking — that to have one must give — is so diametrically opposed to the special love relationship's thought system that it could never be upheld. Separation is vital in its being the "fuel" that fear transfers into hate, that this relationship so seeks to hide. Operating from the ego interpretation of the relationship's purpose (to hide guilt) instead of the Holy Spirit's interpretation (to discount guilt's validity) is key to sustaining these special relationships. It is for this reason that the Holy Spirit must be invoked so that special relationships can be transformed into holy ones. There's no question that this inner separation we feel and the corresponding special relationships that follow are the reason that these relationships are so individually and globally prevalent in our society.

Moreah Ragusa

The Dynamics of Attraction

We are always attracted to others to transcend or enhance the unexpressed and undeveloped parts of our own personality. Up to this point, we have discussed them as our perceived lacks. For instance, when I first met my current husband, I noticed within him an incredible level of patience in teaching new tasks to my young sons. At that time, I did not feel that I had the same level of patience in this area. It was one of the very key parts of his personality that I was interested in. Patience was not something I had experienced in my own childhood; therefore it was an unexpressed need. As the relationship continued and I further healed my own mind, the patience that naturally follows when we become one with our authentic identity, emerged. Consequently, this strength began to manifest within me also.

In the special love relationship, what is masked is that the ego attraction toward a specific partner exists in order to permit us to study that strength, to observe how it is achieved, and then to "steal" it. The hidden, unexpressed parts of ourselves that our partner has, are used at first by the ego to confirm our lack, and then as we develop those strengths, the ego dictates, "Through your development this person has nothing left that you want. Therefore, you no longer owe them anything, either. (The breaking of the pact!) You do not need to fill their lack because they no longer fill yours. Obviously, then, it is time to go and find another who will hide your guilt."

Rediscovering Your Authentic Self

At the beginning of any relationship, the ego will attract us to the one who can fill a lack that we feel exists within us, and the ego will feel temporarily empowered by our ability to do the same for them. As shown in this "loving" relationship, the hate is then hidden beneath the conscious mind. In contrast, the Holy Spirit reminds us of a principle, or law of mind, that will ultimately place cause and effect in proper order, in that we cannot perceive in another something good or bad that we do not have within us also. This truth is brutally used by the ego that states, *"To see a stain in another is the only way to receive absolution for yourself."*

Or, just as heinously, if the ego detects our heightened level of responsibility for our thoughts and the acceptance of this law, it whispers, "A character flaw seen in another is the reflection of that same flaw within your despicable self."

The ego, having been caught in its earlier attempt at playing savior, now works passionately to convince us that it is no longer the other person who is a guilty sinner, but we ourselves. The ego hopes, once again, to drive us to our knees in shame of our disgraceful self, to again bow before the ego and ask for a solution. This would no doubt start the cycle again. However, if we are able to maintain our strength and follow the still small voice within, we will be led to the realization that neither the perceived guilt within ourselves, nor the guilt perceived in another, is real. The acceptance of this realization then summons the beginning of the end of the ego's vicious control dramas that so impact our lives.

As shared previously, I recognized within myself a lack of patience in relation to teaching my children new tasks. My husband, who soon noticed this, was quick to point out my weakness. At that point, I was faced with a choice to either perceive his comment as an attack, or I could decide that he was bringing this to my attention to help me strengthen the quality of patience. In keeping with my passionate inner desire to heal the belief in separation still within my mind, I chose to believe that all incidents were coming my way to assist me in that healing. (My perceived need to heal does, however, indicate a belief that I am still lacking in some way). Consistent with the belief that my husband was there to help, I made the decision to perceive his comments as the latter of my two choices. Since I have a preconditioned defensive nature, I need to be constantly aware that I can exercise my power of choice by receiving my husband's comments through either love or fear. Due to my upbringing and being molded by the defensive responses of my parents, I will naturally have the tendency to respond in the same defensive way. Comments from my husband or others can trigger one of my past defense mechanisms; hence, I must work diligently to keep those mechanisms at bay.

Rediscovering Your Authentic Self

Through the Holy Spirit, we will be reminded that the strength we saw within our partner from the beginning was perceived by us because we already had that strength within us.

Moreah Ragusa

Healing Our Wounds and Filling the Void

Our ego is relentless in telling us to perceive our partner's comments as an attack. Even if it was my husband's intent, through a comment, to show me that he had strength and I didn't, the decision about how I want to use that comment is still up to me. Living through the embodiment of the holy relationship, I would perceive the comment as an opportunity to strengthen my personality. In a special love relationship, I would see his comment as an invitation and as an opportunity to exercise my "right" to attack in response. I would then make a decision to either attack immediately or to "file" this information away, to use it more viciously later.

When we begin to authentically heal an underdeveloped part of our personality, our partner's ego may quite possibly respond with outrage. This is because the ego has the belief that our new strength has been attained unjustly. The ego believes that we have stolen our strength from our partner. Because of our growth, we will no longer be willing to play the game of guilt. In response, our partner's ego will start signaling to end the relationship before anything else is taken or revealed about their guilt. Through the rising in awareness or awakening of one or both parties, what actually occurs is that instead of two halves being maintained as an illusory "one," two "wholes" are being cultivated. Because the foundation of the special love relationship is to maintain the belief in two halves, which maintains the guilt, this transcendence, born of recognition of our innocence, will signal an attainment of independence that will be perceived incorrectly as a "threat to love."

Interestingly, what this threat, by its nature, causes us to question is whether it was love in the first place. Of course, as has been revealed, it was not love but hate that maintained the relationship. This horrifying realization will cause us either to change our belief in our self, which will perpetuate the change in foundation from fear to love, or we will run to find another partner to remain safe in the toxicity. Although, by its nature, real love does threaten the continuation of the special love relationship, it also affords us the opportunity to finally heal the infected wounds that the ego insisted were there, which will allow the holy relationship to emerge. The Holy Spirit, as the great transformer of thought, will have revealed to us that our being healed of the belief that we were ever guilty, recognizes Its reality and success. Through the Holy Spirit, we will be reminded that the strength we saw within our partner from the beginning was perceived by us because we already had that strength within us. We did not recognize this, however, because that strength was lying dormant. The ego is terrified that we might awaken to this realization! As we awaken, this change in perception is revealed to dismantle our guilt, signaling the beginning of the formation of the holy relationship.

Moreah Ragusa

Transcending The Ego

Perception lies in the domain of ego rather than spirit, which equals truth and knowledge, therefore, it is perception that requires healing. Perception is a way in which the ego signals to us through the filter of guilt that we are not whole and perfect. Consequently, when our ego perceives that within us, we are lacking a particular strength, its primary goal is to either hide that fact or, in the role of savior, rob those strengths from other people. Our ego's hope is to bring to us a person that can meet our need to help us stay disconnected from the self-loathing we feel. I trust that you can see that the ego is not the foundation from which to enjoy healthy spiritual and emotional well-being. Nothing can get us into trouble faster than our ego! It is important to recognize that in order to transcend the ego's effect on us, we must thoroughly understand what it is, what is does, and why it does it.

The ego continually keeps us searching for love while it secretly schemes to prevent us from truly finding it. In fact, at the very moment a relationship develops to the stage at which love's presence is recognized, the ego signals us to run. Love, which means innocence and acceptance, is a dangerous proposition for the ego. It is crucial to recognize that the ego actually prevents us from knowing its position at a conscious level of awareness. The ego takes on the role of hero as it continues to sabotage love. The ego believes it is maintaining its role as our savior by endlessly seeking and attracting people who possess qualities that we do not have, so that it sustains our incompleteness.

Rediscovering Your Authentic Self

To illustrate this, let's look at the type of pattern that might occur if I were lacking in willpower. I would be desperately attracted to a person whose willpower is plentiful. Initially, I would admire my new partner's willpower, and, through observation, I would try to understand his skill as I attempt to acquire it for myself. In doing so, the ego communicates to me that what I am attempting to do is robbery! This is true, because the ego is incapable of understanding that I could nurture and obtain willpower on my own through self-awareness and practice. In addition, my partner's ego will also perceive my attainment of willpower as a threat, for that would mean that I no longer need him to fill that need. This will cause terror within him, as it violates the agreed-upon pact. No matter how authentically or honestly I acquired my strengthened willpower, he will view it as a threat to his own. An important point here is that my ego will prevent me from being consciously aware that this strength of willpower still exists in my partner. If I carry on blindly, meaning that I'm not aware of what my ego is withholding from me, I will continue to follow this destructive pattern.

It is possible that I can bypass my ego taunting and its avoidance of love. Through perseverance, I will recognize that I can nurture a desired strength within myself, by correcting myself, by setting out specific tasks, and then accomplishing them. If I am successful at cultivating a higher sense of authentic willpower, my ego will equate my success with its own weakness, and it will become outraged. The relationship with my partner may continue as a result of my higher sense of authentic willpower, provided his sense of self is rising also. In the special relationship, our ego tolerates the joining of bodies, but never the joining of minds. The ego calculatingly encourages us that to join minds would mean that we would expose the anger, guilt, and hatred that so pervade our mind. The ego threatens us with the loss of any relationship, should these undesirable emotions and characteristics be revealed through a joining of minds. The ego viciously promotes within us the idea that the joining of our minds would be the end of us. The reality is that through the joining of minds, we are acting naturally and re-establishing our identity, which finally transcends the ego. Because the ego's foundation relies on keeping us separated from union, which is correctly perceived as the dwelling place of the Holy Spirit, the ego does not encourage the union, as this would signal its end. In this sense, the merging of minds is correctly perceived by the ego as dangerous.

Rediscovering Your Authentic Self

When we are willing to have our special relationships transformed into holy relationships, we are truly seeking to lay down our defenses.

Moreah Ragusa

Summary of the Special Relationship

The special relationship relies on our acceptance of sacrifice, which induces anger and powerlessness within us. The cause of powerlessness is a result of the power others have over us, which results in guilt. Because the idea of separation encourages us to continually feel guilty, the ego tells us that our only way out from guilt is through the belief that we must perceive it in another. The Course tells us that if our love to the Sonship is limited, or is directed at only a part of the Sonship, then this lack of love brings guilt into our relationships and consequently makes them unreal. The Course further states that if we seek to separate out certain aspects of the Sonship and expect these parts to meet our imagined needs, then we are attempting to use separation to save us. This begs the question of how, then, it is possible to prevent guilt from entering. For us to experience ourselves as separated and alone is to deny the oneness of the Father and His Son, and thus to attack reality.

The foundation of the holy relationship is that there is only one love, and all people deserve that love equally. The Holy Spirit reasons that it is impossible to perceive something of value, strength, weakness, or undesirability in someone else unless we already possess it ourselves. Through Its unified awareness, the Holy Spirit invites us to forgive qualities in others that we dislike. It does this in the hope that, by knowing we can forgive others, we might become willing to forgive such qualities in ourselves. It is clear to see that others become the source of our own personal salvation. There is a wonderful line in the Course that states *"We are free to save ourselves, by saving others."*

The holy relationship is nurtured by the Holy Spirit's thought system. A building block of this thought system is that for us to "have" and "keep," we must give. Similarly, as mentioned, to recognize something in another, we must also possess it. The Holy Spirit continually reminds us that, in reality, we are always wholly innocent. Each of us can restore our peace by staying focused on reality. We are not always able to act from innocence, but it is our mission to do so. To reveal this to our awareness is the goal of the Holy Spirit, which is always operating within the holy relationship.

When we are willing to have our special relationships transformed into holy relationships, we are truly seeking to lay down our defenses. Also, we are willing to become vulnerable, to expose and therefore heal the parts of our self that have been tattered and torn. Through trust in our Holy guide, we become willing to accept our strengths and weaknesses and do not project our wounded psychological perceptions onto others. Further, we take full responsibility for our own feelings and ask for help in forgiving our perceptions of our own and others' past mistakes. No longer do we believe that we are at the effect of loveless behavior. What we are really asking for is to begin again. In the holy relationship, we continually strive to live in and through the holy instant. We surrender the fear of joining our minds, which will result in authentic communication between the two. We live in the "now," allowing the past to be undone in the present. We are taught through the Course that the only thing wholly true about the past is that it is not here now! This is the key that delivers us our salvation. Just imagine the power this can bring to your own life if your slate can be wiped clean and the story can be rewritten, reorganized, and revalued by you.

Finally, through love, we are able to recognize that all the events in our lives are manifestations of inspirational thoughts and actions to heal ourselves. Our personal responsibility is accepted so as to make each of our relationships a holy encounter. We accept that, ultimately, it is our responsibility to commit fully to each of our relationships, which means that we share our honest feelings through kindness. In doing so, we are promised that our relationships will remain harmonious and will never conflict.

Moreah Ragusa

Finding Our Inner Power

That people have been assigned to particular roles, as in the special hate (the enemy) relationship and the special love (the savior or idol) relationship is undeniable. The premise is that we have, like Dorothy in The Wizard of Oz, experienced a trauma. In the story, Dorothy and her house are sucked up in a tornado that comes to rest on and kills Dorothy's most feared enemy. This scenario reflects the fact that a vehicle had been created which allowed Dorothy to hide from her feelings of guilt, for wanting to get rid of the old woman who is later revealed to be a wicked witch. Her enemy is portrayed as a bitter, decrepit old woman with a hooked nose, who can't stand Dorothy's dog, Toto. The fact that guilt causes us to become separated from reality is unquestionable, and becomes the actual foundation for the story. As is demonstrated within the tale, Dorothy dreams that she and her dog Toto are in a magical place reflecting heaven, which no one in their right mind should ever want to escape, except that, after a while, she begins to get homesick. Consequently, she begins to search for an escape from what was first perceived as a sort of heaven, but then, through feelings of entrapment, quickly converts to an experience of inescapable hell. However, through her search to find the way home, Dorothy begins to discover her dormant power.

Interestingly, through her desire to return home, she comes into contact with her latent power through seeking within, and magnifies the powerlessness she feels through seeking without. Her

Rediscovering Your Authentic Self

journey begins alone, but she soon attracts others who feel lost also. In this depiction, her perceived shortcomings are each revealed in a particular character. The Scarecrow, who is seeking intelligence, the Tin Woodman, who seeks a heart, and the Cowardly Lion, who searches for courage, are shown to reflect parts of Dorothy's unconscious, which reveals her belief in not having enough intelligence, sensitivity, and courage. For each character, the personality weaknesses they individually feel are compounded by the recognition of how truly lost and powerless they feel inside to correct the problem.

For each of these characters, their respective lack and loss seems hopeless until they are directed by the Munchkins of Munchkin Land to go to Oz and seek out the Wizard. Dorothy and her new friends are told that the Wizard can fill all their lacks and needs. They are promised that their freedom and wholeness is certain to be attained by following the yellow brick road. Searching for the Wizard seems paradoxically comparable to how at times we feel that there is a special someone who will save us.

While journeying down the path, they meet the Wicked Witch of the West, who expresses an insatiable urge to revenge the past accidental death of her sister, the Wicked Witch of the East. She reminds Dorothy of the falling house, which crushed and killed her sister. Dorothy's guilt is then substantiated and fuels what Dorothy perceives as a justifiable desire for revenge. The Wicked Witch seeks to stop at nothing, and she intends to prevent Dorothy and her friends from finding the one who can set them free. Intriguingly, yet unbeknownst to the group, the many obstacles that the Witch places before them afford each character an opportunity to demonstrate that they, in fact, already possess the strengths that they wish to find in another. After much running and fear, the final confrontation between the Witch and the terrified Dorothy and friends occurs. Through what seems to be an accident, they discover that the Witch's vulnerability lies simply in being dowsed with water.

The realization that the terrifying Wicked Witch of the West turns out to be nothing more than a bar of green soap, which is vulnerable to something so attainable as water, is truly inspirational. The comprehension that our greatest fears can be melted with love, as is depicted by the water, is shown to have properties that inherently wash away our guilt. Finally, following the death of the

Witch, they arrive in the Land of Oz, and stand before the castle. In an ominous voice, they hear the Wizard speak, who at first rejects them. Through determination and persistence, they receive approval to enter. Then, in great anticipation of the help they still feel certain to receive, everything begins to fall apart.

Dorothy and her friends uncover the Wizard's deceptive ways. They realize that the idolized Wizard used nothing more than an amplifying system, projector, smoke screen, and bullhorn to attain his grandeur. Apparent was his need to hide his fear that he was a nonentity. He then is revealed to be an illusory inflated image of a desperate, tiny, and powerless man. Completely disheartened and believing there no longer is hope for salvation, the Good Witch from the East appears. Finally, with the compassion and mercy of love itself, the Good Witch from the East reminds Dorothy that she still has on her feet the shoes that were "placed there" to guide her to the path that leads to her home. Revealed then, is the truth that all that is needed to return home is already with Dorothy. Just by clicking her heels three times, she is finally able to experience her liberation. The memory of the observer is then jarred, as the "finale" shows Dorothy in the process of awakening, to discover that, in reality, she was never lost.

The characters in Dorothy's dream are, of course, dream figures, but so, too, are the characters in our ego dream. Like Dorothy, we people it with our own projected fear and guilt as she did, and then forget that we are the creators of the story. We, like she, seek out both special hate and special love relationships in order to avoid our guilty self. We awaken as we realize that the objects or dream figures assume direct proportion to the fears that we are experiencing. When we are dreaming, all this orchestration is forgotten, thus we act accordingly. Once we pour on the waters of truth, the seeming reality and illusory images dissolve "into the nothingness from which [they] came..."

My unquenchable thirst for truth, and my incessant desire to know my Creator, led me to deeper and deeper questions and answers.

Our Relationship to God

Do you agree that life is about relationships? Whether it is your personal or business life, relationships can be the key to progress, happiness, and success. What about your own personal relationship with God? We are in relationship to our God in the form of our parents, children, mates, peers, friends, work, environment, homes, money, and even material possessions. The question we are so commonly asked to examine by principles in the Course is, what is it for — what is the purpose of the relationship? This is a powerful question to explore because we have already discussed that the world of form is reflecting the world of thought. We can move from that foundation into this topic. Each of the above-mentioned people or things that we have a relationship with reflects back particular beliefs about ourselves and the corresponding rules that govern our lives. Quite simply, these rules set the stage by which we live.

My personal relationship to God has undergone many transformations throughout my life. At times, I saw God as a parental figure who loved me unconditionally, while at other times, He appeared to be a God who would scold me for my inappropriate actions and bless me for appropriate ones. I saw Him as the judge and decision-maker of my life's experiences. At times, I even feared Him as a punitive God. I truly believed that I was becoming holy through the hardships I endured, and to some extent, I believed He was a testing God. All of these beliefs were reflections of my ego perception of God and my limited understanding of love. At times, I

Rediscovering Your Authentic Self

was very angry with God, and I told Him so. I believed that I was being tested to see how much I could endure. What never crossed my mind was that it was my own belief system that was creating my misfortune. What this revealed, then, is that my relationship to God was, in fact, my relationship to myself. My ability to communicate with Him was in direct proportion to my ability to forgive both Him and myself for our mistaken identities.

    I saw the phrase "God never gives us more than we can handle," and this enhanced my perception that God was outside of me, which enforced my feelings of separation and abandonment. Finally, through the deep feelings of pain, I reviewed the beliefs that laid the foundation of my understanding of God. My intuition revealed that these were not actually my own beliefs, but rather predominantly those of my mother! This was the dawning of awareness for me that the beliefs we hold in our lives are actually the beliefs of our parents, our culture, and the society that raised us. On the surface, this may appear obvious, but as life unfolded, I took it one step further and began to question these adopted beliefs in many areas of my life. My unquenchable thirst for truth, and my incessant desire to know my Creator, led me to deeper and deeper questions and answers. For the first time, I felt as though I personally owned the answers that now undoubtedly reflected new truths. I now remembered the childhood perspective of love that I had inherently known as being rightfully mine.

Moreah Ragusa

Our Relationship to Our Parents

My relationship with my parents evolved over time, especially my relationship with my father, who left my life when I was seven and did not return until I was thirty. After he returned, it always amazed me how, in his presence, I could quickly be reduced from being an empowered, successful adult and parent to a helpless little child. As well, because of my father's absence during my childhood years, I suffered from issues of abandonment, particularly in relation to males. Throughout my life, I desperately sought the approval of male figures, with the underlying belief that if only I behaved properly, they would not leave.

To this day, I am most attracted to men whose physical attributes resemble those of my father. On an energetic and archetypal level, however, my marriages have been to individuals who are like my mother. Whenever I was attracted to men whose defenses reflected my father's, they would ultimately leave me and enhance my beliefs about male abandonment. This continued to happen until I healed my belief in abandonment. The healing occurred through my acceptance that I, through my thoughts and beliefs, had created my own life. Naturally, in the absence of my father, I had a need to create my ideal of a father figure to heal the pain that I had felt because my father had not been there to guide and protect me in my early years.

My mother was raised as a gypsy and was truly a gypsy in nature. Congruent with her culture, she was quite simply a survivalist and did whatever was necessary in any given moment without any regard for future consequences. She was an incredibly strong-willed woman. Her mother had died when she was three, and from what she told me in my youth, my mother herself was also raised in a horribly dysfunctional home. Psychologically, she was not well and suffered from many disorders stemming from her own serious issues of childhood abandonment. My parents had a volatile relationship filled with rage and violence. Both of them desperately sought power and control in the marriage.

My mother constantly sought the approval of others in order that she might extinguish the feelings of abandonment that touched her life. She was highly suicidal, but I came to realize that her attempts to take her own life were manipulative in nature. Through my own suicide attempt, I discovered the level of courage required to succeed in such an act of desperation. My mother's absolute survivalist nature, in combination with her genius ingenuity, did not lend her either the courage or the desperation necessary to end her own life. As a youth, I assumed the role of caretaker of my mother. This role was reflective of my soul nature. Through close observation of my family history, I came to realize that my soul had chosen a path of self-reliance in this lifetime. Self-reliance is a logical choice for a child or youth faced with a situation where both parents are unavailable on emotional, psychological, and physical levels to provide love, protection, and support.

My mother was a deeply compassionate person, and a mystical seeker. In many ways, she was ahead of her time. In the same age group as actress Shirley McLean, she was most likely studying the same books. With a mother who was so clearly devoted to seeking the truth of God, it is no wonder that I have chosen the metaphysical path. My mother's life had been filled with pain, stemming from a belief system based on victimization and martyrdom. One could say that she suffered from an out-of-control personality. To cope, she learned to manipulate, lie, and steal, if necessary. In her compassion, she founded the "Lethbridge Aid Society," which, to my knowledge, is still operating today. Through her desire to serve humanity, she brought people's awareness to the need to feed the hungry, underprivileged, and less fortunate in Lethbridge, a southern Alberta community.

Moreah Ragusa

Unfortunately, I have not seen my mother for a great many years due to her choice to both deny and abandon her family. I do, however, send her my love and peace daily, and remain grateful to have chosen her as a maternal role model in this incarnation. Through my mother, I learned of our responsibility to find God, to serve humanity, and to question the rules. Most important, I learned that, no matter what, with God I can survive anything!

Rediscovering Your Authentic Self

By operating through the filter of love rather than fear, we can consciously work with these archetypes.

Moreah Ragusa

Transcending Archetypal Patterns

I see attributes of both of my parents in my own makeup. Some of these attributes are strengths, while others are the defense archetypes that I attempt to transcend on a daily basis by using them in positive ways. By operating through the filter of love rather than fear, we can consciously work with these archetypes. Self-reliance is a powerful lesson for any soul to live through. The trap of the self-reliance archetypal pattern, in its negative form, occurs when we are unwilling to take help from others for fear of abandonment. Self-reliance in its positive form comes from understanding that the self is not a single identity hanging out there on its own, but is rather a Sonship. Through my own life experiences, I have indeed transcended this archetype from the negative into the positive. Because I have succeeded in transcending this archetypal pattern and have a higher goal to help others transcend similar patterns, Heaven continuously sends me people who themselves are trying to transcend this same archetype. When a person is caught in the negative side of the archetype of self-reliance, their fear will result in turmoil that is covering issues of abandonment and a deep sense of being out of control. Interestingly, this lack of control actually triggers the need by the ego to provide a reasonable substitute, and it does so by seeking to control others. Conversely, on the positive side, self-control through a developing will allows us to take steps in a healthier direction.

Rediscovering Your Authentic Self

What about the archetype that is founded on *sabotage*? In the positive, the sabotage archetype is used as an opportunity for us to strengthen our willpower. In the negative, the sabotage archetype fuels our feelings of inadequacy.

The *victim* archetype in the negative continually tempts us into a state of helplessness. This is undeniably the ego's favorite. In the positive, however, this archetypal pattern affords us the opportunity to be liberated as we finally take ownership of what we create in our life's experience. Through the healing of the victim belief, we are absolutely reinstated as the co-creators that God created us to be.

Then there is the *prostitute* archetypal pattern. This archetype seduces us through fear into self-abasement. In the positive, it gives us the opportunity to follow our guidance in spite of the fear. It reminds us that we have the power of choice, meaning we can actually say no.

The *child* archetypal pattern tempts us to live in denial of our part in creating a situation. In the positive, this archetype invites us to take responsibility to conduct ourselves in an adult manner.

Eventually, we make the observation that all defense archetypal patterns are, of themselves, neutral. It is our perception, past experience, and choices that define the archetypes' power or the lack thereof. Freedom can therefore be reinstated through consciously noticing these patterns rather than allowing them to contaminate our experiences.

Through understanding my parents, I am better able to understand myself. One message is clear: The parts of my parents and myself that I would prefer not to see reflected back to me, are the very parts of me that still require healing.

In my counseling practice, my favorite phrase is, "If you can feel it, you can heal it." This refers to the awareness that a loss of energy is being detected within our bodies when we experience feelings of anger or being upset. This indicates a loss of power that usually stems from an unconscious painful memory. Without exception, an upset feeling is the result of a painful memory. We can overcome this pain by taking complete ownership of its presence within us. We are invited by this challenge to simply stay with the feeling of powerlessness when it occurs. Conversely, we can compound our problem by projecting it outward, which usually means that we seek the cause of our problem in another person. Staying with a feeling when it occurs helps us to regain any power we may have otherwise displaced. This will, of course, agitate our ego, but will delight the soul.

    Indeed, we are able to finally heal places in our memory that reflect childhood pain. We can complete any perceived unfulfilled moments in our memory by filling in the gaps with actions we can take today, in the present. If we perceive that we were not hugged enough in our youth, we can decide to hug lots starting today. With great success, I have used this method in my own life to fill in the gaps. A powerful tool that I use in the present to heal the past is to give parents and siblings the support, on an emotional or physical level, that they were previously lacking. In turn, this stimulates them to reciprocate, feeling filled with the love that they have received from me.

I knew that the silent agreements of keeping our individual weaknesses hidden had ended.

Moreah Ragusa

When Is It Time to Leave a Relationship?

    A high percentage of my client readings and counseling sessions address questions about whether or not it is time to leave unfulfilling or abusive relationships. Often, a client hopes that I will provide an answer to this life-altering question. Although I will not give them the answer, I am happy to discuss with them the Course principles to better empower them to make a loving, conscious decision.

    The decision to leave a relationship usually engenders a great deal of pain. Primarily this is so because we begin to reflect on the broken dreams of an unrealized future. My recognition of this truth comes from my own personal life experiences, as well as from my counseling. For me, the pain always lessened, and at times even ceased, when I dealt with the decisions of leaving the relationship on a moment-by-moment basis. Any decision to leave a relationship would heighten my awareness that I was walking into uncharted territory, and this awareness was bound to bring up my guilt and fears of inadequacy. Through this process, I was fully aware of all the times, places, and situations where I had surrendered my power to my partner. I could never decide with whom I was most angry for this surrender; was I angry with myself for giving away my power, or with my partner for accepting it? I knew that the silent agreements of keeping our individual weaknesses hidden had ended.

Rediscovering Your Authentic Self

As I look back on my decisions to leave a relationship, there is a common denominator. I became aware that the art of self-love was dormant during the relationship. I was solely responsible for this. I further realized that if I had stopped loving and respecting myself in a relationship, I could not possibly have either respect or love for my mate. The price tag for the absence of love in this circumstance is resentment. My first step in the decision to leave a relationship was the decision to practice self-love and self-respect. I could then determine if the relationship could sustain this influence. In each of my own cases, the relationships could not sustain the influence of my heightened self-love and respect. I also acknowledged my personal responsibility to heal myself, which I had previously thrown upon another. We find out who really loves us when we decide to love ourselves first.

For me, the second step in deciding to leave a relationship was to determine if I could love my partner enough to accept them exactly the way they were and continue the relationship. Once again, I discovered that the answer was no. It is not my right to command that a partner change to suit me, but I realized that it was my right to change myself. Through the termination of each relationship, I grew. I knew I had to assess which parts of my personality were contributing factors to the dissolution of a relationship. It was then necessary to make a personal commitment to work on those parts to prevent them from sabotaging my next relationship. In some areas, I was successful, while in others it is an ongoing process.

I arrived at the decision to leave each of my relationships by asking myself whether the relationship was truly reflecting how I wished to be treated. In addition, I realized that we had both been influenced by the facade of love through the perceptual lens of "you only love me if I..." When the answer to the question if I had been treated appropriately was no, I recognized that I was being treated exactly the way I had been treating myself. Now, because of my decision to treat myself with love and respect, only two questions remained. The first was to see if my partner could grow enough to reflect my heightened level of self-worth back to me, and if so, the relationship would continue. The second was that if my partner was not willing to change, and therefore could no longer reflect my new self-worth, the relationship was over.

Moreah Ragusa

Each time I ended a relationship, I made the conscious choice to remain a friend to my partner. I made it clear that although we were no longer sharing a partnership, I was still willing to be kind. I knew that the way I treated my partner following our separation would be directly reflected in the dynamics between new people who would enter my life, and myself.

It was a tremendous relief for me to discover that the end of a relationship did not necessarily mean it was a failure. Remember that *A Course in Miracles* assures us that, quite often, relationships end because one or both souls have accomplished what they had come together to learn.

So how do we determine when it is time to release ourselves from a relationship? I often suggest to clients to look at the situation from a new perspective. If this were your son or daughter in this relationship, would you want them to stay in it? If the answer is no, it becomes apparent that the love and respect the client projects to their son or daughter is not extended towards themselves. In this case, I will often suggest that the next step is to sit down with their partner and share the fact that they are considering letting go of the relationship. It is an act of love to allow our partners the opportunity to change and grow. If a partner makes the decision to do nothing to continue the relationship, then the answer is clear, and it is time to lovingly exit. If, on the other hand, the partner is willing to explore how both parties can take individual responsibility to heal their perceived guilt, fear, and lack, the door will open to allow change and growth to happen. This, in turn, will provide the opportunity for the relationship to continue.

In these situations, communication between partners is vital. It is not fair for us to make decisions that involve our mate without their contribution. When we are afraid to share necessary information, it is usually because we have already made our decision on some level. At this point, we can contaminate the opportunity for a miracle by projecting how we believe the other person will react, before we actually have their input. If we have done this, it is not too late to reverse the cycle when we become cognizant of what we are doing. We are still able to return our minds to where the error occurred, and then turn our minds over to the Holy Spirit to receive the atonement.

Rediscovering Your Authentic Self

The recognition of our mistakes and the undoing of those mistakes become the cornerstones of holy relationships. These new relationships can and should outshine the original ones. Too often, honest communication only begins when the relationship is about to end. This occurs at such a late point because it seems as though there is nothing else to lose, so we may as well tell the truth. If a relationship gets to this stage, it is unfortunate, but often it can be the turning point where restorative action can heal the relationship. When couples come to see me because their relationship is in danger of breaking up, I always advise them that, more than ever, this is time to share their fears and any other information openly. Only then can decisions be made with any degree of intelligence and awareness.

Ultimately, any decision to leave a special relationship is based on an open and understanding heart. As a society, we have been programmed to end a relationship and simultaneously close our hearts at such a time. Consequently, our heart begins to close as directed by societal beliefs, followed by a tremendous heartache and heartbreak. Somehow the heart knows that to surrender a relationship does not mean that it must also surrender the love that was attached to it. If only the heart were left to its own wise devices, it would stay open and lead us to a gentle and caring letting-go.

It is normal to feel the need for some form of guarantee that a relationship will last a lifetime, but this cannot always be true. Even when we play by all the right rules, as we do in the holy relationship, and we love with an open heart and mind, partnered lifetime relationships are not always a part of the divine plan for us. The guarantee we receive from the extension of love is that the moment we give it, we are blessed in knowing that we have love, and therefore it is ours to give. Love does not possess, so there is no guarantee that any two individuals will stay together to the end of their life. The Course teaches us that when the learning/teaching balance is perfect, and the practice of real love and forgiveness is operating moment by moment, a lifelong relationship will likely occur. However, two consciously evolving souls who have sustained a holy relationship may nevertheless occasionally re-evaluate whether they still desire to walk down the same path in life. The choice not to do so is then guilt-free and equally supported by the Universe.

Moreah Ragusa

The question that naturally presents itself is, what do we do if only one of the two partners wants to end the relationship? In such a case, it is necessary to assist the partner who is hurting and struggling with their fears. It is crucial that we provide love and support to our partner when we leave the relationship. We must not forget that the Holy Spirit is still active in the relationship even as it ends. Ultimately, what we give to this grieving partner is what we will, in turn, receive. It is important not to take unresolved issues from a past relationship into future encounters. Patience is key, as is an understanding that fear needs to be brought to love. In our society, the loss or ending of a relationship is usually seen as a failure. From the perspective of *A Course in Miracles*, however, the way in which we leave a relationship is the decisive factor. Once again, love is the key to unlocking the door to a healthy and happy future.

My husband and I review this question each time either one of us makes an individual soul decision that affects our careers. It must be of importance to our souls to determine whether or not they are destined to be together in the future. Neither one of us has any guarantee of what the future holds for us, nor do we need to. We are both okay with trusting that each day, we fully participate in and nurture each other's growth. We accomplish that goal by taking personal responsibility for our unhealed issues. We no longer individually try filling the perceived lack in each other, but rather call on the Holy Spirit to heal these unexpressed needs in ourselves. What we can do, on a daily basis, is to continue communicating and sharing our dreams. We do this to determine if we wish to continue to merge our individual dreams into a shared life together. Up to this point and into the future, my husband and I place outcomes in God's hands.

The more committed we are to our own personal growth and the healing of our own childhood wounds, the more we free up our children to fulfill their own soul's mission.

Moreah Ragusa

Our Relationship to Spouse and Children

Perhaps you've heard it before that no one can hurt you like family can hurt you. Often, our spouse or our children can "push our buttons," meaning they trigger the wounded places within us. These scenarios are opportunities for us to get in touch with the raw wound, as well as every other wound that is related to it. It is extremely important to identify and heal these wounds in ourselves first before we attempt to correct the issue in others. The more committed we are to our own personal growth and the healing of our own childhood wounds, the more we free up our children to fulfill their own soul's mission. Each generation works on these wounded archetypal patterns and heals a portion of that archetype and then passes on the remainder to the next generation. The more committed we are to healing those wounded responses in ourselves rather than passing them on unhealed, the quicker the family as a whole will become freed from those patterns.

We may have a tendency to want to correct our children when they trigger a wound within us, without doing our own healing first. This is described in the Course as being the action of "the unhealed healer." The "unhealed healer" is typically a person who continually criticizes and points out other people's faults. An unhealed healer has not yet recognized why they themselves are upset. By having our buttons pushed, we are presented with the

Rediscovering Your Authentic Self

opportunity to accept the atonement for ourselves and to get in touch with our feelings of guilt that unconsciously drive a particular nature. The unhealed healer's nature is to be chronically critical of others.

Moreah Ragusa

Healing Archetypal Defense Mechanisms

In my life, I have played intimate roles in the victim/martyr archetype and consequently have personal scar tissue in that area. Those who act out this role will inevitably invite me to illuminate that wound or "button" and again tempt me to fall prey to my role. Or, I can hold my own through forgiveness. One of my daughters often uses the role of victim as a coping mechanism. Her behavior reminds me of the times in my own life when I was powerless and dramatically affected by the victim role. When this happens, I simply go to the place inside my being and feel the feelings. I do not run from my feelings or judge them. I call on the Holy Spirit to once again bring healing to the memory of my role as victim. I recognize that when an old memory comes up, it is presented for me to heal it. A choice is required when this happens, and I choose to use this opportunity to once again acknowledge the healing that is underway.

A helpful thought that has kept me from the playing out the "I/they" drama is to recognize when someone is irking me and whisper to myself, "Just like me." For instance, I sometimes notice a person who "makes mountains out of molehills" — a version of victim-consciousness that has been demonstrated and adopted within my life. Instead of becoming prey to my ego's judgment, I say to myself that the person can react in ways that are way out of proportion — just like me. That we are going to get in touch with our defense mechanisms is undeniable, but how we choose to deal with these situations is key to unlocking the door to a healthier future.

Was Jesus tempted by such defense mechanisms or archetypal patterns in His life? Absolutely; He had to be. It was His ability to transcend these temptations that gave Him the power to demonstrate single-mindedness. This is the meaning of what the Course so emphasizes, namely, "your brother is your savior." Jesus could not have demonstrated the "rising up" unless first He had surrendered the laying down of His physical life. When we are given the opportunity to get in touch with the minefields in our memory, we are able to regain the power that was there before the painful experience occurred. It is not necessary to get in touch with each and every experience we have been through. The Holy Spirit within our minds is fully aware of all the linking patterns related to a memory and effortlessly heals them simultaneously. For example, a belief that repeatedly brings us pain, such as, "I'm not good enough," will again and again be healed at different levels of our acceptance of self-love. One of my own stories will help to illustrate this further:

My husband owns and operates a heavy truck dealership. From time to time, he is detained from being home for dinner because his clients want to socialize with him. In the past, whenever this happened, I would fall apart. My husband normally calls me just as he is leaving the dealership, allowing me just enough time to prepare dinner for the family. Once in a while, he will call late, perhaps when he's already sitting in the driveway, just to tease me. Quite often, those are also the days when he brings me flowers! Occasionally, he is delayed and calls to inform me that he will not be home until seven or seven-thirty because a trucker arrived late and wants to chat. In the past, this news would sink deeply within my head, leaving me feeling defeated.

The response my husband received from me was a deafening silence. The energy that would leave my body and rapidly travel through the telephone line was seeking a victim to strangle. I could hear the fear and frustration in his voice because he did not understand the depth of my upset. Even I didn't truly understand my upset, so it seemed impossible to explain it to him. This pattern continued for years. Often, I would be having a wonderful day until, suddenly, I was sure that one of my angels had directed some trucker to enter my husband's office at 5:30 just to set me on my own course of healing! No doubt my husband dreaded making those calls to me. Finally, one day, I'd had enough. I decided that I needed a miracle, so I made a conscious decision to trace my feelings to identify what was triggering the rage I was feeling. I went within, and heard the question.

"What do you feel when he calls to say he's going to be late?"

"Helpless," I answered. (*Anger because our pact was broken*)

"Why do you feel helpless?"

"Because it seems as though he cares for his work more than he cares for me." (*Abandonment*)

"What if he does care for his work more than he cares for you; what then?" asked the inner voice.

"Well, that means that I'm not good enough," was my answer. (*Guilt*)

"Good enough for whom?" the guidance questioned.

This one got me thinking; without a doubt I do believe that I am good enough for God, so why do I believe I might not be good enough for my husband? (*The point at which I was willing to take ownership for my perceived lack — up to this point, I had looked to him to fill this lack.*)

"Why do you think he cares more about his work than he cares about you?"

"I don't know, I think it's because I don't believe that he could love me as much as he loves his work."

My inner guidance asked, "Why are you so upset with him when he calls and he can't help being late?"

"Because that proves that he loves his work more than he loves me." (*Projecting my beliefs onto him*)

"Why do you think that?" the inner voice questioned.

"Because if he really loved me, he would tell those selfish truckers that he wanted to get home for dinner and he couldn't stay and chat with them." (*The attempt to make someone else the cause of my pain*)

"What if he had said that, but also had to acknowledge that he was the owner of this dealership and needed to honor the commitment to his customers as well as the commitment to you?"

Rediscovering Your Authentic Self

(The final acceptance that what we give to others we must be willing to receive)

This was the statement that made me understand. My perception of the whole situation had been backwards. Due to the fact that I suffer from control issues with my husband, I knew that somehow this was related to my backwards thinking. Further, I recognized that I held the beliefs that love had to be proven to be real, that love was not without cost, and that it was selfish of the truckers to want my husband's time. I completely ignored that this was exactly what my special agenda had been. The truth was that I had been living from the effects of these beliefs for many years, and so I was projecting those beliefs onto my husband, and then getting mad at him for my beliefs. Does this sound insane? Absolutely! My ego's belief that my husband may love his dealership more than me was symptomatic of an inner belief that he couldn't possibly love me as much, because I didn't. What a revelation that was! Oh, what we can create when our ego's beliefs drive our imagination!

In reality, all the things I was feeling were not true, and the untruths were spinning off and affecting other areas of my life. All of this was awaiting my recognition and healing — one does not happen without the other. I returned my mind to the time of my thinking error and then confessed my belief system to the Holy Spirit. I took responsibility for my thoughts, and a sense of peace overcame me as I atoned from these beliefs. I couldn't wait for my husband to get home that night so I could share the revelation. He was grateful that I had come to my senses, but I'm sure he still had doubts about what my response would be the next time he would call. When he did, I simply "forgot" to respond the way I had responded in previous incidents. Remember that I had asked for a miracle before going through my healing process, and I had received it. In the up-and-coming replays of this event, I was simply grateful that my husband was safe, I was fine with it, and we were on our way to once again upholding the dynamics in our holy relationship.

Moreah Ragusa

Nurturing Our Children's Self-Esteem

Expectation and projection can also cause considerable pain in parent/child relationships. One day, a client came to me in search of tools to help her relate to, and interact with, her teenage son, Adam. Susan and her husband, Greg, were financially well established, and it was relatively easy for them to provide for the material needs and desires of their son. Over time, however, they discovered that in spite of their strong material support, they were "losing" Adam to drugs and alcohol. Bewildered by how this could be happening, first Susan and then Greg sought counseling.

My first suggestion was that their son's increasing level of addiction was partially their responsibility. They agreed, telling me that they had been aware for years that Adam had been "smoking up." They had believed that, because he was determined to use the drugs and they would not be able to stop him anyway, it was safer that he didn't feel the need to hide his habit from his parents. They felt that honesty between them and their son was very important.

I suggested to the couple that treatment for their son would have to include the whole family. They agreed, and we began family counseling as well as individual counseling. For Adam, the motivating factor for using drugs was that he felt good while "high." From this reasoning, I concluded that when he wasn't using drugs, he must be feeling sad, angry, stupid, unloved, or not good enough. At

Rediscovering Your Authentic Self

first, Adam didn't make the connection, but after discussions with the family, it became clear that this was indeed how he felt.

Adam was intensely protective of his parents as successful, loving people and role models. In addition, he repeatedly expressed that he knew they expected much more of him. This expectation was felt in all areas of Adam's life, and he had deduced that he always needed to do better, or be more. Through our joint exploration of the situation, however, he realized that they had never actually said the words "we expect more," and yet the energy of expectation was unmistakably laid as the foundation of their parent/child relationship.

It had taken several years until Adam's addiction took hold and began depleting his desire to do things and accomplish goals. His school grades plummeted, he partied to the early morning hours, and his performance level in the various sports that he played, dropped.

One day, I suggested to Adam that he could simply choose happiness, and that it wasn't dependent on anything external. For Adam, this simple truth was a revelation, because he had associated happiness with achievement. Since he had learned that any achievement was always open for yet greater achievement on an unending inclining scale, he had felt that happiness was almost impossible to attain.

For Susan and Greg, the realization that they had always placed a need on Adam to live up to their increasing expectations, was a turning point. They clearly recognized that through their actions, their son was unconsciously getting the message, "I'm only good enough if I fulfill today's goal." It finally became transparent for them that their son believed that he was not already good enough.

In this story, we clearly see the importance of believing in the inherent perfection of our children, and of communicating to them that they are already perfect in identity. As parents, our primary function is to cultivate and nurture our children's self-esteem. In addition, it is vital that we not identify our children with the actions that they participate in. Remain aware of the fact that negative actions are calls for love.

When children are continually reminded that they are beautiful, powerful beings, they are far less likely to seek outside themselves to attain external power.

Moreah Ragusa

The Holy Role of the Stepparent

Before this role, I humbly stand in awe,
For no more difficult a task can be embraced.

To stepparent is a heart endeavor, to say the least.
The guilt and constant wonder if you are fair.

To expand one's heart to open, yet not possess;
To guide and influence, yet not manipulate and control.

To nurture a friendship,
Then be expected to switch roles to parent,
Through the decision to join a mate in a committed relationship.

To at first begin by wisely modeling emotionally detached discipline,
And then, through the dynamics of attachment,
Be tempted to neglect that skill.

To wonder — if they were only mine.
To recognize that children are like guests in your life.

To temporarily miss the experience of a young child's adoration for its parents,
Until finally one day as an adult — that same child recognizes the depth of your love and commitment.

Rediscovering Your Authentic Self

To pick up the pieces from the dysfunctions of the natural parents,
To observe clearly what would be the answer, yet feel silenced by genetics.
To recognize that as a stepparent, your voice is not always asked for.

To give and give and give, and then feel invisible and unappreciated.
To be taken for granted, and in spite of this, still know that it's you who will need to pioneer this difficult parenting role.

To shape a life by choice, to love another as your own, yet have to share them.
To expand your awareness of love's gift — reflected in the eyes of a child.

To love and let go; to honor all of the other relationships in this child's life.

Before the selfless works of the stepparent — I stand in awe,
thus remaining certain of the power of love.

    The role of the stepparent is truly an incredible endeavor to accomplish. In this lifetime, I have not personally been tested to experience this role. On the other hand, I have observed the stepparent role in the dynamics between my husband and my children, and have directly experienced both the positive and the negative consequences. It is because of many painful life experiences around stepparenting that I feel qualified to address this issue.
    In the beginning stages of our relationship with our partner's children, we usually do beautifully. Just as in the beginning of any relationship, we focus on and recognize the beauty, the strength, and the innocence in ourselves, which is then reflected back to others. Just think about your own situation, and you will recognize that the reason you fall in love is because of the way you've felt about yourself while in the presence of another person. As new love begins to envelop us, we accept our greatness, at least for a while. In the beginning stages, we have no past experiences, conditions, or benchmarks with these new people. In the early stages of a new relationship, we rightfully live in the now. We may begin to perceive

dysfunctions in the relationship, but we are still unsure of, yet compassionate towards, these dysfunctions and their causes.

When the stepparent adopts the role of disciplinarian in any form, this role is not emotionally charged at that point. There is still a healthy separation between the stepparent's personal issues and those of the child. In these beginning stages of the parental relationship, the stepparent is quite often a brilliant disciplinarian. In future situations, it may be extremely helpful to look back at these periods and remember our own feelings and behavior. During these early times, stepparents are able to assess situations without allowing personal emotions to trigger their responses. They are still able to stay "unattached." At this point, they are willing to embrace their role without knowing the child's past behavior.

However, with the passing of time, a memory file is built as a result of discomforting experiences with the children, which begins to change the dynamics between them and the stepparent. In their simplest form, these memory files go to work and engage the archetypes of guilt and judgment. The stepparent then gets in touch with their own childhood wounds, and this ultimately involves traditional parent/child relationship patterns. The stepparent will feel guilty for falling into this pattern, which will fuel a vicious cycle between parent and child. This cycle leaves both of them feeling powerless.

As we have explored at length, relationships are built upon either love or hate. In the special relationship, the unexpressed needs of each partner are being projected outwardly, and only at times being fulfilled, creating a pendulum effect between these crippling dynamics. This is when the stepparent's own wounds or "buttons" are pushed, causing an outward projection because of his or her own archetypal patterns, and the result of these patterns begins to be felt.

The classic mistake is that the stepparent embraces the belief that the cause of their upset is in the present, and therefore with the child. This is an illusion, as something else is actually happening. A mirroring effect is occurring, and with it comes an opportunity for the stepparent to get in touch with their own childhood wounds, so that they might be healed. The biological parent/child relationship is the most critical relationship to the soul, and consequently the role of the stepparent often becomes doubly fused in emotion. The archetypal patterns of biological parents are in action in the biological parent-child relationships, and this also holds true for stepparents and children. It is for these reasons that the role of the stepparent becomes so difficult.

Moreah Ragusa

Love Asks No Reward

The role of stepparent truly challenges our understanding of love. Love does not possess in any way. Love gives itself freely, knowing that receiving love depends on its being given. Love does not need to be proven in order for us to believe that it was received. This is a fundamental truth that we often overlook in all of our loving relationships. This truth becomes magnified with a stepparent, and often leaves them feeling powerless because of the seductive belief that children can only fully love two parents.

We must be reminded once again that love is not an emotion or sentiment. However, our emotional body works as a filter, predetermining the amount of love that we will allow to flow for any individual. We can acknowledge that different emotions arise based on our experiences with people, but the emotions themselves do not refer to the level of love's presence. Intensity of emotion is merely a gauge of how much love we allow to flow through our hearts. Love, being perfect, gives itself fully and completely every time it is offered.

In the parenting role, we need to closely examine our understanding of what love is. Over the past eight years, I have observed my husband fulfill his role as a stepfather with conviction. I watch him impart endless hours of emotion, guidance, financial support, and leadership as he seeks to model a positive image of fatherhood. Through the fulfillment of his role, we are both able to better understand the emotions that trigger stepparents into psychologically dangerous areas where they attempt to replace a biological parent. I can't help but feel compassion swell in my heart as my husband describes to me his feelings of insufficiency that arise when my sons leap into the arms of their biological father. The emotional response mechanism that my husband experiences at such times is to shut down and to close his heart, as he begins to feel vulnerable and separated from the love that he has been sharing with his stepsons.

The role of the stepparent will continually challenge our belief systems in what it means to truly love someone. This role is currently so prevalent in Western societies that I suspect it is a major contributor to the awakening of human consciousness.

We must realize that we are able to love many people simultaneously. The belief system of the ego-driven special relationship is to separate certain people out and share love with them exclusively. This is a painful endeavor. It is true that a stepparent will not receive due recognition from a child for the love, commitment, and devotion they've offered to them until the children are grown and have become parents themselves. During the upbringing, however, it is the responsibility of the biological parent to give thanks to the stepparent for their part in rearing the child on a day-to-day basis. It seems that my husband's most dramatic downfall in his relationship to my sons is guilt and the feeling of being unappreciated.

What a stepparent often fails to recognize is that even a biological parent at times doesn't particularly like the behavior of their child! It is critical that we separate the child from the behavior. Children are not what they do. For the stepparent, these feelings of dislike will create deep feelings of guilt and resentment. For the parent, unwanted behaviors are seen simply as reflections of themselves or the other biological parent. Both stepparents and biological parents must realize that any dislikes they experience in connection with a child are reflective of parts of themselves which are yet unhealed. For the stepparent, these feelings of guilt become a powerful charge of resentment. In turn, these feelings will taint the stepparent's ability to love the child now, and consequently, to love the child in the future. The stepparent's belief might be that the cost of loving this child is too great. At this point, the biological parent can assist immeasurably by helping the stepparent to remember that their resentment stems from their judgment, from the past, and from some fear-charged belief rather than from love. When a couple is capable of having this type of discussion, it has an extremely positive impact on their loving relationship as well.

Respect is a natural out-picturing from a person who feels loved, uncontrolled, and cherished.

Moreah Ragusa

Nurturing **O**ur **R**elationships

It is important for a stepparent to have time alone. It is also important for a stepparent and the biological parent to find some time alone on a regular basis. This will further nurture their relationship to each other, as well as their relationship to their children. Often, split families can find time when children are spending time with their other biological parent, but there are other ways of finding time together as a couple. This can be accomplished through requesting the support of family or friends. Try to find another couple that is willing to share the responsibility of an extra set of kids for an evening or weekend. Make reciprocal arrangements with their children. Make an agreement to do this once every couple of months, so that both couples are given some free time. If neither option is possible, you can still create time alone through teaching your children boundaries. It's okay for mom and dad to retire for the evening at 7 pm!

Another important factor that helps to nurture the relationship dynamic in a blended family is for the stepparent and child to spend time alone. All too often, the biological parent does not allow the space needed for bonding to occur between stepparent and child. This has been a powerful tool in our blended family dynamics. My husband often shares with me the closeness that he is able to achieve with my children in my absence. He expresses that the children react differently to him in my absence, and he has revealed that they rely on him in ways in which they would not rely on him in my presence.

Rediscovering Your Authentic Self

Children quickly learn which strings can be pulled on the biological parent that will not work on the stepparent. It is important for the children to respect both their parent and stepparent equally. Respect is not something that can be requested. Rather, it is something that is given freely to someone who loves us. Respect is a natural out-picturing from a person who feels loved, uncontrolled, and cherished. The relationship between the stepparent and child will flourish if the stepchild feels safe in communicating their feelings honestly. A command for respect will often tear down this communication. To respect somebody means that you listen to them, and honor and acknowledge the feelings they have. Respect is not born from a belief that the parent has more power. In fact, the more empowered our children feel, the more willing they become to be respectful.

Surrendering Feelings of Guilt

It is very helpful for both the stepchild and the stepparent to not take things personally. Both roles are fused with the unfortunate belief that anything that goes wrong stems from their individual role. If this belief is the foundation of the relationship, there are bound to be problems because that belief will be reflected back to them. This belief system also initiates the role of victim, which will fuel anger and resentment. Stepparent and stepchildren must diligently surrender any feelings of guilt. Both parties can learn that they are guests in each other's lives. In fact, from this standpoint, there will be more respect between them. When we attempt to flex our muscles, we will receive a defensive response. This type of scenario eats away at a relationship. I often suggest to clients with a blended family that they allow the children to set out what they feel are appropriate disciplinary actions for the mistakes that they themselves have made. This is particularly helpful between the stepparent and the stepchild, as it diffuses the feelings of guilt that are so prevalent in this relationship. I also suggest the same for the stepparent who has made a mistake. Ask the child what they feel would be an appropriate "penance" for your mistake. This approach quickly diffuses the power struggle that so often affects this family unit.

The stepparent needs to recognize that it is detrimental to a child to feel guilty for loving either of their parents. If a child is forced to feel guilty for loving his or her parents, the long-term effect will be outrage. Subsequently, it is also possible that the child will

Rediscovering Your Authentic Self

become completely alienated from the instigator of such contamination. The instigator might be one of many individuals affecting the child's life, such as a parent, stepparent, aunt, uncle, grandparent, or other close family relation. It is natural for the child to have different feelings for the stepparent than they have for their biological parent. The feelings are different because they have had different experiences with each. Neither the child nor the stepparent needs to feel guilty for these feelings.

Because our feelings are so charged by past experiences, we must learn to evaluate them and question their authenticity in the moment that they surface. We must learn to let feelings of the past be surrendered to the Holy Spirit so that we might experience a holy instant in the moment. The success of the relationship between stepparent and child ultimately rests on the fact that we are not what we do. What we do is only a temporary reflection of a current state of mind. This will not guarantee that we will be totally safe from certain actions and their effects. It does guarantee, however, that those effects will not be charged with emotions from the past.

Trust between biological parent and stepparent in the disciplinary arena is critical. If the biological parent does not trust the disciplinary acts of the stepparent, then this issue needs addressing as quickly as possible. If there is a lack of trust between the partners, then agreements must be made to nurture their trust.

In our blended family, I have struggled to trust my husband as he was raised in a family where strict conformance was expected of the children. He always listened as a child — or else! Fear is a powerful motivator of children's behavior, but it is certain to cause repatterned defense mechanisms for the child in the future. This approach is a learned behavior that will haunt future generations, if it is not surrendered to love.

I do not want my children to be afraid of my husband, so I have "policed" him on several occasions when I have recognized his highly emotionally charged response. The key to my trusting his disciplinary response is in direct relation to the emotion with which he fuels his disciplinary measures. When he is emotionally detached, I trust.

Moreah Ragusa

Love in Abundance

What does it mean to be a spiritually based, blended family? It means that we believe there is more than enough love to go around for all members of both sides of the family. It means that we set boundaries and adhere to those boundaries for the psychological well-being of the family members. In the spiritually based, blended family, we understand that different rules will apply in different homes.

We must resist any temptation to try to impose our belief systems onto the other parent's household. As parents, we must also resist the alluring temptation to ask the children probing questions in order that we might place judgment on the other parent or their house rules. Our goal is to communicate honestly, sharing all the information that is required to make fair decisions for both parties.

As parents, we recognize that although we have left a marriage partnership, we have not abandoned one another as people. When it comes to dividing up visitation time or even property, we can make a wise decision to divide equally and then offer the other party first choice of which half they would like. Another tool that has been used with great success within the blended family network is to surrender any expectations of the other party's actions. We live by the rule that "life works," which means that we understand that what we give is what we will receive as we surrender our need for justice or vengeance.

In the area of financial maintenance and the blended family network, the children must be the winners. The financial status of both parties needs to be honestly evaluated to reach this goal. This means that if one parent is in a financial bind, we do what we can to ease that pressure. This does not mean that the financial responsibility of either biological parent can be released. It does mean that we deal with the situation honestly, and if we have less or more to give, we give it.

When offering gifts to the children in a blended family dynamic, fairness is the key. If one side of the family is financially more affluent, then the benefits of such affluence are to be contained within the affluent home. This ensures that the other children who are not of that marriage will not feel deprived. In the blended family, we use all spiritual principles taught through *A Course in Miracles*. The principle that will bring the most success is, "Do unto others as you would have them do unto you."

It is through gift-giving in the blended family dynamic that so much pain can be experienced. Some family members need to "walk in the other person's shoes," and take the time to consider the effects of their actions when giving gifts. An ill-timed gift, or a gift that is out of balance, can dramatically increase the stress on an already tested family dynamic. As parents, we can keep extended family members informed by honestly communicating to them how their actions can affect the whole family. It is critical to remember what the children's goals are within the blended family dynamic. Children are far less interested in the financial gains or even the losses than parents realize. They are much more interested in creating peaceful, guilt-free, and loving relationships between all their family members. It is difficult if children feel like "pawns" when the parents are playing them in attempts to gain power from one another.

In a spiritually based, blended family, one or more of the parent figures will be more interested in the psychological well-being of the children than in acting in accordance with societal rules. Spiritually based parents do not view their loving actions as a sacrifice; they see such actions as a demonstration to their children of how love really operates and expresses.

As spiritually grounded parents, we trust that our children have chosen both sets of parents for specific learning opportunities. We therefore can allow those opportunities to come into their lives. To be spiritually propelled within our family means to accept one another as we are. Once again, it means that we take ownership of our feelings and that we acknowledge that if we can feel it, then we can heal it. From this perspective, we are capable of recognizing that all the events in the blended family dynamic are there purposefully for the growth of each family member. We then encourage our families to operate on the power of faith rather than fear.

Rediscovering Your Authentic Self

I have come into your life to experience your love and for you to experience my love.

Moreah Ragusa

Our Relationship To Outer Relationships

It's interesting to note how we can change our personalities when we bounce back and forth in daily relationships with peers, co-workers, and friends. The driving force in these scenarios is competition. The belief that there is never enough to go around is the foundation of competition. Is it any wonder, then, that we feel such a need to compete when we live in a world that seems to say we're not good enough unless we make it to the top? Who cares if I don't win first place in the provincial or national cross-stitching contest? Right from the time we enter the school system, we are taught to strive to be the best. This is a dangerous message to give our children because the flip side of this belief is the implication that they are not already perfect.

As we awaken to who we are, we become more accepting of the strengths, weaknesses, and undeveloped parts of ourselves and others. We need to learn to release our judgment upon these undeveloped areas, recognizing that within our souls, we have all that we need to accomplish our life's mission.

My husband and I know of an elderly gentleman in the trucking industry who has not completed more than a grade-nine education. He began his journey as a truck driver and eventually was given the opportunity to buy a dealership. This dealership has been awarded the accolade of Top Dealership of its type in North America

Rediscovering Your Authentic Self

and is recognized to be one of the most profitable dealerships in North America. As you might expect, the owner is extremely wealthy. He likely has no understanding of algebra or how to do fractions, but those are not the skills he needs in this lifetime.

Parents and teachers need to relax with their children and send them messages acknowledging their perfection rather than highlighting their incompetence and continually teaching them to strive. Striving occurs naturally when a child is cherished. If we are told that we are perfect and wonderful, which is our authentic identity, we can accomplish all things through embracing that reality. As a consequence, achievement happens effortlessly. Success comes from empowerment. Empowerment lends itself to learning, and then teaching, the cosmic laws of love.

As mentioned earlier, a favorite phrase in my home is "life works." What this phrase says is that we can stand aside and let life's cosmic laws unfold. This is the way our heavenly Father treats us. It is an effective way to teach children that they are capable of creating form through their thinking. Our children need to know that in order to receive, they must give, and that all other people are a reflection of themselves. These are powerful universal truths that will effectively guide our children through their school years by generating feelings of empowerment. "To do unto others as you would have them do unto you," is a powerful foundation upon which to build a family. It engages every-day common respect, which is a gift that is all too often forgotten.

The things that we love in another person are a reflection of the things we love about ourselves. It is wise to keep focused on these positive reflections rather than on the reflections of our weaknesses. I remember the first time that I met a dear friend of mine, she had the nicest teeth I had ever seen and a smile that was vibrating with joy. I absolutely loved to watch her speak. At that time in my life, I had a mouth full of crooked teeth that inhibited and prevented me from smiling nearly as much as I would have liked to. I realized that what I loved in her I was actualizing in myself. A year or so after the beginning of our friendship, I was fitted with braces. I was told that, because I was an adult, the process of straightening my teeth would be a lengthy process of two-and-a-half years. To my delight, this prediction was wrong; it only took one year. I believe that it took considerably less time because I continually visualized

Moreah Ragusa

myself with a beautiful smile and said thank you to my teeth for yielding to the braces. Since I began learning the Course teachings, I have sought out the strengths of others rather than their weaknesses. As a result, I naturally see more of my own strengths.

If we could just surrender our possessiveness and our separateness and remember that all is one!

Moreah Ragusa

Remembering Our True Identity

It is amazing how readily we forget our true, divine identity and instead identify with jobs, titles, roles in society, and even things! For instance, many people seem to slip into a different identity when they are behind the steering wheel of their car.

I remember getting my first car. I was only a teenager, and my parents agreed to put me on their insurance policy so that I could afford to drive. At that time, we lived in a small town, and I went to school in the city. For months, I drove around absolutely convinced that I was an extension of my car. I was so excited by this newly acquired sense of freedom. Of course, this freedom must have originated from within me or I couldn't have experienced it. I felt absolutely omnipotent when I was driving.

What happens to our personality when we get into our cars? Why does the car become an extension of us, and why do we believe that we own the road? Road rage stems from the belief that we should already be at our destination and that everyone else is preventing us from getting there. What a helpless state! Do some people act as if they owned the road because they pay more taxes? Or maybe it's because they believe they're running out of time, as the concept of eternity has not yet become a foundation of their life.

And what about the rules? We are bound to become prisoners of the driving ethics of others if we are unwilling to be flexible with right-of-way regulations. If we could just surrender our possessiveness and our separateness and remember that all is one! I always wave a thank-you to the person who is letting me enter the

Rediscovering Your Authentic Self

lane in which they drive. This lane does not belong to them any more than it belongs to me. Keeping this awareness as a foundation when I'm driving helps me to be courteous to others. As a result, they are courteous to me.

We will greatly enhance the quality of our driving experience if we become more committed to suspending our judgment of others. When I encounter a person who is driving particularly slowly in front of me, I say, "thank you." I realize that because the Universe loves and cherishes me, there must be a reason for this speed. I don't go on and on trying to figure out what their problem is. I just accept that every person, even the slow one in front of me, is exactly where they're supposed to be at exactly that moment in time. I remind myself that this is God's party, and I'm simply one of His invited guests. This is the same approach I take when I have to wait in line. These situations are often opportunities to communicate with one another, and we simply don't take advantage of them as they arise. Let's start!

Moreah Ragusa

Our Relationship to Prosperity

Money is like the body — neutral. It can be used for holy or unholy purposes. It is an effect rather than a cause. It is the love of money that becomes dangerous. In the Bible, there is a line making reference to the fact that it is harder for a person in pursuit of money to enter Heaven than it is for a poor person. This is not a statement blessing poverty. It is a statement that makes us aware that if we pursue power on a physical level rather than on a spiritual level, attaining Heaven will be more difficult because attaining Heaven is an internal matter. This is simply because we usually don't focus our attention in the right location in order to attain peace. Peace is an "inside" job.

Often, people believe that financial independence will create power, freedom, peace, and happiness. However, we learn from the Course that these liberties are inherited rights of our being, and that we should not struggle towards them. This explains the parable of the rich man in constant pursuit of money, who finds it difficult to attain Heaven. By definition, "to struggle to attain" reflects that we lack in the belief that we already "have" these inherited rights. In summary, our ego is searching for idols, to fill a perceived lack that, in reality, does not exist.

Our relationship to money is directly related to the relationship we have with our self-worth and ourselves. Our relationship to ourselves is our relationship to God. Ultimately, we will discover that God is our source, substance, and supply. God is prosperity, and we were created from the abundance that is God.

Consequently, we begin to understand that our prosperity consciousness is directly related to our ability to be in contact with our God-given identity. Our sense of self and self-acceptance is a reflection of our beliefs and directly affects our self-worth.

This does not necessarily mean that people who are financially prosperous are always kind, generous, and loving people. It does mean that these people truly believe they are worthy of receiving prosperity. I have known some abrasive personalities who bully through control and manipulation, and who are extremely asset-rich people. True wealth is the external manifestation of a person who fully understands who they are. From self-love comes self-worth, which ultimately allows a person to picture out this inner knowing. From this, we receive the opportunity to manifest prosperity in our lives.

A question I always ask when communicating with a client who is seeking a higher level of prosperity consciousness is, "What is your resistance to your current level of prosperity?" This is an important question. The answer is intimately linked to our desire to prosper, and reveals the intention behind that desire. This is crucial to understand. If one desires prosperity in order to seek some reward, such as happiness or love, then this is the wrong reason.

Freedom, happiness, love, and abundance are inherited rights that belong to the children of God. By pursuing them, however, we disown these inherited attributes, mistakenly believing that they are not already ours. People who know on an inner level that these attributes are rightfully theirs will simply reflect them on an outer level. Most people see this backwards. They will look at a wealthy person and believe that her financial independence is the reason for her freedom. I want to clearly remind them that in accordance with the laws of mind, the freedom that this person has came first from within. The money followed to reflect and support the level of freedom that was accepted within that person.

Now here's something to consider that goes against everything we've been led to believe in our society. Prosperity is something that is accepted, not created. We were all created prosperous, brilliant, loving, and giving people. What affects our ability to reflect these inherent rights in our lives are our life experiences, which are quite often related to our upbringing — those things that were demonstrated to us and that we were exposed to in our lives.

As children, we may have watched our parents struggle and strive. As a result, we will have learned to believe that struggling and striving is the way to succeed and accomplish financial success. If we had parents who lived by the cosmic laws of love, we will feel safe and accept that we are co-creators of our universe. This does not mean that every person who is aware of their identity will automatically experience financial prosperity in their life. For some people, prosperity is not related to money. Mother Teresa believed that her prosperity was reflected back to her in the faces of the children and people whom she helped. Once again, the cosmic rule, "As you think, so shall you experience," prevails.

Rediscovering Your Authentic Self

If self-worth is a determining factor in one's ability to create prosperity, it's time to remember who we are.

Moreah Ragusa

Creating Abundance

Personally, I think of money the same way I think of air, which is to say that it is here for all of us to use, and return without restriction. We are never told that we are allowed fifteen trillion inhalations of air and then we'll run out. Money, like air, is here for all of us to use. It will be in our experience temporarily, and will then be lovingly shared with others. I absolutely refuse to take personal ownership of the money that is flowing through my life. Rather, I prefer to remain open to the full expanse of the abundance available to me. In so doing, I increase the level of abundance that I experience.

It has been my experience that taking ownership of money limits me as to what I'm allowed to experience. I'd rather say "what is mine is yours, and what is yours is mine." This is a win-win situation for everyone. I choose not to separate my thinking from that of the Holy Spirit — to once again hold true the consciousness of "all is one." When I see a person touched by an increase of prosperity, my heart revels in joy because what they have done is a model to me that prosperity is around us and open to those who will accept it. I see these people as demonstrators of inherited rights that also belong to me. I do not see them as violators of, or threats to, my inherited rights.

If self-worth is a determining factor in one's ability to create prosperity, it's time to remember who we are. Our beliefs about time are often linked to our ability to create financial wealth. "I don't have enough time," is not a statement I make. There is more than enough

Rediscovering Your Authentic Self

time to accomplish all the things that my soul has set into my life's experience. This I trust.

I am reminded of a popular saying that is a favorite among successful individuals: "If you want something done, give it to a busy person." What this means is that busy people have become very adept at working with time and using it to their benefit. They hold the belief that there's more than enough time to accomplish all things that enter into their experience. Successful people understand that new opportunities are around them all the time. They acknowledge that opportunities arrive because they can be accomplished. Sometimes, it is said that successful people are good time managers. It may seem ironic, but because time does not exist, there is nothing for busy people to manage. This approach in itself cultivates the freedom that these busy people enjoy, and thus it increases their prosperity.

Successful individuals have realized that moment-by-moment living is arrived at through trust. They trust that all things are possible in due time. They are not fixated on the belief that there is only one time for one thing; instead, they remain open to many possibilities. When we think we are all-knowing, we restrict ourselves. When we detach from absolutes and keep our eyes, ears, and minds open, life is able to flow through us. Consequently, our natural, inherited greatness can be reflected back to us.

Moreah Ragusa

The Unhealed Healer

An unhealed healer is a person who recognizes guilt rather than innocence in another. He or she is afraid to accept that their sense of failure is nothing more than a mistake in their perception about who they really are. We are reminded that it is the function of the Holy Spirit to judge, not ours. The premise of the thought system that the unhealed healer operates from is to correct others. The unhealed healer does this in order to deflect their attention away from their own sense of guilt. The very fact that a person recognizes fault in another defines the unhealed healer.

In our role as miracle workers, it is our conscious effort that allows us to see our own innocence first and then the innocence of others. However, the unhealed healer will recognize innocence in themselves, but will not offer that innocence to another. They feel that their innocence is present because the guilt lies with the other person. Operating from this premise, they fan the flames of a misinterpreted understanding of forgiveness. An unhealed healer will feel that she is forgiving someone else for their mistake because she feels holy enough, or enlightened enough, to do so. Forgiveness given honestly should not engender feelings of power; it should engender feelings of relief. Forgiveness becomes unnecessary to a miracle worker because they operate from the deep awareness that only love is real, therefore, there is nothing that needs to be forgiven. The miracle worker chooses to forgive the mistaken actions of others in recognition of the fact that their forgiveness will release them from their own mistakes.

Rediscovering Your Authentic Self

The unhealed healer is apt to talk about negative energy as if it were real, and to give warnings of falling prey to the "dark side." An unhealed healer will completely overlook the fact that the dark side is an illusion that has no power unless we fuel it with our own fear. On the other hand, a miracle worker recognizes that fear is a delusional belief that tempts us to believe in it, rather than believe in love. An unhealed healer is quick to criticize and police the actions of people around them. They will be very focused on the mistakes of others rather than nurturing the healing of their own mind.

The way to deal with an unhealed healer is through defenselessness. This does not cause one to be a martyr or a doormat. Quite to the contrary, it demonstrates true power. Martyrs and doormats are archetypal patterns that need your agreement in order for you to fulfill them. Defenselessness, on the other hand, empowers you in living the truth of your innocence, which is what we all seek to better understand. To take a defenseless role with someone who is operating in the role of the unhealed healer does not take away the truth of your innocence, but rather reflects it.

To defend against, or react to, an unhealed healer's comment is to give them credibility and treat them as real. It is wiser for us to quietly acknowledge that we have received input from an unhealed healer and then ask for the Holy Spirit's intervention in the relationship. When we are in a relationship with an unhealed healer, we must recognize that the unhealed parts of this individual are being projected outward, and they can only be engaged through our defensiveness. The only decision that we can make is the one between being right or attaining peace, within and without. We will ultimately come to understand that whenever we claim peace, we are right!

Moreah Ragusa

Part Four

The Purpose of The Body

Part Four - *The Purpose of the Body*   241
    Understanding the Body   243
    Balance   245
    The Purpose of Illness   247
    Magic vs. Miracles   253
    The Forming of the Body   257
    The Seven Chakras   259
        Chakra One   261
        Chakra Two   264
        Chakra Three   268
        Chakra Four   270
        Chakra Five   271
        Chakra Six   273
        Chakra Seven   274
    The Seven Chakras Working Together   277
    Addiction   281

Understanding The Body

A Course in Miracles teaches us that the Holy Spirit uses our body as a learning tool. The Course says that it was not God who created our bodies. Our bodies were made by our sleeping minds as a reflection of our individual desires to oppose God's will for us, and therefore to live our lives in a state of separateness from Him. This state of separateness is counter to our reality as created by God. Separateness creates guilt and fear that result in various forms of defense mechanisms, one of which is the body. We could say that our bodies are material barriers that we erected around ourselves to protect our minds from openly communicating with others and with God.

The Course teaches that we think we hate our bodies, but what we really hate is our minds. We hate our minds because of the perceived guilt that we detect within them. We are taught that the body itself is neutral and its health is reliant on the health of the mind.

The very same universal principles that we are taught in ACIM will reflect directly through the body according to the information that the mind perceives. In reality, the body does not exist outside of its purpose to help us learn the proper use of our minds. Therefore, in this section, we will explore the relationship between the energy and information that is stored within us, and our physical health and well-being. As mentioned previously in the book, it is particularly helpful to think of our body as our best friend. Our body continually out-pictures the signals of the mind, and in so doing, it allows us to become aware of our thoughts. This is why the Course emphasizes that the body is a learning tool. A misuse of mind will be reflected in the body as some form of discomfort or illness.

The Course is very clear and strict in its approach that an awakened mind transcends the body. It continually reminds us that in the absolute present moment, the body does not exist. Science reveals that the body is a river of energy and information that only *appears* to be solid. Congruent with the theories of quantum physics, the Course emphasizes that the experience of the body's presence comes from the mind's desperate desire and belief in its own existence. The ego's goal is to keep our attention on that which is effect (the body), rather than the cause (mind), lest we heal the mind that gave rise to the body. Our experience of the body is a reflection of the mind's thoughts that are continually moving between past and future tense. In other words, we have a memory and a desiring anticipation of the body within the mind that is projected outward. This teaching is the foundation of why there is no order of difficulty in miracles. In any instant, all we are is love. It is the perception that we are anything but love that gives rise to the experience of the body.

Moreah Ragusa

Balance

Health is the natural state of balance, while imbalance gives rise to sickness. Balance means that the elements of water, fire, space, earth, and wind that create life — both physically and non-physically — are in perfect proportion to each other in sustaining life. Each of these elements has natural specific properties that reveal its purpose. For example, water is cooling and amalgamating; fire, created through friction, is hot and illuminating; and space is the distance that seems to separate objects and the manifest from the un-manifest. Each element has a natural function, and the interaction of these elements gives rise to the physical universe.

Remember that purpose and meaning are indivisible. We have, up to this point, explored at length the fact that thought creates experience. Thoughts, like elements, have purpose. When the purpose of thought is to conceal rather than reveal, then an illusory truth will manifest. However, we must remain aware that long before we see or experience the effect of an underlying imbalance, it may already be present. For instance, we all inhale or ingest impurities, such as viruses or bacteria, yet only some of us experience certain effects in the subsequent hours, days, weeks, or even years. So why do some of us become susceptible to impurities while others don't? The answer lies in the domain of identity and the appropriate order of cause and effect. When we think impure thoughts or come into contact with either mental or physical impurities, we must seek for the natural balance that will correct the problem.

Rediscovering Your Authentic Self

Spiritually, we are taught to atone, which means to regain awareness in who we authentically are. Because the physical body is the effect of the mind, it must mirror the corrective thought. This is why prayer and meditation are considered so important in alternative healing disciplines.

Moreah Ragusa

The Purpose of Illness

Sickness is one of the most convincing witnesses to the ego's case against God. It seeks to prove that we are not at the effect of God, but rather at the effect of the body. Once again, it seeks to distort the true order of cause and effect. ACIM teaches that sickness results from a sick mind that projects its illness onto the body. In doing so, it is able to keep our attention towards healing in the body, from where it can never originate. It seems as if we have many conflicts within the mind to heal, but we are taught that, in actuality, there is only one: the conflict between the ego and God. We are reminded, however, that no such conflict really exists, because God, being Truth, does not recognize something that is illusory. The ego, however, considers this "war" to be very real, and it works diligently to make us into the "soldiers" of this battlefield. As long as we buy into the belief that we are a body separate from God, we will experience the effect of that thinking.

The fundamental conflict stems from the belief in separation that continually enforces our guilt. Sickness is the projection of the guilt we feel, onto the body. This dynamic is the same one that we explored in our discussion of relationships in Part Three concerning the way in which we project our guilt onto others. For this reason, martyrdom is often revealed in those who possess the spiritual maturity not to displace their hidden feelings of guilt and project them onto others, while completely overlooking this same dynamic at play against their body. The ego in its viciousness works diligently to keep us from discovering the guilt we suppress within the mind, so that we will remain its hostage. The ego uses three tactics to maintain

Rediscovering Your Authentic Self

the projection of guilt. It does this to keep us from self-discovery. It protects itself from the consequential healing that our progressive questioning would induce.

First, the ego decides that by attacking ourselves, we will compensate for our sinfulness. It deduces that, through an "unspoken" agreement with our Creator, it can punish us so that we can avoid God's punishment. Those of us who are parents often see this dynamic at play in our children. For instance, a child will accidentally break a dish or spill a drink. The child will feel guilty, and, rather than just confess the accident, they will tell you they have decided that they no longer want to play and instead are going to clean up their room — and make dinner! The Course states: *"Illness is a form of magic. It might be better to say it is a form of magical solution. The ego believes that by punishing itself it will mitigate the punishment of God."* (T-5.V.5:4-6) The suffering of the body then becomes the price we pay for the sins we perceive in the hope that this will appease God's insatiable need for revenge. If we once again reflect on the concept, "defenses do what they defend," then we recognize that this suffering merely sustains the guilt that the ego so vigilantly drives home.

Second, the ego is not yet satisfied that we be victimized; it continues onward in search of a scapegoat.

> *Whenever you consent to suffer pain, to be deprived, unfairly treated or in need of anything, you but accuse your brother of attack upon God's Son. You hold a picture of your crucifixion before his eyes, that he may see his sins are writ in Heaven in your blood and death, and go before him, closing off the gate and damming him to hell.*
>
> *A sick and suffering you but represents your brother's guilt; the witness that you send lest he forget the injuries he gave, from which you swear he never will escape. This sick and sorry picture you accept, if only it can serve to punish him. The sick are merciless to everyone, and in contagion do they seek to kill. Death seems an easy price, if they can say, "Behold me, brother, at your hand I die." For sickness is the witness to his guilt, and death would prove his errors must be sins. Sickness is but a*

Moreah Ragusa

"little" death; a form of vengeance not yet total. Yet it speaks with certainty for what it represents. (T-27.I.3:1-2;4:3-9).

Here we see the ego's tactic at work: First, it projects the guilt onto the body, then continues on to find the responsibility of this sickness with another. When we honestly search our hearts and minds, we can always find someone who we feel is to blame for our misery. The ego is ruthless in its non-selectiveness as to who might serve the goal; dead or alive, someone else must be at fault.

One morning, just months following a failed attempt to heal the shattered and torn relationship between myself and my daughters and their stepmother, I was meditating. Suddenly, I began witnessing a vision of being nailed to a cross. Immediately, I concluded that my daughter's stepmother must be the one doing the nailing. Quite to my surprise, however, I saw myself as the crucifier, and her as the one taking away the hammer. What a revelation that was for me! After years of experiencing her to be the assailant, I was finally healed enough to recognize that, although I was the recipient of her great unkindness, which was due to her insecurities, I had completely overlooked my own. What this vision revealed to me was that I was ready to heal the belief in our separate identities. It demonstrated the last-ditch attempt of my ego to maintain its belief in the need for guilt and separation between myself and this person, who had finally agreed, through communication, to try to heal our relationship.

The third use for sickness that the ego dictates is as "a defense against the truth." In the Course we read:

> *Sickness is a decision. It is not a thing that happens to you, quite unsought, which makes you weak and brings you suffering. It is a choice you make, a plan you lay, when for an instant truth arises in your own deluded mind, and all your world appears to totter and prepare to fall. Now are you sick, that the truth may go away and threaten your establishments no more. (W-pI.136.7).*

Truth is, of course, the reality that we are spirit, innocent and unified with God. The more we evolve and awaken to this identity, the more the ego will search to prove us wrong. One of its most

Rediscovering Your Authentic Self

conniving tactics is to make us sick. I had such an experience while on a business trip with my husband. I was thoroughly enjoying endless hours of reading the Course by the poolside. One evening, while reading, I suddenly began having an anaphylactic attack that appeared to come out of nowhere. I had experienced this condition on two previous occasions, each following an over-exertion during my training for a relay race. At that time, I had learned that it was due to my body's experience of too much stress. The stress came from the feelings of competition that the ego engenders.

To put it simply, my mind was experiencing itself as being in danger of defeat, and consequently, it felt attacked. The difference with this case was that I was not running; I was reading. To the ego-mind, the threat was just as real. It perceived the presence of truth as being so threatening that it attempted to prove me to be a body rather than spirit. I recognized its goal immediately and prayed. At the insistent urging of my husband, I then took two antihistamines. I subsequently fell asleep. I awoke in the morning exhilarated and honored that the Course was properly perceived as the ego's most feared opponent! The ego thus concludes that, if we are in pain, this makes the body real. If the body is real, then spirit can't be. In deducing this, the ego becomes safe from what it perceives as truth's "attack."

Obviously then, illness has a purpose. In Course terms, it is *"a method, conceived in madness, for placing God's Son on his Father's throne."*(M-5.I.1:7) Sickness reinforces the belief in separation, which rose up to enforce our insurmountable guilt. Instead of examining whether or not we are in fact guilty, the ego wants to validate the guilt, and therefore insists that the perpetual cycle of attack and guilt is the only way out.

Through this exploration, we can see that in the world sickness is no different than any of the ego's other games to maintain its existence. We have already explored at great length the concept that the physical world is nothing but a projection of an underlying idea of separation. Thus, the body is only carrying out the wishes of the mind, but it does not have any creative power in itself. The Course states: *"Only the mind is capable of error. The body can act wrongly only when it is responding to misthought."*(T-2.IV.2:4-5), for *"...sickness is not of the body, but of the mind. All forms of sickness are signs that the mind is split,..."*(T-8.IX.8:6-7)

Moreah Ragusa

Any resistance that we feel to this statement reveals our allegiance to the still persisting belief that we are at least in part attached to our body identification. In keeping with this concept, we believe the body to be self-directed and vulnerable to outside forces. We therefore seek for these outside forces to "heal" the body. Within the parameters of the laws governing the ego world, our bodies are vulnerable. Therefore, the laws of sickness and the laws of medicine — meaning any remedy aimed at the body rather than at the mind — do hold. Yet the reason they hold is due to our belief and conviction in them, not because they are true. This will be explored in detail in the next section, in which we discuss Magic vs. Miracles.

In one of my favorite books, *Illusions* by Richard Bach, we meet the Messiah, who is disguising himself as the barnstorming pilot of a 1928/29 Travel Air 4000. His name is Donald Shimoda.

Throughout the story, he defies the laws of time and space. He flies never needing to refuel, creates lunches at will, and never needs to clean his windshield from bug splatter. The reason he can do this is that he doesn't associate himself with the physical world. When we associate ourselves with the physical world, we are also at its effects, whereas when we don't, we are not.

Another story is that of a conversation held between Bishop Berkeley, and Samuel Johnson, the eighteenth-century British man known for his writings on metaphysics. They were said to be debating Berkley's belief that the material world is illusory. To make his point opposing what Berkley believed to be true, Johnson slammed his foot into a tree. Yelling out in pain, he exclaimed, "So much for an illusion!" What Johnson, and many others who have been perplexed by this illusory world failed to recognize, is that his foot was just as big a part of the illusion as was the tree. His nervous system simply responded to the mind's direction. Being within the ego's world, his body was perceived to be at the effect of its laws and consequently felt pain. Only when we truly believe in the power of miracles and that *"I am under no laws but God's"* (W-p1.76), will the effects of the ego's world disappear. We are reminded again that **"Miracles reawaken the awareness that the spirit, not the body, is the altar of truth. This is the recognition that leads to the healing power of the miracle."** (T-1.I.20)

In Course terms, sickness is understood to be of the mind and not of the body; therefore, the mind that wishes to bear witness to the separation is the mind that needs healing. Since it takes two people to witness separation, it also takes two individuals to witness sickness, one who believes himself to be sick and another who will support that belief. The Course states: "*No mind is sick until another mind agrees it is separate. And thus it is their joint decision to be sick.*" (T-28.III.2:1-2)

Once physical symptoms appear and I join with you in the belief that you are sick, I attest to being sick also. Since sickness is the manifestation of the belief in separation, my support in the belief determines that I, too, need healing. When I have fallen asleep with you, I can no longer wake you; therefore, I must call on the Holy Spirit to heal my perception. By definition, in accepting the atonement for myself, I accept it for you also, and the result of this joining is healing.

Moreah Ragusa

Magic vs. Miracles

As we have explored, sickness is the result of guilt that gives rise to a split mind. For this reason, healing must occur within the mind first. In the Course, we are taught that mistakes can only be undone at their source. What constitutes magic, therefore, is when healing is being pursued at a level of effect rather than cause. It is to attempt to heal a problem where it is not, and this action is based on error. Magic "spells" are remedies that focus on the body rather than the mind. These interventions won't work because the lack of forgiveness that is the true cause of the illness is left unresolved.

"*All material means that you accept as remedies for bodily ills are reinstatements of magic principles.*" (T-2.IV.4:1) This includes traditional and alternative treatments such as surgery, medication, acupuncture, massage, vitamins, herbs, laying on of hands, and aura manipulation. "*Physical medications are forms of 'spells,' but if you are afraid to use the mind to heal, you should not attempt to do so.*" (T-2.V.2:2) The reason these remedies and therapies are classified as magic spells is because they focus on the illusory solid body rather than accept the reality of spirit. This does not mean, "*that the use of such agents for corrective purposes is evil*" (T-2.IV.4:4), as some spiritual and religious sects would imply. When a person is too affected by fear's hold to abandon the ego's commitment to guilt, seeking the healing of the Holy Spirit can induce an even greater level of fear — the idea seems overwhelming to many. In such a situation, the Course suggests that "*it may be wise to utilize a compromise approach to mind and body, in which*

Rediscovering Your Authentic Self

something from the outside is temporarily given healing belief. (T-2.IV.4:6)

As we have all experienced, such magic does work at its own level. A Tylenol will relieve a headache, and surgery will remove obstructions and repair organs and tissue. The mistake that we make, however, is that we ascribe healing properties to them, because these methods do not heal the cause that birthed the problem. When we believe in magic agents, we slam the door to the power of the miracle to undo the guilt that is the true culprit. In doing so, we protect the guilt from the healing power of love, which again supports the shame we feel for supporting the belief in separation. The vicious circle that the ego describes can once again be seen: In denying the power of the mind to create the sickness, magic denies the mind its true power — the power to heal itself through the Holy Spirit.

True healing always occurs through the joining of minds and the practice of forgiveness of the belief in separation. In order to be healed, we must look past the symptoms, no matter how grotesque they appear, to the spirit beyond the body and accept that this spirit is one with us. As long as we perceive guilt within ourselves, we will project it outward, either onto our bodies or onto another person with whom we form one of the special relationships.

Because we live in the world of separation, we see how the world of the ego has an effect on us. As long as we see ourselves as being of this world, rather than of the world of love, we remain susceptible to guilt. But when we are sick, the last thing we need is more guilt, particularly once we have learned of the reasons why we get sick. If we fall prey to the cruel ego criticism while we're down, we get twice the hit. Rather, it is wiser to view our sickness in the same way that we should view all forms as fear — realizing that fear is "just a call to love." Being gentle with the self, we can celebrate the discovery that this sickness is revealing a cornerstone of guilt now surrendered to the love of God.

I have directly experienced illness teaching me how my past emotional suffering is used to make another person feel guilty for hurting me. I had been the receiver of malicious untrue gossip from a particular person for years. Then, one day while discussing the character traits of this person with a dear friend, I heard the Holy Spirit say, "Stop talking about this person; these issues are in the past." I chose to ignore the warning and again heard Its voice, "Stop talking about this or you will get sick!" Still, I chose to ignore this warning. Immediately as I hung up the phone, I began to feel a sore throat, and within half an hour I was flat out on my back with flu symptoms.

Completely denying my part in the sickness, I fell asleep. Hours passed, and then the question was finally asked, "Why am I sick?" Without hesitation, the voice within me answered: "In gossiping, you have done to this person what they have done to you. You knew the destructive effect that this had on your life, yet you proceeded. You separated yourself from her in order to project out your guilt. In doing so, you brought the past pain into the future. In this act, you secretly wanted her to suffer the guilt of her unkind action, in order for you to embrace the role of victim. You did this so that you might be exonerated from the guilt you've felt. Thus, your part of victim was assured in the situation."

This was the personal experience that taught me how the ego uses the body as a means to ensure the separation. Once I was given this clarity, I atoned, and a few hours later was returned to perfect health. I have learned since then that the form an illness takes is directly related to a particular form of "unforgiveness" within ourselves that needs healing.

In Summary

The Course emphasizes that the Holy Spirit can use all worldly forms to fulfill Its healing purpose. It can use "idols" or "forms" that were made to hurt and separate, or to heal and join. The Course teaches: *"They [idols] become but means to which you can communicate in ways the world can understand, but which you recognize is not the unity where true communication can be found."* (W-pI.184.9:5) In other words, all true communication comes from union with each other and God.

Healing occurs when two or more individuals join in the name of the "Christ" — the real identity that corrects all illusion through the forgiveness of our perceived guilt. This joining reflects the miracle, which attests to the correction of the belief in separation. The act of joining restores the proper order of cause and effect, which promotes healing. "Joining of mind" can include the joining of the Holy Spirit. Therefore, we do not necessarily need the presence of another individual to accomplish healing within ourselves.

It is the first step in giving back to cause the function of causation, not effect. It returns the cause of fear to you who made it. Thus is the body healed by miracles because they show the mind made sickness, and employed the body to be victim, or effect, of what it made.

The miracle is useless if you learn but that the body can be healed, for this is not the lesson it was sent to teach. The lesson is the mind was sick that thought the body could be sick; projecting out its guilt caused nothing, and had no effects.
(T-28.II.9:3;11:1,4,6-7)

And so we are taught that forgiveness heals because it joins what the ego separated. The idea of sickness is replaced with the idea of the miracle, which testifies to the healing of the love of God. This memory of God's love is identified as the end of dreams of sickness and pain.

Our purpose, we are taught, is to heal. We are shown that forgiveness undoes the ego's plan for justifying anger, and healing reverses the ego's plan to make us what we are not. Through sickness, we are encouraged to invest in an identification with the body rather than with spirit, and this supports the guilt we seek to get rid of. We are reminded, *"All sickness comes from separation. When the separation is denied, it goes."* (T-26.VII.2:1-2) This happens through *"Uniting with a brother's mind [which] prevents the cause of sickness and the perceived effects. Healing is the effect of minds that join, as sickness comes from minds that separate."* (T-28.III.2:5-6) Healing occurs as we accept the atonement for ourselves, because in doing this, we do not give support to someone's dream of sickness. We are reminded that as we heal, we are healed, and that very specific opportunities will be presented that will reflect the form of "un-forgiveness" in ourselves that needs healing.

The Forming of the Body

The deepest understanding of Body, Mind, and Spirit washes away the belief of separation on earth. Spirit is equated with God, and is a three-fold manifestation. Spirit is one with God, the Christ Mind, which reflects the Spirit, and the body that reflects either the belief in the ego or the Christ Mind is the manifestation of God. Each of these are aspects of the Divine that, when properly understood and identified in their order, can and do express love. The battle between God and the ego does not really exist. As in a set of magnets, the ego is identified as the love that pulls away, while Christ is that which moves towards itself. It is, however, always up to us which of these we want to experience — that which will attract love or that which repels it. The body as a reflection of mind is not really solid. Rather, it can be defined as condensed consciousness.

In many of the ancient Eastern religions, the body is depicted as the tree of life. This illustrates that the body is subject to certain laws which govern its internal energy and information systems. In Ayurveda, energy and information that are self-referring are defined as intelligence. *Ayurveda* means "The Science of Life," and in Ayurvedic terms, intelligence is thought of as Spirit. Intelligence is in every atom of our cells, and in this section we will discuss the healthy balance of energy required to support wellness. There are seven specific energy and information centers that are commonly known as *chakras*. We will explore these to further understand how our thoughts affect our health.

Rediscovering Your Authentic Self

Life force energy is the unification of five elemental forces of intelligence that are intertwining to be the expressers of the physical universe. They are: fire, water, air, space, and earth, and they, in addition to the chakras governing fields of energy and information, are what forms a body. Individually, we experience the elements as senses: sight — fire, sound — air, taste — water, touch — space, and smell — earth. The body can be experienced through the amalgamation of these five senses, which are, in their very nature, designed to perceive and mirror the five elements of the universe. Although the chakra system cannot be seen with ordinary sight, those who have awakened their spiritual sight can see it. The life force energy, information, thoughts, and memories are gathered and therefore determine how each chakra expresses this energy. Chakras can be read like a book by an individual with intuitive ability. It is important to emphasize that our memories are not only present in the chakras but are, in fact, in every cell of our being.

The chakra, however, is the storehouse of the memories and experiences since the beginning of time, which includes our entire physical evolution. There are at least seven chakras reflecting cosmic laws within the mind that are reflected through the human body. The chakras can be thought of as databanks governed by and through specific laws of love. When the mind is used appropriately by adhering to the proper use of these cosmic laws, our health is maintained.

Moreah Ragusa

The Seven Chakras

We will briefly discuss here the chakras and the laws they reflect. However, a more in-depth understanding can be gained from the book *Anatomy of the Spirit* by Caroline Myss. The chakras can be defined as the "spinning wheels of life," which adhere to specific cosmic laws that help us to embrace authentic power. Each chakra spins at a different rate, creating a specific sound, vibration, and color in the individual's auric field. Misuse of the laws that the chakras reflect can be seen as energy and information in the auric field. When I see this information coming from a person, I can usually link it to a past painful memory that the person continues to fuel with their daily life force energy. This results in the chakras' becoming contaminated through improper use of mind and through the misuse of the laws that reflect love. The chakras can be consciously cleared through the intervention of the Holy Spirit, and through meditation.

When I began to do Angel readings for people, I soon discovered that there were specific belief systems that triggered illness or malfunctions within their bodies. Because I'm wise enough to know that there are other teachers around me from whom I can learn, I began to study Caroline Myss' information to better help me understand what I was seeing. I became fascinated by her discovery that the symbolic Judaic tree of life and the ten *Sefira* (principles), which join to create the Sefirot, as well as the Catholic Sacraments, are expressions of cosmic laws or divine principles that move

Rediscovering Your Authentic Self

through the human body. Not surprisingly, I discovered that the way in which Caroline Myss suggested that healing might occur was indeed congruent with the principles of *A Course in Miracles*. We must recognize that we do have the right to detach ourselves from belief systems that fail to serve our highest good. In light of these opportunities to re-direct ourselves, we will briefly explore the chakras and the information contained within each of them.

Moreah Ragusa

Chakra One - All Is One

The first chakra is located at the base of the spine — it is often referred to as the *sacral chakra*. It is red in color and is energetically the densest. The law that governs the information here is "all is one" or "do unto others as you would have done unto yourself." The misuse of this command results in the loss of power and will eventually create illness. This is the chakra that, through the culmination of the five elements, vibrationally appears to manifest creation on a physical level. In the Judaic tree of life, this is the dwelling place of the *Sefira Shekinah*. It is female in its energy and governs our individual beliefs in time and space. It is through this chakra that we are connected to our Mother Earth. This chakra stores the information that encompasses our measure of "twelve," that is, twelve disciples, twelve hours in a day times two, twelve months in a year, and the twelve archetypal patterns that we have incarnated to transcend.

Contained in this chakra is the Catholic sacrament of baptism. This sacrament contains the belief systems we were born into and which therefore were imprinted upon us. It asks us to accept the family we were incarnated into and to understand that they have been specifically chosen to help us fulfill the mission of our soul. There are times in our lives when we resist following through with personal dreams due to a fear of "what will they say or think"? Such resistance occurs, and can be detected in this chakra region. Through the sacrament of baptism, we are initiated into our communities, which include our church, community, friends, and ethnic orientations. Because guilt is a powerful block to the guidance that we can receive in these areas, we must learn to transcend it. Guilt that stems from this chakra is expressed from the fear of betraying our familial and societal teachings.

There is a pulsing that resides in this first chakra that continually encourages us to share spirituality in a group setting. This is an innate need within us. Caroline Myss has brilliantly asserted that kids form street gangs to "act out" in ways that include body-piercing and colorfully died hair, in an attempt to express this starved spiritual need.

This first chakra also contains "the rules." These are the rules that have been set to control outcome — the family standards in

Rediscovering Your Authentic Self

addition to the social and religious expectations that are set in order to maintain conformity. This is also the house of the victim-consciousness archetype that continually seduces us to feel powerless. It continually tempts us to believe that we are at the effect rather than the cause of our life experiences. As a result, epidemic illness stems from the misuse of this "all is one" chakra. So how do we get out of this cycle? The powerful antidote, in order to maintain our health, is to be responsible for how we think. Because thoughts are vibrations and we live in a magnetic, self-referring universe, we must begin to think from an identity that is congruent with our authentic self. Therefore, it is important to remember that we attract that which we think we are.

When we are plugged into — meaning we want to adhere to — a specific disposition, this first "all is one" chakra will generate a desire spiritually to be a part of a group rather than pursuing the divine individually. The first chakra will encourage a person to be part of a congregational setting. Conversely, an individual who is not plugged into the first chakra may be more inclined to pursue spiritual studies on their own. In evolutionary terms, this group chakra was critical as we were once safer, and had a better chance of physical survival, in group dynamics. This principle is still valid today because, as people, we can at times function better and feel safer when we live and adhere to a specific set of rules. Whenever we choose to join a specific group, such as *Mothers Against Drunk Driving*, or a cancer or diabetes research group, we fuel this group with our own life force energy. As a result, we become individually susceptible to the effects that the whole group will experience. This is true for both the positive and negative experiences that the group may encounter. Does this mean that we should not join groups? Not at all, but it does mean that we are to remain conscious of the beliefs that the group holds and be willing to be at the effect of those beliefs.

What this and all the other chakras offer is the realization that there are certain governing rules that help us to have a healthy physical experience. It is important to be aware of the fact that these rules automatically engage when we are asleep or unconscious of our spiritual reality that is both unbounded by a body and eternal. What we are to discover is that these rules or laws can also be consciously bent to free first ourselves from the belief that we are bound and temporal, and then, to free the collective of human consciousness.

This awakening will result in the end of the belief that we are separate from God, which, we are taught, was the idea that gave rise to the body in the first place.

The manifestations of bending the rules are miracles, which operate in time and space yet are not of them. We are meant to live in the world while consciously knowing we are not of it — we only appear to be. If we become victim-oriented, we are adulterating the law of "all is one," because it means we have reversed cause and effect and separated from the whole. When we remain a perfect facet reflecting the perfect whole, we are honoring this chakra. One of the primary goals of this first chakra is that it will test our ability to maintain a healthy sense of self while in a group setting. What this means is that we are to learn not to project our suppressed feelings of guilt onto another, not to try to free ourselves by judging and condemning others, and finally, not to seek out someone other than God to fill our feelings of lack.

Rediscovering Your Authentic Self

Chakra Two — Honor One Another

The second chakra, located in the reproductive region, and often called the *reproductive* chakra, holds the command of "honor one another." This chakra, orange in color, is the relationship chakra. This is also the place where all our struggles for power that originate from our loss of identity are recorded. The information stored here records our relationship to the external world, which we look to for power, including money, power over others, and power in the area of sex. Interestingly, as our sense of power increases, so does our sex drive. This is because we have a social belief system that imprints in us the belief that power equates to freedom. Freedom, in turn, allows us to break the rules, which also include socially and ethically set morals. This is why presidents of corporations, and of countries, are so susceptible to acts of infidelity and also why they are often pardoned and their trespasses overlooked.

The second chakra is male in energy and is the seat of "foundation." Foundation is the base upon which everything else is built. Through examination, we discover that everything in life is in relationship to another — our relationship to God, our children, our job, our body, and so on. The second chakra is the center that questions our faith in our power, and therefore it becomes the foundational bricks that each of these relationships is built on. Its Sefira name is *Yesod*. In Catholicism, this is the sacrament of communion, which requires us to honor one another. In addition, I see these teachings to be congruent with the principle taught in *A Course in Miracles* that says that "only love is real."

This chakra asks us to treat all life with reverence, as we acknowledge that all the individual parts of life support the whole. To put this in perspective, we can look at the body. An old cell must die in order that a new one may be born. When a cell refuses to die and builds a kingdom unto itself, it becomes destructive to the whole. This is called cancer.

When we are confused by the actions of others, we are asked to send love rather than pass judgment. In addition, we are also encouraged to make our own decisions and to release our fears about relinquishing any societal and family rules which governed us, but which no longer reflect who we believe ourselves to be. I remember an example from my childhood: My mother's gypsy nature led her to believe, and to teach her children, that a broken mirror meant that the family was now cursed to seven years of bad luck. In keeping with the principle "as you think so shall you be," this superstition did have an effect on my mother, but I knew instinctively that it did not have to affect me in the same way. All I needed was for that idea to be challenged by my authentic identity. Because I believed that an accidentally broken mirror could not become a cause in my life, I broke the childhood spell. In breaking rules, we discover what friends or peers think about our actions or about us. One of my clients made me aware of a beautiful line that I have come to embrace: "We truly find out who our friends are when we begin loving ourselves first." When we make the decision to love ourselves first, we can explore what sets of rules we can break to allow love to rule rather than fear and judgment.

Because this is a relationship chakra that is the center of our reproductive system, we store information here that relates to our ability to create and give birth to both ideas and children. This is the place where our creative ideas are recorded. In addition, this chakra is where I usually find the residual effects of a person's decision to abort a pregnancy. It also records any dreams and desires that were aborted because of fear, guilt, or judgment. Consequently, this chakra logs our ability to honor ourselves while we honor others.

On the relationship side, we must remember that God is within us. Therefore, we are asked to seek His presence in the people we meet. Further, we are asked to communicate with one another through the Christ Consciousness. Christ Consciousness asks us to function on the premise that all is one, and that therefore we must "honor one another." This is the center that really questions our beliefs about what love is and does. The belief that love always involves some type of sacrifice is predominant in our ego mind, and so all memories reflecting this belief are stored here. We need to remember that the only sacrifice required by love is the sacrifice of the ego.

As conscious beings, we are continually encouraged to seek internal rather than external power. The snag is that our society and its belief systems have taught us that external power creates freedom. This leads us in the wrong direction as we fall prey to the need to control others in order to attain power. People who have an incessant need to control others create contamination in their second chakra, which leads to imbalance. The second chakra also records information concerning our vitality and physical strength. Memories of sexual abuse, issues around money, and any financial failures are all recorded here, and can be healed only through taking responsibility for all the events in our life. As ego-deflating as it is to accept that there is a reason for even the grossest levels of unkindness with which people treat each other, we will not heal until we join with God in forgiving both our perpetrator and ourselves for our part in the relationship. A deeper understanding always follows forgiveness if we ask.

When we receive a new idea, we will filter it through this chakra to check out the "cost." This concept will be explored in depth in the next section, "The Seven Chakras Working Together." Whenever we hold past painful memories, we fuel them with energy that we could use towards more positive and productive purposes. We are stealing energy from our precious life force to fuel these painful memories. This illustrates how, if we hold too many past painful memories, we truly do not have enough energy to run our bodies on a day-to-day basis. The energy required to maintain such memories is drawn from cell tissue connected to the information center for that chakra. We've all heard that thinking — and thus living — in our past is dangerous to our bodies. This is the reason.

The act of confessing shameful experiences from our past is a powerful catalyst for allowing healing to begin. One day, I was explaining to my client Marcy how we use a particular amount of our daily life force energy in order to be healthy. She sat in awe as I watched the light go on for her regarding a past phenomenon she had experienced, that she knew was of great importance but that she fully understood only at that moment.

Marcy had been experiencing menstrual flow complications and severe pain for years. She had been in a rocky relationship and had become pregnant. Due to the circumstances, she decided not to tell a single soul that she had become pregnant and terminated the pregnancy. Years later, she met her current husband and felt so safe with him and his nonjudgmental nature that she confessed her pain-filled secret.

She shared with me that as she was confessing, she could feel warmth in her entire body that she believed was coming from his gentle understanding. But she now realizes that the warmth must have been actual energy flowing through her previously dammed-up system.

Here is how I explained the financial accounting of energy and health to Marcy: Let's say each day it costs twenty dollars to run our bodies, and each day we are given one hundred dollars. We will then obviously have a surplus of eighty energy dollars to spend each day. This will be enough to finance future dreams and desires. Now here is the important thing to become aware of: The past that you have not released, for whatever reason, will cost you energy dollars each day to maintain the wound. Over time, more and more energy dollars are taken up until finally you are in debt. Once in the hole, your cell tissue will provide the dollars necessary to maintain the wound. In Marcy's case, therefore, the pain that she had experienced in her reproductive center ended with her confession and her ability to forgive herself.

Chakra Three — Honor One's Self

The third chakra, yellow in color, pulses out to "honor oneself." This chakra is located in the central region of the waist and is known as the *solar plexus* chakra. The solar plexus is a complex of radiating nerves at the pit of the stomach, and the chakra that sits in this area is highly sensitive to signals from the environment. If we are approaching any situation that could be dangerous on either an emotional, physical, or psychological level, the third chakra will send us a warning.

From this chakra, we must learn to love and cherish ourselves. This teaching is congruent with ACIM as we are invited to accept and own our individual perfection and innocence. We must all learn to lead our lives from a strong sense of self-acceptance. To help us in doing so, this power center continually encourages us to forgive ourselves for the misperception we hold of both others and ourselves. For this reason, I predominantly find a warehouse of guilt in this chakra region. In this chakra, we have both the female and male energies and information coming together.

The Judaic tree of life names these Sefirot as *Hod and Nesah*, which are "the predominant qualities of God." In the female energy as *Hod*, which means "Majesty of God," we are asked to confirm our personal honor code — the personal vows and morals that we believe support love. On the male side, this Sefira is called *Nesah*, meaning "endurance." The learning and accepting of these qualities are in part what this chakra employs. This center is where we learn of endurance, and it is often attained through physical illness or an extreme life challenge.

In the Catholic faith, this is the center of confirmation. This means that we become committed to our own personal growth. We are self-accepting of our strengths and our God-given talents. This chakra is also the center of integrity, which is the way we choose to live our lives when nobody is looking. From this center, we must learn that it is all right to break the socially implemented rules that govern the illusionary world. It is from this center that we learn to adhere to the laws of love rather than the laws of man.

The third chakra is the home of intuition. The more self-love we can access and accept, the more intuitive this center becomes. Our relationship to ourselves is also our relationship to God, and it is by expanding this relationship that we are able to heighten our intuitive abilities. The energy pulsing in this area is commonly referred to as the "gut feeling." This sensation is one that most men connect to. From this chakra, we learn to run our dreams by our faith rather than by our fears. When we are living our lives through intuition, which we were all created with, we are allowing energy to guide us — not matter. Decisions are made with our heart that works congruently with our mind.

This is the chakra of self; therefore, our self-esteem issues are recorded here. Anytime we attempt to accomplish a goal but experience a perceived failure instead, we record the information from that experience in this chakra. Along our path in life, if we have ever received information implying that we were not good enough, good-looking enough, or lovable enough, then these memories were recorded in this area as well. Learning to forgive ourselves is synonymous with a healthy self-esteem, and we can improve our ability to forgive ourselves through the undoing of our past painful memories.

It is important that we grow in our understanding of our authentic self, because as that understanding increases, so does our power. As our sense of self increases, so does our ability to understand deeper and deeper levels of truth. Like water, truth seeks its own level. This means that the more able we are to integrate and express ourselves from a higher level of understanding, the more we become able to recognize universal truths that reflect cosmic laws.

Chakra Four — Perfect Love

This chakra is located around the heart, and it is a connecting chakra. Through the *heart* chakra, we are encouraged to experience the giving and receiving of unconditional love. This chakra connects the top three chakras to the bottom three. It is a powerful emerald-green chakra that pulses out perfect love. For Catholics, this is the sacrament of marriage, and in the Judaic tree of life, the name of this Sefira is *Tif'eret*, which means beauty. The energy flowing from the heart center is female in nature, and it encourages us to experience feelings and to acknowledge our emotions rather than to deny or ignore them. People who are unable to express heart energy will eventually suffer from heart problems, which, in the extreme, can manifest as heart attacks. In the heart center, we are asked to act from the foundation that only love is real.

In our lives, the first marriage we must honor is the marriage to ourselves. Once again, we explore the understanding that our relationship to ourselves is our relationship to God. I often suggest to people to create marriage vows to honor themselves. Most people will find this to be an incredibly difficult task. Often the question is, "Where do I begin?" I suggest that people include words such as integrity, honor, self-love, and forgiveness in their contracts, as well as the promise to follow through on commitments made to the self.

Following our marriage to ourselves, we are able to honor our marriage to our mate. If we do not first love and cherish ourselves, we will become resentful of the love we feel we are giving to others at the expense of ourselves. This heart chakra continually seeks harmony and balance. It is such a powerful chakra that it stands alone in the center of the tree of life. The heart energy chakra has a strong electromagnetic force that pulses out into the world. This healing force truly has the ability to heal the world. Jesus was a powerful demonstrator of this heart chakra at work. It is through the heart that we learn compassion. Through the expansion of this heart center, we begin to recognize that love is divine power. What most contaminates this heart region is the inability or unwillingness to forgive others and ourselves for past mistakes.

Moreah Ragusa

Chakra Five — Thy Will Be Done

The fifth chakra is located in the throat and is baby-blue in color. This, the *throat chakra*, is our will center. Here, once again, the two Sefirot energies of male and female come together. The female side in the tree of life is the *Sefira Gevurah*, meaning "judgment," while the male side is the *Sefira Hesod*, meaning "mercy." The will center is located in the throat and is directly connected to what we say. Because the power of words is so intense, we are encouraged to use judgment and mercy whenever we speak. In this center, we learn that we should only say about others what we would have them say about us. When we are faced with a situation where we must make choices, the energy of judgment asks us to use divine understanding. The energy of mercy asks us to speak with compassion and love. The teachings from *A Course in Miracles* ask us to trust our will to the Holy Spirit, which is in constant awareness of who we are.

The Catholic sacrament here is confession. Confession is a powerful tool toward stopping the inappropriate use of our thought energy. This center asks us to be responsible for what we think and say. It's important for us to be aware that, whenever we judge a person or situation as unworthy of our experience, we actually deposit a part of our life force energy in that situation. We are continually encouraged to pull our life force back from situations and people whom we have judged. Take a moment to consider the difference between *judgment* and *discernment*. To judge someone or something means that you believe that a certain person or situation should not be in your experience. To use discernment means that, although you do not fully understand all of the components of an experience, you release the person or situation to be who or what they are, but do not currently choose to have them in your life.

The fifth chakra asks us to accept all experiences in our life as learning opportunities. We are required to trust that painful events in our past are meant to be surrendered to the Holy Spirit for purification. The will center is so powerful that if it is not governed, it will seek out a substance to govern it. For example, if we think of our heart as the mother and our mind as the father, we can identify with our will center in the middle as being our child. If the mom and dad don't work congruently together, the child will run rampant. A rampant child will seek externals to govern it. These externals are known as addictions.

Our will power is directly linked to our identity. When we suffer from the belief that we are separate and alone, our will is fueled by defense mechanisms. The ego's use of our will always leaves us feeling powerless so that the ego might rescue us. The ego continually pulses with the belief that something outside of ourselves can bring us satisfaction. When we remember who we truly are, our will is powerful in its defenselessness. There is only one way to govern this chakra center effectively, and that is through the union of heart, mind, thoughts, and choices.

Developing our authentic will is the essence and root of the spiritual journey. Remember that the whole idea of being separate from God arose from the insane belief that we could oppose God's will, which is love. We come to understand that the surrendering of our will is the wisest and, in eternal terms, the only choice we can make. When we follow our will and not that of the Holy Spirit, then our will is driven by the ego thought system. To follow "Thy Will" — the will of the Holy Spirit — is congruent with the "all is one" teachings. Because God knows perfectly who we are and what our worth is, to surrender our will to Him invokes knowledge and understanding.

It is through this will chakra that we learn of the power of choice. The choice that we are encouraged to make is one where we surrender judgment to God, and accept the Holy Spirit's function of mercy for our own lives and the lives of others. People who suffer from control issues can quite often develop problems associated with the will center in the throat. I have often found people suffering from thyroid dysfunction due to their incessant need to control others, which is reflective of their deep feelings of being out of control themselves. Thus, control over others is sought in the misguided hope of returning a sense of control to their own being.

Moreah Ragusa

Chakra Six — To Seek Truth

Mind clarity through wisdom is what this chakra, located at the brow, embraces. Like the third and fifth chakras, this indigo-colored *brow chakra* is an information Sefirot that is a combination of male and female energy. On the female side of the Tree of Life, there is understanding known as the Sefira *Binah,* and on the male side, there is wisdom known as the Sefira *Hokhmah*. This chakra is a favorite of mine, and for me personally, this is a highly developed chakra. What we are required to do through this chakra is to trust God to lead our life, no matter how things may appear on the outside. We are encouraged to trust the love-founded inner world rather than the fear-prone, illusionary outer world. With this chakra open and developed, a person has made the decision that energy precedes matter.

This chakra represents the Catholic sacrament of ordination, which means that we are asked to ordain ourselves and accept what our community has called us to do. Our community has the capability to see particular strengths that we have that we don't always recognize or value as important. We will be called to give service back to humanity through this strength, but for many people there will be a resistance and diminished valuation of their particular service. Through God's blessing, however, we are called on by Heaven to fulfill our soul's purpose. This is the contact point between God and the human mind — Supreme Intelligence and human consciousness. It is in this center that we take sheer life force energy and transform it into thoughts and ideas. From this chakra, we are continually encouraged to seek the intentions that lie beneath our thoughts and that ultimately result in our actions. This chakra, often referred to as "the third eye," is the seat of the imagination, which consequently is the road to Heaven. Those with a developed sixth chakra have clear sight, which is also known as clairvoyance.

It is through clarity of mind that we are able to bring the subconscious into awareness. This clarity allows us to heal the shadow side of ourselves, namely our ego. Here we see a link with ACIM principles that encourages us to become increasingly aware of how and what we are thinking. "As you think so shall you be," is the principle inherent in the sixth chakra.

Rediscovering Your Authentic Self

Chakra Seven — I Am As God Created Me

The *crown chakra* is where divine energy comes in and is transferred into thoughts and form. To those able to see chakra energy, the seventh chakra is identified by a royal purple glow. It is located in the mid-brain at the top of the spine. It pulses with the knowingness that "I am as God created me." Again, this chakra involves the two energies of male and female, or the manifest and un-manifest coming together. The Judaic Tree of Life makes reference to this chakra as the Sefira *Keter*. This center reveals our enlightenment and transcendence of the belief in separation.

In Catholicism, this sacrament represents extreme unction — the releasing of the dead. This does not necessarily refer to a dead person as much as it refers to the releasing of the past, and of illusions, including the belief that we are bound by time and space and at the effect of the physical universe. When this chakra is well developed, we are able to "raise the dead" or, in other words, release the past — that which has had power over us. We are then released from the person or situation that held us back from accessing or expressing our full capacity, and we can fully be who we are. To live in the moment is what keeps this chakra clear. It is from this center that we are able to complete the fusion between human consciousness and God consciousness. From this center, we are able to experience perfect love.

Actualizing the seventh chakra allows us to use our intuition not only for ourselves but also for others. It is when we actualize this chakra that we are called by Heaven to work on a community, or global, level. One of the requirements for fulfilling this task is to have completely learned to release judgment. We must learn to step aside and allow the Holy Spirit to use us for the fulfillment of God's plan. This is literally the source of "miracle mindedness." We live through this chakra center when we are able to accept and harness the power of who we are. We use this power not only for our own transcendence but also for others. When a person experiences an "awakening," it is at this center that their opening and actualizing occurs. Through this opening, we experience a sense of oneness with each other, with nature, and with God. We have all experienced inspired moments, and these moments come directly through this chakra center. People that are living from their seventh chakra believe that energy comes before matter, which means that they have discovered that the inner world is the world of truth. Because of their clarity, these people access and share a higher love and do not hold a private agenda for other people. They live from total acceptance, as they no longer suffer from the illusion of separateness.

Every new idea we have automatically gets measured.

Moreah Ragusa

The Seven Chakras Working Together

The seven chakras work congruently with one another as information is shared and sent back and forth among them. All form began from an idea, and ideas are manifested through the combination of thought and desire. To illustrate, let's say that I had the idea of starting a new business. The idea in itself is not enough to manifest it into a form. Desire is needed to back the idea, and what will challenge my desire is my fear. From nothingness came the "new business" thought, so at this point, I'm using my sixth and seventh chakras. Every new idea we have automatically gets measured. The "cost" of the idea will have to be filtered through every chakra system to determine whether or not to proceed with the idea.

Here is an example from my own life: one day, while meditating, I received the idea to realize a long-held dream of establishing a wellness center. In my meditative state, I simply accepted the idea as coming from the God within me and trusted that any obstacles I would encounter would be jointly met. The following hours revealed the process that we undertake at lightening speed with every new idea we ponder. A wellness center idea, as any other creative idea, begins at the seventh chakra — "I Am as God Created Me" — the center of divine consciousness. Divine love will guide this idea into the sixth chakra "to seek truth" in the center of mind clarity. I will then imagine the wellness center and see how it can be used for the purpose of healing our belief in separation.

At this point, I may or may not see any reasons why the dream can't manifest. For each person, this is directly related to their current level of faith. If no insurmountable obstacle dawns, the idea will continue to move down into the fifth chakra — the seat of "thy will be done." I will decide that if my will is joined to God's will, the dream can be born. At this point, fear may start to arise because verbalizing my dream to family and friends will bring to the surface any past and current beliefs I hold that will test my ability to see the dream through. If, on the other hand, I am able to turn the dream back over to God with the intention of "thy will be done through me," then the dream will continue on. If, however, my ego dialog begins chattering away about how I never finish what I start because the saboteur within me reigns, the idea will die.

If I have only some doubts concerning the idea, it will continue into the fourth chakra. As the idea of a wellness center moves through the fourth chakra, all obligations of this chakra will rise up. For instance, I will question how this idea will tax what I view to be my marital responsibility to my husband. In addition, I will think about how it will affect my "marriage" to myself. Both these marriages and the respective vows made will be tested against the idea. It should be noted that, until we hit the third chakra, we do not usually anticipate the physical "costs" of manifesting our dreams; instead, we encounter only spiritual and psychological ones.

If the idea still seems feasible after measuring it up against these highly individual beliefs, then it will be passed on to the third chakra. As this idea enters the intuitive third chakra, it will explore my ability to "honor self" and will therefore focus on this center of confirmation, which relates to my relationship to God. Now the manifestation of the wellness center will challenge me in all areas related to my personal material circumstances. This chakra is the place where all ideas of self-image and the responsibility of that image are recorded. These ideas will include having less free time, questioning my ability to start a business, and magnifying all fears about keeping accounting in good order. Will I be able to lead staff and govern all overhead costs? Will I be able to maintain balance? And will people even use the center or will they think I'm crazy? Most of all, I will question all my intuitive abilities and my current beliefs in my ability to fulfill my part in the plan towards healing the belief in separation.

Again, if the idea is sustained, it will journey downward and be pondered in the second chakra, which is the chakra of external relationships — "honor one another." Therefore, I will ask, what will my husband think? If he doesn't support the idea, will I leave him? Will he leave me? Can I afford to support both the center and myself? If not, what will I sacrifice for the dream? What will my father think? Will he banish me from his life? Then the more apparent physical debts that the idea entails will be measured against it. Who will clean my house? Do I need a cleaning person? Will my children have to suffer? Will they need to be tutored if I'm not there to help with homework? How much money will this idea really cost? What will the birth of this idea cost? And what will aborting the idea cost? Finally, what is my purpose in creating the center?

If, to this point, the idea has been sustained, meaning that my faith still precedes my fear, it will make its final movement through the principles inherent in the first chakra where, if it successfully passes, it can finally be seeded in the soil of manifestation. The first chakra — "all is one" (honoring the tribe) — would challenge my current beliefs about what the family as a whole and the community think. How will that affect how they view me? Am I conforming or breaking out of a set role? If I do break away, will they abandon me? Will there be anyone to help? Finally, how much time will it take to set up the center — days, weeks, or months, and where should the center be located?

Each of these possible "costs" will be questioned, and if the answers come from a joint effort with God through faith, the idea will be executed. If I am able to see the opportunities that present as a result of making these changes, I will move forward. If, on the other hand, fear predominates, the idea will return to the mind and soul from which it arose and surface at a later date. When an idea is part of a our soul's mission, it will keep arising, and not fulfilling the idea can often lead to illness or depression.

To magnify this powerfully transformative realization, I would hold the idea and make a decision as to whether or not I felt I had enough self-discipline (fifth chakra) and willpower to see my dream come to fruition. If I felt I did, I would next move the idea through my heart (fourth chakra) and get a sense of feeling around

Rediscovering Your Authentic Self

the idea, and if once again it felt positive, I would move the idea downward. Next, the idea of a new business would come into my third chakra, to test my sense of self-worth or confidence and explore my "who am I?" belief systems. The second chakra (power) comes into play next, examining how my idea will affect my relationships, how much money it will take, and what other people might think of me. If the idea of starting a new business passes my fears thus far, the final test will be in the first chakra, that is, what will my community and family think? If I am able to transcend any fears at this level, my dream can manifest itself if I maintain my desire.

We go through such a process with every decision we make. It happens at lightning speed, and we are normally unaware of it. When we feel powerless, separate, or afraid, we begin responding through one of our chakra systems where we will arrive at reasons why we feel justified in our choice to abort the idea. As we heal, we transcend the fears that reside with the appropriate power centers of each chakra. Reflecting a law of transcendence, power and the opposition to power are always equal; therefore, our authentic power continually grows.

Moreah Ragusa

Addition

It seems that part of the human journey involves some form of addiction. At a certain point in our lives, we discover that a substance, a belief system, or an activity outside of our self has become, at least in part, the source of our happiness. Personally, I have experienced addiction in a number of areas, including addiction to cigarettes, exercise, caffeine, overeating, starvation, diet pills, and sugar. Overcoming these addictions was possible through the lending of strength from a higher power, which was within me but not of me — the power known as God. What I came to realize through my own personal journey is that the propulsion of each of these "fixes" was a desperate inner desire for peace of mind and happiness. Despairingly, however, neither peace nor happiness was ever sustained through the use of these addictions. Following temporary feelings of reprieve from the "hit," the hell within my guilt-ridden mind would return. It seemed like an unending vicious cycle of guilt and shame that would forever entrench me. Ultimately, I realized that my ever-expanding guilt was due to the way in which I had attained temporary feelings of happiness — by giving in to the craving that arose from the addiction.

I was in search and need of a way to stop this wheel of suffering. Therefore, I discovered that the more I was able to deal with whatever the addiction was, moment by moment, the more unveiled became the relationship between self-forgiveness and freedom. I learned that the more guilt I surrendered, the more unchained my true will became and, therefore, free from outside forces. This breaking free set the stage so that my authentic willpower could finally emerge. Again, I saw the inseparable link between guilt and my intense desire to deny or stuff it. This was the pattern that birthed the ego. Subsequently, as my level of self-love began to increase, so, too, did my willpower.

My self-love was wholly reliant on learning to accept my true identity as an innocent, holy, perfect child of God. I needed to remember that *"I am still as God created me"* (W-pI.94.3:3). Finally, it was through forgiving myself for past mistakes that I was able to allow the Holy Spirit to fulfill its part within my mind. I had prayed, actually begged, God on several occasions to stop the madness. I desperately wished for a pill or the immediate "just do it to me" answer that everybody seemed to know except me.

What I discovered was that the journey of developing my willpower was an intricate part to my awakening process. I was finally able to walk away from my self-abusive, addictive patterns through joining my fear-ridden mind with the transcendent power of the Holy Spirit. I began to accept the reality that I was not what I did in my past, but was, in fact, still the innocent being I was created to be. I was then able to receive the healing power of God. It would not be a pill or an easy-fix answer to put all of the insanity away. The key to my freedom was authentic self-acceptance and acceptance of the loving God who created me. I surrendered with the awareness that of myself, I could do nothing but transfer one addiction for another, but with God, all this would stop.

What I eventually had to understand and accept was that the happiness and peace I sought to attain elsewhere was already inside me. I decided that, from then on, my happiness would no longer be reliant on the outer experiences or events occurring in my life. For the first time in my life, I realized that I had a real choice. I could either continue to see events and occurrences through the eyes of the victim, which nurtured my need for the addiction, or I could choose to see them through the eyes of a conqueror. Through embracing the role of conqueror, I began to perceive the challenges and reasons for turning to my addiction as being the actual opportunities to overcome the addiction. In other words, any roadblocks or challenges to sustaining an addiction are truly the raw materials required for us to overcome them. For instance, if a person is an alcoholic and their job is the most important thing to them, then compassionately the Universal Intelligence will place their job in the balance. The job will be placed in the balance in order to offer the individual enough willpower to give up the addiction. Likewise, if I want my son to do his homework before all other activities, I will place his favorite activity, which is playing computer games, in the balance. If my son neglects his homework, he will be suspended from playing for a few days in order to help him remember his homework. In my own case, I recognized early on that I was being tempted by the saboteur archetype, and that my personal power would increase each time I did not succumb to its temptation.

Oh, how I remember clearly the very last cigarette I inhaled! For quite some time, I had been tossing back and forth the concept that I no longer needed to smoke. I had asked the Holy Spirit repeatedly to enter my mind when I could feel the grasp of past conditioned responses taking hold of me. The Holy Spirit always responded to my invitation with an inner dialogue that reminded me of my own preciousness. The still, small voice within me would question what it was I believed the cigarettes could give me. I always responded with the same answer: "It will give me whatever I tell it to give me." "Yes," the inner voice responded, "remember also that if you did not believe it would give you anything, it would not."

I knew this statement was true because several times over the years I had tried to retract my belief that the cigarette could offer me anything and therefore it didn't. The question, then, is why was this working sometimes, while on other occasions it felt nearly impossible? The answer to this question was revealed through my better understanding of my individual, versus my unified, willpower.

I remember desperately wanting a cigarette, yet not having any in my possession. I drove to the nearby gas station and bought what would be my very last package of "smokes." I battled between my higher and lower mind as I took out one lone cigarette. I asked the Holy Spirit for help, and the still small voice suggested that I go ahead and have the cigarette, only that I should include the Holy Spirit in the process. I was stunned by this response. How could I possibly invite the Holy Spirit to smoke? Well, I did, and as I lit that final cigarette and began to inhale, a deep sense of peace and calm overcame me. Something deeply powerful had just occurred. I recognized that the desire to have a cigarette was at its deepest level a desire to be unconditionally loved. Since the Holy Spirit loved me so much, It was willing to join me in my addiction. I was able to toss that last smoke out the window and never look back.

Throughout my different addictions, there was a direct relationship between my level of willpower and who I believed myself to be. What I discovered was that all addictions were ultimately the same. The foundation of all addictions was the desire to understand and accept who I truly was, to fill the perceived lacks within me, to numb out the pain of the past, and to finally feel innocent. Each of my addictions was a desperate attempt to fill the perceived separation that my ego insisted was there. The healing of each of these addictions ultimately came through my realization that neither the separation nor the void really existed. Consequently, I learned that the freedom from addictive parts of my personality was attained through better understanding the power of my authentic being. I realized that the driving force behind my addictions was my ego, as it continually commanded me to find something to fill the void it perceived in me. Through my inner search, instead of finding a void, I discovered a fullness within myself that was somehow able to implode and bridge the higher and lower states of mind, unveiling my internal unification with God.

My liberation was eventually achieved through forgiving myself for past mistakes. I had been walking around feeling like a guilt-ridden sinner who deserved to be punished or killed. If the world wouldn't punish me, I would find somebody who would. That somebody always turned out to be me. Then, after awhile of feeling even guiltier, I would become outraged by my self-abasement and would "seek out" another to hate for the pain I felt inside.

Does this sound familiar? In the area of addiction, we can once again see the Vise-Grip hold that the ego has on us, if we allow it. Our freedom comes from the joining of our hearts and minds in making choices that should reflect and nurture our authentic identity. Through learning the principles of *A Course in Miracles*, I came to understand that happiness was an inherited right that belonged to me through my creation. I began to comprehend that my happiness was a decision, and that I was given the freedom to accept or reject it. Finally, my mind was lit up with the realization that both peace and happiness are states within me that I simply needed to claim.

I believe that my personal journey through the world of addiction occurred for many reasons, none of which is to be minimized. However, the area in which I think my experience can most be used as a tool for the Holy Spirit is in compassionate understanding. Through the many years of working with clients, and from the feedback they have given me, I have discovered that the healing from any addiction is always permanently accomplished when we join with the Divine. The shape that the addiction takes has no bearing on the Holy Spirit's understanding of the root fear that underlies all addiction and of the truth that once we remove the belief that the addiction is necessary for our happiness, our freedom is restored. The size, shape, and degree of difficulty of the addiction, and the relationships that the addiction has affected, can all be managed in the understanding that, in reality, there is no order of difficulty in miracles and in the sight of the Holy Spirit.

Each and every person, each and every experience has played a part in my salvation.

Part Five

Expanded Consciousness

Part Five - *Expanded Consciousness*   287
Perception vs. Knowledge   289
Reincarnation   293
Karma   299
Grace   303
Self-Love   305
Prayer   309
Illness and Healing   311
Prayer and Our Relationship to God   313
To Begin Again   315
The Final Analysis   319

Perception vs. Knowledge

The Course teaches us that knowledge is truth. Knowledge stems from a whole and perfect mind. It is equated with reality, which is defined as that which is changeless. Perception, on the other hand, lies in the domain of changing experience. The part of the mind that "perceives" is the part that believes itself to be split and apart from its Creator. It is also the level of mind that perceives itself as separate from that which it observes. Once again, the analogy of when we sleep and dream becomes our point of reference. Remember that we are all the characters of the dream and we experience ourselves through those characters.

Well-known spiritual teacher and author Dr. Deepak Chopra brilliantly explains how each and every sentient being, whether animal or human, perceives its world differently. The snake, for instance, experiences its world through vibration, through smell via the tongue, and the heat energy emanating from the material world that produces ultraviolet light, in order that it can distinguish between its prey and the environment. A dog, on the other hand, experiences the world through a keen sense of smell and sound, yet is limited in the color spectrum to black and white. This awareness can help us to become cognizant of the fact that each creature experiences life differently. The way each species interprets the world of energy and information depends largely on the sense receptors it possesses. What we perceive is not fact, as is demonstrated when we see a skyline meet and appear to touch the ocean in the distance, or when we watch as a plane seems to shrink and disappear into nothingness as it flies away into the distance.

Rediscovering Your Authentic Self

Even our sense of vision is subject to such phenomena, as we all have learned to correct the upside-down image of the external world that is cast upon our retinas.

Similarly, the science of psychology has explored the hidden psychological distortions that influence the way in which we perceive the environment and the people around us. Respected psychologists such as Sigmund Freud have shown systematically that the world we experience is not as it seems — that our individual perceptions and past theoretical understanding of reality are greatly affected and, at times, dramatically distorted by unresolved issues. These problems are often unrecognized within our awareness, and consequently are projected onto the external world. These hidden complexes then become the filter through which we view people and situations and, as such, they often reflect our unconscious needs and fears. The fundamental process through which our needs and desires affect our perceptions is underway at all times, both in normal relaxed situations, and during times of unusual stress.

We continually interpret the information that is fed to us via our sensory receptors. Such interpretations are based on past experience, due to the nature of the split mind that birthed them. In fact, without the past we cannot perceive, for we have no basis or reference point to organize and understand the insurmountable amounts of sensory stimuli that come to us. Take an apple, for example: Without past experience, I would not know if it is sweet or sour, hard or soft, or whether it could fill me up. Furthermore, the apple's purpose will differ. If I were a fruit farmer, that apple would be my livelihood, but if I were a teacher receiving an apple from a student, it would become a sign of affection.

When we explore this and other examples, we can safely admit that perception is neither constant nor stable. Even the bodies we see appear to be solid and fixed in form, yet we know that on a quantum level they, too, are a river of self-referring energy and information. Indeed, we have all had different experiences, and our opinion of those experiences is directly related to the way we view them. Our prior experiences, therefore, become the filter through which we view all that follows.

Perception is a relative phenomenon, because of the mind that gives rise to it. It does not reflect a picture of what is constant and absolute. *"Perception is a continual process of accepting and rejecting, organizing and reorganizing, shifting and changing."* (T-3.V.7:7) Perception, therefore, cannot reflect a stable picture of the world that surrounds us. Rather it becomes an interpretation of the world we occupy, which becomes in effect an "unreal world." *"Perception always involves some misuse of mind, because it brings the mind into areas of uncertainty."* (T-3.IV.5:1)

We are taught through Course principles that we cannot deem reality based on our experience. However, we are taught that our perceptions are capable of coming so close to truth that knowledge, or God, can then take the final step towards our awakening. Knowledge is equated to love, truth, light, and the Christ Mind. Perception, on the other hand, lies in the domain of the mind's perceiving itself as being split. The split refers to the mind that perceives itself as being apart from what surrounds it, as well as being apart from that which created it. Knowledge, on the contrary, is wholly cognizant of the fact that no separation or split has occurred.

Knowledge is the mind's natural state prior to perceiving itself to be split. Although, through the Holy Spirit, knowledge still remains within the mind, it is not always being actualized. A split mind denies its Creator and knowledge, and thus it believes that it needs to learn. When we have attained or, more factually, *remembered* knowledge, learning is no longer required. It seems that at its most fundamental level, the human journey is one of transferring perception into knowledge. The way I help clients to connect with this statement is to ask them how they go about proving their particular gender to the rest of the world. Usually the response is that they don't. Outside of the fact that they may conform to gender-specific clothing standards dictated by society, no attempt is made to prove their womanhood or manhood. That is exactly my point. When we have attained something, we no longer exert energy in order to prove it. When we attain the awareness that all is one and only love is real, we will have attained mastery.

Rediscovering Your Authentic Self

The initial daily lessons of the Course are designed to help us undo our false beliefs. What we are being reminded of is that if we think we know, we are not teachable, while if knowledge is present, learning is futile. It is for this reason that we are so encouraged to turn our minds over to the guiding knowledge of the Holy Spirit within our minds. The Holy Spirit's function is to transform perception into the final step before knowledge is attained. In consideration of the memory of who we are, God must take the final step. What does this final step mean? I believe that the final step is our complete surrender to love. We therefore awaken to discover that we never left our Creator, we only dreamed that we had.

Moreah Ragusa

Reincarnation

I believe that the reason most fundamental Christians struggle with the concept of reincarnation is because it is seen as having a past, present, and future. The fear within this doctrine is that if and when people have another life or another chance, so to speak, they will not be willing to do their best in their current life. Once again, we recognize that imbedded in this idea is man's desire to govern people.

In *A Course in Miracles*, we are taught that time does not exist outside of this moment. The Course allows its students to either believe or disbelieve in reincarnation. I believe the reason for this is simple. It is reminding us that we have only ever had an eternal "now." There is a wonderful line in the Course that tells us that the entire idea of separation occurred and ended in an instant. It explains further that every single event since that instant has been a replay of the attempt to make the separation real.

When I do readings with people, information that does not experientially belong to this lifetime is drawn forth from the soul. I'm quick to acknowledge that all lifetimes that this soul is living are being experienced now. Once again, what I'm trying to have the person understand is that they are totality, and therefore they are still now experiencing on some level all of the experiences that they have moved through.

We are not our experiences; our experiences are simply reflections of thoughts that we uphold. The physical world arose in order to show us what we think. Because mind is totality, we have

Rediscovering Your Authentic Self

the capacity to experience all things. What we measure as time is the change that occurs between the experiences we remember. This is why total peace and total freedom are restored to our awareness when we are living in the moment. When we totally accept the concept of *all is one* and that we are the totality of this physical universe, we are better able to understand that all the experiences we have lived through have been toward a common goal. The goal was to discover that separation from God could never have occurred.

If this idea seems to break your conceptual mental boundary, then you are closer to understanding why we have made an agreement of measuring change through past, present, and future tense. The concept of living hundreds of lifetimes in this instant literally blows our minds. The ego's response is to shrink down our total reality to one that we can better deal with on an individual human consciousness level. In my own personal journey of awakening, I have discovered and accepted that time works vertically rather than horizontally. This idea means that in the very instant I was being born I was also dying, and that through memory I could experience these events. What we come to accept is that we are the immortal beings God created us to be. This allows that we are capable of experiencing every experience we've ever had or will have, *now*. As our awareness expands and we are able to use our unlimited Christ Consciousness, we are better able to embrace this concept and eventually even live by it.

To better help you understand this concept, let's say I am at a stop sign, and before me are four choices. The first choice is to proceed straight ahead. With this choice, I would encounter certain people and experiences along the path. Let's go back to the stop sign, and this time I will choose to turn left. Again, I will travel down the road, this time meeting different people and experiences than I had encountered as I moved straight ahead. If I go back to the stop sign again and this time turn right, once more I will experience a different scenery and different people that will also result in different thoughts. I have one more choice to make if I return to the stop sign. If I turned around heading in the opposite direction, I would again have different experiences and encounter different people and therefore experience different thoughts. If, in fact, I made all of those choices, then the information from all of those choices is inside of me. In reality then, in any given moment, I can call up and relive any of those paths.

Collectively, however, we have made time-space agreements in order to shrink down our reality, but in achieving higher states of awareness, those agreements can be broken. What we want and have been conditioned for is to have time work on a continuum. It is true to say that we have choice one, choice two, choice three, and choice four, but since we have made all of those choices, it is also true that they are all occurring right now.

One might now ask, "what if I had only made one choice?" Then in that one choice I will have been given the opportunity to meet all of the people, encounter all of the experiences, and have all of the thoughts I would've had through the four paths. The choice was up to me as to whether to divide the experience, which always offers a lesson, into four directions, or to do it on the one path. It is because we are totality that we are so willing to go through the experiences that we go through. We do this in order to experience our self-referring nature and, through experience, to remember our divinity and unbounded totality. In other words, absolutely any experience that we can have originates from who we think we are. And since we are everything, everything is open to our experience. Through this journey, we will discover the experiences that reflect our magnificence back to us, along with those experiences that do not. What we will ultimately come to embrace is that our experiences reflect back to us who we think we are. So moving back to the stop sign once again, we realize that each and every one of those choices can be layered one on top of the other, and we can recognize that they are, in fact, all happening right now.

To illustrate the reasons why some souls may choose suffering, let's suppose that I have spent many lifetimes evolving and minimizing the impact that the ego-oriented mind has over me. Then I decide that I still recognize within my soul a yearning to see if I can look to God to fill all of my desires. I want to discover if I can be happy and at peace, even while living in a situation of impoverishment. By necessity, then, I will be born into such an environment in order to test and fully experience my current level of faith and trust in God. In my decision to live a life of impoverishment, I also offer others the opportunity to show compassion and reach out to help minimize or eradicate poverty from someone's life — in this case mine. I will, however, need to choose if I eventually want to be freed from this experience, or if it serves my soul to remain in this particular situation. Because we do not know the reasons why people choose the lives they lead, we need to be careful not to judge. One of my mentors, Dr. Wayne Dyer, explains this so well when he says that suffering is a part of life, but so is the desire to end suffering. God, accepting all things, allows both, knowing that they both end in Him.

Many people fear the idea of reincarnation. They believe that if reincarnation is real, then it means that we might be less willing to live an honorable life this time. Their fear is that if we have another kick at the cat, so to speak, why do it now? The answer to this question is simply that to not live honorably is painful. When this pain increases too much, we will seek a higher truth and return home to our reality and our identity.

The fear of reincarnation comes from our need to implement human justice rather than trusting that life works. And that life is God. When we believe that God is life, then we can trust, we can surrender, and we can observe.

From the foundation that we have been building upon, we can experience the principles of the Course. Principles such as to receive one must give; as you think so shall you experience; and through these works we release our need to police the Universe. We become more willing to know that each and every person is given the right at that stop sign to choose the path they want to travel. We also come to accept that upon each path are specific learning opportunities that encourage the awakening of our souls. Spirit is continually seeking balance, and this balance is already within us. We are eternal beings, so the time in which we want to learn of our perfection is up to us. Neither the past nor future exists, simply because what is eternal is eternally now. It is interesting how often we fail to recognize that our entire life has in actuality always been lived in the moment.

It is through memories of our travels down a particular path that we are given the illusion of the past. So what we need to remember, even when using our memory, is that we are still using it in the now. We are taught through the Course very specifically that it is crucial to our peace of mind that we learn to use our memories wisely. Those things that we can remember through love are eternal.

Moreah Ragusa

On the other hand, it is important to remember and recognize that memories experienced through fear are hallucinogenic and can be lit by the light of truth and shone away.

We must always remember that we are beings of service, and it is through our service to others that we are able to expand our awareness of our identity. We continue to write, direct, and act our script so that we will come to know our own magnificence. We must remember that people in our lives, the soul "characters" that we choose to play parts in "our script," are lovingly fulfilling their roles.

Rediscovering Your Authentic Self

Only the thoughts we think through love are true and can have an eternal effect on us.

Karma

Thoughts never leave the mind of the thinker. *A Course in Miracles* encourages us to think only through a mind of love. These thoughts will always be reflected back to us. Similarly, ideas that are generated through fear are also capable of creating experiences that reflect those fearful thoughts back to us. This is the universal process known as *karma*. Karma is the cyclical motion of memory and desire. Mind is eternal, and through the trillions of experiences we have moved through, we have had thoughts that we perceived to be true. These thoughts, in turn, must be reflected back to us. For example, if we hold the belief that we are victims, this belief will be reflected back to us through experience. An entire lifetime can be spent acting out this belief, which will create additional karma for the soul. Following the surrender of the soul's body, these "victims" will remember who they truly are, and once again write out a life script to heal their belief in victimhood.

From this, we recognize that the preponderance of what we think about creates karma. This is why *A Course in Mir*acles is so committed to teaching us that we are responsible for what we think. The application of the Course principles can collapse karma, or experience, because these principles are designed to help us learn how to discriminate between thoughts of love and imaginings of fear. Consequently, the Holy Spirit is able to reverse the physical laws that are meant to reflect all thoughts.

Rediscovering Your Authentic Self

> Atonement corrects illusions, not truth. Therefore, it corrects what never was. Further, the plan for this correction was established and completed simultaneously, for the Will of God is entirely apart from time. So is all reality, being of Him. The instant the idea of separation entered the mind of God's Son, in that same instant was God's Answer given. In time this happened a very long time ago. In reality it never happened at all. (M-2.2:2-8)

Only the thoughts we think through love are true and can have an eternal effect on us. Therefore, a miracle is meant to reflect this truth back to us. Thoughts that were born from fear and that we believed to be real must be undone. Remembering once again that only loving thoughts are real, we can undo those fear-generated thoughts by changing our thought patterns. It is the soul's mission to incarnate until this goal of undoing is accomplished.

Eastern religions see karma as desire and experience. They believe that by getting in contact with our identity, our source and center, we are able to dissolve unwanted desires or karma. This is easy to understand since karma is another word for *cause and effect*, and we are truly only at the effect of love. When we get in touch with our identities as being wholly innocent, and can hold that identity for longer periods of time, we can dissolve thoughts created by our mistaken identities. This is why in the Eastern religions meditation is revered and recognized as a powerful tool toward enlightenment. The more time during a day that we can remember who we are, the more accepting we'll become of our authentic identity. The Course strongly supports the value of meditation, and it also goes a step further by encouraging us to apply the principles of love that result in miracles moment by moment. What the Course illuminates in our minds is that each and every thought we think has the power to take us straight to Heaven or to hell.

The twelve archetypal defense patterns we discussed in the section on relationships tempt us to believe that we are something other than who we are. Yet, transcending these patterns becomes the pathway home. When we believe that we are anything outside of love, we create painful karma. When we believe that we are the innocent, perfect children of God, and accept the fact that, ultimately, we are one being, we are able to create joyous karma. It's our choice!

We continually discover that life is truly about owning our identities, and we will all come to realize that every lesson we have ever been through was a lesson in love. The ultimate goal of every lesson is self-acceptance, which results in "all is one" self-love.

Karma is equated to thought and the desire to experience that thought. Desire should not be seen as a hindrance towards becoming karmically clear. What Heaven is really watching for is the time at which all our desires are reflective of our authentic identities. In addition, the intentions that lie beneath these desires are of equal importance.

Grace means that God is awake and has never lost sight of His children or their worth.

Moreah Ragusa

Grace

Grace is a reflection of truth. The grace of God simply means we accept that our thoughts and experiences that were propelled by fear do not exist outside the dreaming mind. Grace means that God is awake and has never lost sight of His children or their worth. Ultimately, it is through accepting this as truth that we are able to understand why there is nothing for God to judge, and there is nothing within us for God to punish. To live in grace means that we accept the atonement for ourselves, and accept others who have temporarily fallen asleep. It is through accepting grace that we are better able to understand the true meaning of forgiveness. God is merciful, so receiving and accepting His mercy is living in Grace. To be merciful simply means that we recognize truth in the midst of illusion. When our evaluation of who we are is tainted by fear, we may find it difficult to believe that our mistakes could be undone so simply. We tend to be fixated on living our lives through the rules of our individually perceived system of justice.

Consequently, it is hard for us to conceive that God is not disillusioned by our perceptions and that He only responds to and through the principles of love. As we become more willing to receive miracles as natural events in our lives, we are able to understand what it means to live in grace.

Rediscovering Your Authentic Self

The journey of self-love, which results in a process of awakening, occurs when we learn, through love, to manage our authentic power.

Moreah Ragusa

Self-Love

It has been my personal experience through counseling people that what we lack most of all in our lives is self-love. It is not hard to understand why this is true, once we understand the ego's thought system. The ego is able to quietly yet viciously attack us by holding us hostage to the belief that we are not who we truly are. The ego's focus is to continually scream out lies that are based upon a perception of separation that will ultimately leave us feeling powerless. The ego ultimately wants us to accept it as our hero.

The foundation of self-love must come from self-awareness. The self that we must nurture is the one that does not unkindly respond to manifested events or experiences born of fear. I am often asked how a person might nurture their self-love. My response is immediate. If you really knew who you were, you couldn't help but love yourself. In keeping with the fact that we are whole and perfect and innocent, we become gentler on ourselves when we make mistakes. Generally I have found it to be those who carry the burden of guilt from the past that are most unable to begin loving self. On a very deep level, we are terrified to accept our identities, since to accept them means that we must accept the higher power that reflects this identity. The journey of self-love, which results in a process of awakening, occurs when we learn, through love, to manage our authentic power.

As we embark upon the first stages of self-love, we are usually inspired to change our hair, buy a new vehicle, get a new wardrobe, or even possibly undergo plastic surgery. This is great!

Rediscovering Your Authentic Self

We begin to believe that we "deserve it." From these initial stages, we become gentler with ourselves, which ultimately nurtures our ability to be gentler with others. From this premise, our guilt begins to diminish, and self-love begins to be restored as the foundation of our thought system. People who learn self-love are "self-full" people. (Not to be mistaken with people who are "full of themselves"!) "Self-full" people are kind, gentle, and compassionate, as they do not seek to be filled by anything outside of God. It is when we feel unworthy, tattered, guilty, and torn that we become vicious not only with ourselves, but also with the people who are in our lives.

Some of the exercises I recommend for people who are trying to nurture self-love are these:

1. Do something kind for yourself each day.
2. Create balance so there is time to honor all parts of your being.
3. Write a letter to God confessing past mistakes you feel you've made.
4. Create at least a twenty-minute period of time each day to simply sit and be.
5. Say thank you when you receive a compliment.
6. Write a list of the qualities you most like about yourself, and write a second list of qualities you wish to transcend.
7. Write a personal honor code to which you will adhere.
8. Strengthen your willpower by setting forth a small task to do each day and then do it.
9. Make a commitment to do something you have always wished to do, and then absolutely follow through on your commitment.
10. Perform some small act of charity, such as giving someone your shopping cart.
11. Review your childhood picture album and send love to yourself at all the stages you felt love was missing.
12. Practice using the word "no" without guilt.

These are just a few ideas to nurture the self-love that you possibly feel you were lacking in either your childhood or adulthood. People who love and cherish themselves and their children are wonderful people to be with, if for no other reason than that they need nothing from you. The destruction of our self-love is directly reflected by the belief that we are guilty and alone. As we learn to live in the moment, and accept the perfection within us, we once again obtain our self-love and peace of mind.

The highest prayer I believe we can pray is that we might know ourselves the way God knows us.

Moreah Ragusa

Prayer

What is prayer? Prayer is the combination of thought and loving desires coming together. We use the same process when we ask anything to come into our experience. Here again, we remember that experience reflects thought; therefore, every thought we think is prayer on some level. Understanding this changes the way we pray. The highest prayer I believe we can pray is that we might know ourselves the way God knows us. Rather than praying for a winning lottery ticket, we might pray to accept the abundance we're created with. Or, a prayer for mental health can transform our prayer for physical health. Our prayer for a new relationship can instead become a prayer to increase our relationship to ourselves. Or to view relationship's purpose differently.

When we pray, we are often asking for help from a level of disempowerment and helplessness. We do not own our responsibility for our thoughts. We are so tempted to ask God to break cosmic laws for what we believe will be our benefit. If we have led a life believing that we are martyrs, then that thought is reflected back to us. By doing so, we are then not able to ask God to take away the effects of our martyr-consciousness. Instead, we ask for healing on the level of mind where the error occurred. A better prayer would be one in which we ask God to restore the memory of who we are to our awareness. We might then have our authentic identities reflected back to us in our experience. It is the function of the Holy Spirit within our mind to undo the consequences and the effects of our experiences on a physical level. For this law to operate, we must first

Rediscovering Your Authentic Self

take responsibility for having made a mistake on a thought level. This is the part of prayer that we most often forget. It is as if we came to God with broken toys while holding a hammer in our hand, in denial that we broke the toy. Compassionately, God's response to this scenario is to offer us experiences that teach us that we have no need for a hammer.

Moreah Ragusa

Illness and Healing

Before we pray for something to come into our experience, there is an important question that we should ask: "What is it for?" The desire for a winning lottery ticket might reveal a belief that having more money would bring us a sense of self or freedom that we did not believe we already had. Our prayer for the healing of a cancer-ridden body might be restated so that we ask for the strength to be able to accept that this condition, too, can be used for our soul's evolution as we surrender our guilt and fear of awakening. We might use it as an opportunity to better understand how our thoughts affect our own health, and that from our innocence comes our peace.

Whenever I work with an individual who has been labeled terminally ill, I ask for guidance in order to understand what their illness is for. It is important for this individual first to accept the diagnosis as it was found, but then to seek honestly within for the highest purpose of the illness. It also is crucial to remember that people are sometimes misdiagnosed and that even that is a step towards uncovering the greater meaning the illness is offering your life. From this deep internal searching, many answers can come, such as those we have already explored. Possibly the illness is as a result of "un-forgiveness," of self or a partner or adversary. Perhaps the illness is a gift which reveals that we have been grossly neglectful of our use of life force energy. Maybe it is a way in which we and others can learn about the power of love and forgiveness, as was the case for well-known author Louise Hay, who healed her cancer in six months, using an intensive program of affirmations, visualization, nutritional cleansing, and psychotherapy.

What is truly important is that we first accept the illness as an opportunity to grow, and to teach us and those who love and care for us that both life and we ourselves are precious. Let me share a story. A few years ago, I watched a documentary about research that was undertaken in order to help the medical community understand spontaneous healings. The researchers took several case studies of terminally ill people and sought to find a common denominator amongst those individuals who had been healed. They found that those who, when diagnosed with an illness, decided to love and care for themselves in ways they had not done before, became miraculously well. One test subject who particularly impressed me was a gentleman who explained that, following the prognosis that he had only six months to live, began to give himself the best of the best. If he had wine, it was the best wine. If he had a cigar, it was the best cigar that money could buy. In all areas, he decided that he was worth it.

Interestingly, in all cases of spontaneous healing, it was the person's forgiveness of the past and a strong belief that the illness did not have power over them that were critical factors in their becoming well.

Prayer and Our Relationship to God

We can transform a prayer for a new relationship, which is usually sought so that we might not feel so alone, to a prayer asking that we might regain a sense of oneness that includes all of humanity. Once again, we might accept that our time with ourselves is a precious gift in self-discovery. Let us be reminded that our relationship to ourselves is our relationship to God, as cake is to icing. When we have our relationship to God as our foundation, all the other relationships in our life are the ice cream on top.

Prayer and meditation are powerful tools to reinstate our true identity to our awareness. Prayer is a way of acknowledging an acceptance of our relationship to our Father. Prayer and meditation bring feelings of empowerment, comfort, and peace to many people. This is true primarily for one reason, and that is that when we pray, we communicate with our Creator and once again establish our oneness. Both scientists and Western medical professionals have studied the power of prayer and its effects on those who are ill. It has been discovered that patients who are being prayed for return to health sixty percent quicker than those who are not prayed for. This is not really so mysterious when we understand that mind is shared. As one of us accepts our totality, all of us receive the benefits. Ultimately, healing is increased because identity is being shared and acknowledged.

Rediscovering Your Authentic Self

We will never find anything outside of ourselves that is capable of giving us a large-enough sense of ourselves to deliver us unto the peace we seek.

Moreah Ragusa

To Begin Again

To begin again means that we accept the grace of God in the undoing of past mistakes and beliefs. It means that we accept our identity and acknowledge the incredible power of the mind. As each of us journeys toward our own awakening and remembering, we collectively create Heaven on earth. We have been programmed by our society to believe that if we plan correctly for our financial and emotional futures while adhering to the rules of the physical universe, we will ultimately be safe. The question is, safe from what? This question brings forth a barrage of responses that tempts our ego to step into the role of hero. The ego will begin to make recommendations of how to be safe and protected, based on the belief system that we are separate and alone. It will encourage us to believe in our powerlessness and diminish the value of the mind as it increases the value of the body. We have all had experiences of setting our mind to a task and through sheer determination receiving the outcome we set out to achieve. And we have all had the experience of attaining a goal yet somehow still feeling helplessly depressed. We will never find anything outside of ourselves that is capable of giving us a large-enough sense of ourselves to deliver us unto the peace we seek. It is important to realize that the search itself was created in order for us to stay very busy attaining rather than just being. That specific something we seek is already inside of us, and it is only in turning within that we will discover that truth.

As we begin again, we recognize that we sometimes make mistakes, and that we need to take responsibility and be willing to

Rediscovering Your Authentic Self

atone for those mistakes. We use each and every life experience as an opportunity to have our beliefs reflected back to us — both the beliefs that serve us, and those that do not. To begin again means living in the now, releasing the idea of both past and future. We must allow new experiences to come into our life, experiences that do not taint the present with our past experiences. To begin again means that we invoke miracles as naturally as we breathe. It means that we learn to differentiate between those who are living from love and those who are calling for our love. We learn to respond the same to both, with love. As we accomplish our goal, we trust that God is both the Creator of life and life itself, and that life works brilliantly without our interference. We surrender our need to judge as we recognize our inability to have enough information to fully assess any situation. We accept all people as they are and respect their sacred journey. We live by faith, and we become the observers rather than the actors within our play. To begin again means that we ask questions from our soul's perspective rather than from our ego. We look at our lives from above, seeking what is the truth within our own belief system. Beginning again means that we are responsible for what we think, and therefore make the conscious choice to think through the higher Christ Mind that we all share.

    The result will be that the constant nattering of our ego that taunts us to find something outside of ourselves will finally end. We will learn to live in the moment, accepting that only love is real, and live from the premise that both our brothers and sisters, as well as we ourselves, are innocent. *"Your resurrection is your reawakening. I am the model for rebirth, but rebirth itself is merely the dawning on your mind of what is already in it. God placed it there Himself, and so it is true forever."* (T-6.I.7:1-3).

Moreah Ragusa

At the journey's end, we awoke to discover that we never really left home.

*In love and peace,
Remember: God Blesses You*

*Namaste,
(I honor and celebrate the place where we are one)*

Moreah

When the mind is used appropriately by adhering to the proper use of these cosmic laws, our health is maintained.

The Final Analysis
(Based on the Paradoxical Commandments by Dr. Kent M. Keith)

People are often unreasonable, illogical, and self-centered;
Forgive them anyway.

If you are kind, people may accuse you of selfish, ulterior motives;
Be kind anyway.

If you are successful, you will win some false friends and some true enemies;
Succeed anyway.

If you are honest and frank, people may cheat you;
Be honest and frank anyway.

What you spend years building, someone may destroy overnight;
Build anyway.

If you find serenity and happiness, they may be jealous;
Be happy anyway.

The good you do today, people will often forget tomorrow;
Do good anyway.

Give the world the best you have, and it may never be enough;
Give the world the best you've got anyway.

You see, in the final analysis, it is all between you and God;
It was never between you and them anyway.

Rediscovering Your Authentic Self

Moreah Ragusa

Before all things manifest, there is an idea. Moreah began her journey as a student of *A Course in Miracles* (the Course) twelve years ago. The power and truth of the concept that all things begin at a thought level transformed her life, and she began teaching what she had learned. She soon became an accomplished speaker and teacher of the Course. As part of her life's work, she envisioned a book that would assist others in the exploration and connection of power and thought. *Rediscovering Your Authentic Self* is a dream made manifest.

As a direct result of practicing the Course teachings, Moreah's intuitive ability soared. Within a very short time, she became one of the most sought-after psychics in her home city of Calgary. Moreah assists her clients by being a communication link for non-physical guides and teachers. She aims to demonstrate that we all have the ability to get help from the loving beings that watch over us. We all have the ability to communicate psychically if we heal the guilt and separation that we feel within our minds.

As a result of her conviction and application of the Course teachings, Moreah has a thriving counselling practice. Moreah recognizes the Course to be altruistic, meaning that in order to receive, one must give. In light of this, she practices as a spiritual psychotherapist — a designation that, according to the Course, refers to any individual who teaches and applies its principles in order to help others on their life path.

Moreah is the president and founder of the Angels Answers Group, which operates as a wellness centre.

Rediscovering Your Authentic Self